The Negotiated Self

The Negotiated Self

*Employing Reflexive Inquiry to Explore
Teacher Identity*

Edited by

Ellyn Lyle

BRILL

SENSE

LEIDEN | BOSTON

Cover image: Mavourneen Trainor Bruzzese, Lakehead University

All chapters in this book have undergone peer review.

The Library of Congress Cataloging-in-Publication Data is available online at http://catalog.loc.gov

Typeface for the Latin, Greek, and Cyrillic scripts: "Brill". See and download: brill.com/brill-typeface.

ISBN 978-90-04-38888-8 (paperback)
ISBN 978-90-04-38889-5 (hardback)
ISBN 978-90-04-38890-1 (e-book)

Contents

Foreword: Advice in this Liquid Midst

David W. Jardine

Miracle: From the Latin *mīrāculum*: object of wonder. *Mīrāculum* from *mīrārī*, to wonder at. From *mīrus*, wonderful. From *smeiros* [(s) mei – PIE – proto-Indo-European] "to smile, to be astonished." Also Sanskrit: *smerah* "smiling." Also Old Church Slavic: *Smejo* – to laugh.

JACKIE SEIDEL, 2016, p. 7

∵

One

No *Foreword* can pretend to usurp or outrun that which it faces. None of us need another summary fly-over. So, I'll begin with this meagre attempt at stepping into the territory of this lovely text.

Such is the trickle of water down a metal chute. Alberta. Spring. Such is an exercise in staring down depressions in the snow. As long as I can remember,

A trickle of water down a metal chute

cutting troughs in slush has been a great locale of enchantment. As a child. Still, old guy, these singing, boot-soaker pleasures. A hand had in having Spring come faster as the released ices shoot their way to water.

Seasonally affected, this, but this is no disorder. When experience is stood over and magnified, it enlarges and enlarges me with it:

> *The more you practice these things, the more accustomed your mind will become to them, and the easier it will be to practice what you had initially found difficult to learn. You will have visions of the Buddha day and night.* (Tsong-kha-pa, 2000, pp. 185–186)

> *One arises from formal meditation and goes about daily activities, seeing the manifestations of the world and living beings as mandala deities. This is the Samadhi that transforms the world and its living brings into a most extraordinary vision. All experiences are taken as manifestations of great ecstasy.* (Tsong-kha-pa, 2005, p. 125, emphasis added)

So, thus, this book names and re-names a "deliquescent move" (Derby, 2015, p. 61): "from Latin *deliquescere* 'to melt away,' from *de-* ... + *liquescere* 'to melt,' from *liquere* 'to be liquid'" (On-Line Etymological Dictionary), a move characteristic of hermeneutic work at is best, which "makes the object and all its possibilities fluid" (Gadamer, 1989, p. 367).

Consider, under this move, this partial, not impartial, list picked *passim* from this text:

> "Co-constructed," "ever changing," "negotiated," "perpetually in progress," "fluid," "fragmented," "fuzzy," "co-authored," "reflexive," "reflective," "imaginative," "multiple," "elusive," "intangible," "fragile," "contradictory," "flow[ing]," "complicated," "interconnected," "felt," "personal," "colonized," "ongoing," "composed," "lost," "re-gained," "unresolved," "ever-changing," "forming and re-forming," "indeterminate," "shadowy," "unknowab[le]," "temporariness," "regenerated," "raw," "visceral," "incomplete," "back-formed," "aggregate," "generative," "nomadic," "re-emergent," "intersubjective," "vulnerable," "becoming," "in the throes," "elaborative," "shifting," "volatile," "contradictory," "unfinalized," "dynamic," "dissonant," "subjective," "self-conscious," "unconscious," "embodied," "process."

This "making fluid" is a sometimes-ecstatic, sometimes-painful, often-both act of restoration and reconciliation as these pages ensue, because it aims at making its object – our lives, our living, our identities – teachers and otherwise – into *what it has been all along*, but what has sometimes taken on the semblances of frozenness, hardness, reification, sedimentation, calcification, capture, or the like. The great shock found repeatedly in this text is that our living has never *been* such a trap, however deeply felt the entrapment. It has always trickled "beyond our wanting and doing" (Gadamer, 1989, p. xxviii).

The unavoidable parallel niggle is that none of these words is exactly right or exactly wrong and this is no remediable error, but in the nature of the task at hand. Every time we might zero in on one of them, they fulfill another old hermeneutic adage:

> Every word breaks forth as if from a center [and] causes the whole of the language to which it belongs to resonate and the whole world-view that underlies it to appear. Thus, every word carries with it the unsaid. (Gadamer, 1989, p. 458)

Zooming in on any one of these terms is instantaneously zooming outwards. Every word radiates outwards into the worlds of its emergence and sustenance,

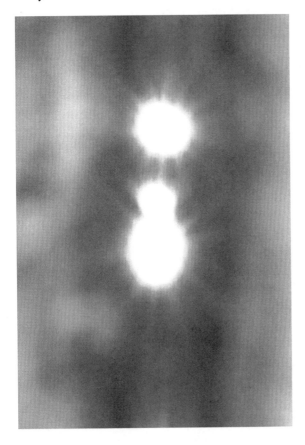

Buddha meditating under spring sunlight, being a magnification of 'A trickle of water down a metal chute'

all its relations, presumptions, histories, ancestries, "to which it is related by responding and summoning" (p. 458).

Look, then. When every word is stood over and magnified, it enlarges and enlarges me with it.

Two

The list of words from this text not only point to deliquescence. They themselves are each precisely that. Each term makes each term open-eyed to that which it aches to, but fails to, quite name:

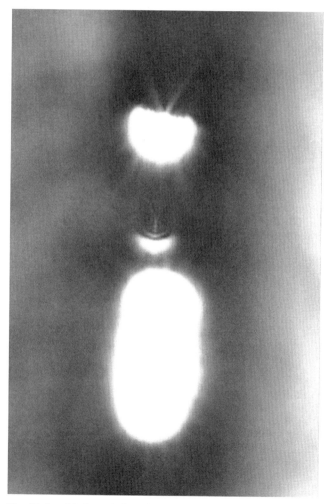

The third eye blinks in slight indigo, being another magnification of 'A trickle of water down a metal chute'

"We can entrust ourselves to what we are investigating to guide us safely in the quest" (Gadamer, 1989, p. 378). Aristotelian dreams, Thomist dreams of *mensuratio ad rem* (Gadamer, 1989, p. 261). That is to say, how to approach this liquid phenomenon must find its measure, not in some methodological assurance or confidence or some goal of "fix[ing] it once and for all in a way equally accessible to all" (Husserl, 1970, pp. 177–178), but *in the thing itself.* We find these swirls of words in this text, these poetic and deeply personal, sometimes painfully intimate outreaches *precisely and exactly because of the deliquescent nature of the thing itself* that *calls for* something adequate to its nature in the express of words:

> Both the one who understands and the thing that is understood "are" his-
> torically, that is, in the process of unfolding themselves over time, and

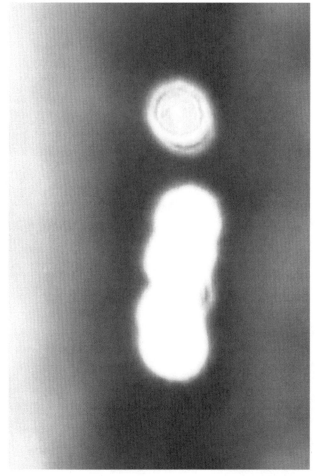

A reciprocal *adaequatio intellectus et rei,* being a further magnification of 'A trickle of water down a metal chute'

neither the one who understands, nor the thing understood "are" statically present [-at-hand] independently of each other. Both "are" in their interactive development. Hence, understand is still a *mensuratio ad rem*, as Gadamer puts it, or, in another traditional formulation, an *adaequatio intellectus ad rem*, except that the "adequation" of the intellect, its measuring and fitting of itself, is never to a timeless thing that always is what it is, some brute fact, "determinable" and independent of the one who knows it. [W]e might better speak of a reciprocal *adaequatio intellectus et rei*, of the temporary adequation of two entities, intellect and thing to each other, each in their particular historical development at the given time. (Smith, 2011, pp. 24–25)

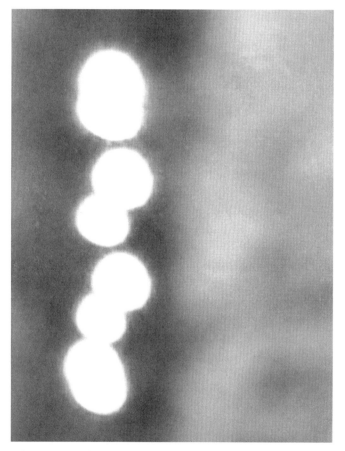

"Like a prisoner whose cell gate has never been locked' being, for now, one last magnification of 'A trickle of water down a metal chute'

Three

> To learn what the path to Buddhahood is, is to learn what the True Self is. To learn what the True Self is, is to forget about the self. To forget about the self is to become one with the whole universe. To become one with the whole universe is to be shed of 'my body and mind' and 'their bodies and minds'. (Dogen, 2007, p. 32)

My thanks to Megan Liddell (2016, pp. 175–176) for spotting a fleeting idea from David Loy's *The World is Made of Stories*:

> Our stories are never finished, and therefore never unfinished. If reality itself is always incomplete, each moment becomes complete in itself, lacking nothing. (Loy, 2010, p. 40)

> Immerse yourself in meaningful, rich and deep work with students and you will forget about finishing it. Teacher, you are never finished, but you are also never unfinished. What matters most is what you do with the very next moment in front of you. (Liddell, 2016, p. 176)

The water's now well down the driveway in the full mix of things, still-ripple and shining in the mixes of road gravel and horse shit and boot prints in the slush and sloosh.

It's why the dogs scurry back and forth when we walk the road. So much dissolved to solve in every whiff. Two great fur saints following the paths of deliquescence.

So, there go the Ravens, my dears, again caught and uncaught on the warm Spring-air foothill uplifts.

To be dying under their wings is a weird miracle.

Meanwhile

Meanwhile, I read my way through this book, feeling much "like a prisoner whose cell gate has never been locked" (Loy, 2010, p. 41).

Meanwhile, too, as per all those gathered in this text, I write my way here to this gathering. This has become my practice, my gate-key. To paraphrase Tsong-kha-pa (2000, p. 211) from a text originally composed in Tibet in 1406, I compose this in order to compose myself over this written gathering.

Tsong-kha-pa said, too, "cultivate love for those who have gathered" (2000, p. 64). Solid advice in this liquid midst.

References

Derby, M. (2015). *Place, being, resonance: A critical ecohermeneutic approach to education.* New York, NY: Peter Lang.

Dogen. (2007). *Shobogenzo: The treasure house of the eye of the true teaching* (H. Nearman, Trans.). Mount Shasta, CA: Shasta Abbey Press.

Gadamer, H. G. (1989). *Truth and method.* New York, NY: Continuum Books.

Husserl, E. (1970). *The crisis of European science and transcendental phenomenology.* Evanston, IL: Northwestern University Press.

Liddell, M. (2016). Thoughts on being neither finished nor unfinished. In J. Seidel & D. Jardine (Eds.), *The ecological heart of teaching: Radical tales of refuge and renewal for classrooms and communities* (pp. 175–176). New York, NY: Peter Lang.

Loy, D. (2010). *The world is made of stories.* Somerville, MA: Wisdom.

Seidel, J. (2014). A curriculum for miracles. In J. Seidel & D. Jardine (Eds.), *Ecological pedagogy, buddhist pedagogy, hermeneutic pedagogy: Experiments in a curriculum for miracles* (pp. 7–14). New York, NY: Peter Lang.

Smith, P. C. (2011). Destruktion-Konstruktion: Heidegger, Gadamer, Ricouer. In F. Mootz III & G. Taylor (Eds.), *Gadamer and Ricouer: Critical horizons for contemporary hermeneutics* (pp. 15–42). New York, NY: Continuum.

Tsong-kha-pa. (2000). *The great treatise on the stages of the path to enlightenment* [Lam rim chen mo]. Ithaca, NY: Snow Lion.

Tsong-kha-pa. (2005). *The six yogas of Naropa.* Ithaca, NY: Snow Lion.

Figures

Notes on Contributors

Cecile Badenhorst

is an Associate Professor in the Adult Education/Post-Secondary program in the Faculty of Education at Memorial University. Her research interests are post-secondary and adult learning experiences, particularly graduate research writing, academic literacies, and qualitative research methodologies. She has written *Research Writing* (2007), *Dissertation Writing* (2008), and *Productive Writing* (2010), and is also co-editor of *Research Literacies and Writing Pedagogies for Masters and Doctoral Writers* (2016).

Melanie Bennett-Stonebanks

is a multiple award winning teacher and has been part of the education community in Quebec for over 20 years where she has enjoyed her role as an elementary teacher, lecturer at McGill and Bishop's University as well as pedagogical consultant at Quebec's Ministry of Education. Melanie has worked to support an understanding and the application of strong pedagogy incorporating 21st century literacy into today's classrooms. Her research focus presently deals with ways of mentoring pre-service and novice teachers through reflexive inquiry and developing effective teaching and learning strategies.

Liel Biran

is an educator at the Lev-HaSharon Democratic School in Even-Yehuda, Israel, and an environmental activist. He is an army veteran with an M.Sc. in Computer Science from Bar Ilan University, Israel, and extensive work experience in the software development industry. Biran now teaches science and technology to K-9 and coordinates educational activities for the early childhood cohort.

Beverley Brenna

is a Professor in Curriculum Studies, College of Education, University of Saskatchewan where her research interests involve literacy teaching and learning, and Canadian children's literature. She is also the author of a dozen books for young people (for further information see www.beverleybrenna.com).

Casey Burkholder

is a faculty lecturer at the University of New Brunswick whose research explores the intersections of gender, identity, DIY media-making, civic engagement, youth, and Social Studies education. She first became invested in the relationships between space, belonging, and civic engagement at a young age when growing up in Canada's North. During her two years as a classroom teacher in Hong Kong, Casey saw her ethnic minority students systematically excluded from school activities and language instruction, and watched as many students were pushed out of the school. She wondered about the difference between the Hong Kong government's policy to include ethnic minority youth in schools and their lived experiences. This question served as the foundation for Casey's Master of Arts work, which she undertook in Educational Studies at Concordia University. In her doctoral work at McGill University's Department of Integrated Studies in Education, Casey embarked on an action-oriented project of creating youth-led media-making about issues of identity, belonging, and civic engagement with cellphone videos (cellphilms).

Amy Burns
is a faculty member and the Director of Field Experience with the Werklund School of Education. Her research interests include non-traditional educational environments and the effects of policy on educational reform. Her primary areas of focus are pre-service teacher education, with an emphasis on the pre-service teacher/partner teacher experience, and educational leadership for staff wellness.

Christine Cho
is an Associate Professor at Nipissing University's Schulich School of Education. A practicing visual artist and a former elementary school teacher, Christine utilizes visual media and critical pedagogy to expand upon diverse ways of knowing and trouble "the way things are" in schools. Her research contributes to current educational conversations on racial, ethnic, and linguistic representation in schools specifically exploring the constructions and understandings of teacher identity, including immigrant teacher aspirations.

Anthony Clarke
is a professor and the co-director of the Centre for the Study of Teacher Education (CSTE) in the Department of Curriculum and Pedagogy, University of British Columbia. His research interests include student teacher mentorship, the practicum, cooperating teachers, and self-study. He actively participates in various capacities often involving new ways of exploring teacher education initiatives.

Julie K. Corkett
holds a Bachelor of Office Management (1992), Bachelor of Arts, honours psychology (1995), Masters of Education in psychopedagogy (1997), Bachelor of Education (1998), and a Ph.D. in Learning, Development and Assessment

(2006). Dr. Corkett has worked as an intermediate and high school teacher and is currently a tenured associate professor at the Schulich School of Education. Dr. Corkett's research interests pertain to literacy, pedagogy, technology, special education, and educational psychology. She has published several peer-reviewed articles pertaining to special education, reading, self-efficacy, technology in the classroom, and chronic illness. She has also published peer-review articles pertaining to English language learning, international practica, teacher performativity, and student responsibility. Dr. Corkett has presented her research at numerous international and national conferences and has been an invited guest lecturer both nationally and internationally.

Kathryn Crawford

is Director of Field Education, as well as lecturer in the area of Learning Theory and Application. She is a doctoral student with a research focus on the complexities of field-institution relationships in pre-service teacher preparation. She is also interested in examining classrooms as environments for emerging pre-service teacher identity, and developing other ways of knowing in preservice teacher learning.

Patricia Danyluk

grew up in northern Manitoba where she spent the early part of her career working with remote First Nations and Métis communities. Dr. Danyluk joined the Werklund School of Education in 2014 after working at the Laurentian School of Education for 10 years. She completed her PhD at Laurentian University, her Master's in Adult Education at St. Francis Xavier, and her B.Ed. at Nipissing University. Patricia is currently the Director of Field Experience for the Community Based Bachelor of Education.

Sara Florence Davidson

is a Haida educator and scholar. She holds a PhD in Literacy Education from the University of British Columbia and has been teaching at the university level since 2014. She also has nine years' experience teaching in the K-12 system at the upper intermediate and secondary levels in humanities in rural British Columbia and Yukon. Her research interests include: Indigenous education; adolescent literacy education; culturally responsive teaching and research practices; and narrative writing and research.

Adrian Downey

is a PhD student at University of New Brunswick in the faculty of education. He is Mi'kmaw and formerly of the Qalipu Mi'kmaw First Nation. His academic interests are in contemporary Indigenous issues, Indigenous knowledges, Indigenous spiritual philosophy, as well as in curriculum theory, white privilege, and arts-informed and Indigenous methodologies. Adrian recently completed his Master of Arts in Education at Mount Saint Vincent University where his graduate thesis, *Speaking in Circles: White Privilege and Indigenous Identity*, won the 2017 MSVU thesis award. Before returning to graduate school, Adrian taught Grade 6 and elementary music in the Cree School Board.

Andrea Dunk
is a PhD student in Curriculum Studies, College of Education, University of Saskatchewan; she is also an Itinerant Teacher, supporting children with learning disabilities, in Saskatoon Public Schools.

Guopeng Fu
is a teaching and learning postdoctoral fellow in the Faculty of Land and Food Systems at the University of British Columbia. His research focuses on teacher agency, especially science teacher agency in curriculum reform settings, in-service teacher professional development, Graduate Teaching Assistant (GTA) professional development, and the Scholarship of Teaching and Learning (SoTL).

Joanna K. Garner
holds a Ph.D. in Educational Psychology from The Pennsylvania State University. Currently, she is the Executive Director of The Center for Educational Partnerships at Old Dominion University in Norfolk, Virginia. Her research on educators' and students' learning, motivation, and identity forms an integral component of the Center's engagement with university and community stakeholders. Garner is an active member of AERA and an outgoing Section Editor for *The Journal of Experimental Education*.

S. Laurie Hill
is an Assistant Professor, Faculty of Education, at St. Mary's University where she is also Practicum Director. Her research interests include pre-service teacher education, specifically the connections between on campus coursework and field practicum experiences. She is also interested in pre-service teacher professional identity, ways of knowing, student transitions, as well as the variety of learning environments that support undergraduate student success.

David W. Jardine
is a retired Professor of Education whose latest books include *In Praise of Radiant Beings: A Retrospective Path through Education, Buddhism and Ecology*

and, with Jackie Seidel, *The Ecological Heart of Teaching: Radical Tales of Refuge and Renewal for Classrooms and Communities.*

Avi Kaplan

is an Associate Professor of Educational Psychology at the College of Education, Temple University, PA, USA. Avi's research interests focus on student and teacher motivation and identity development, with a particular interest in the role of the environment in these processes. His research involves collaborative design-based interventions to promote educators' and students' identity exploration around the curriculum. Dr. Kaplan serves as the editor of the *Journal of Experimental Education.*

Andrejs Kulnieks

is an Adjunct faculty member at Trent University. His research interests include curriculum theory, language arts, literacies, poetic inquiry, Indigenous Knowledge and eco-justice environmental education. His co-edited book with Dan Longboat and Kelly Young is titled *Contemporary Studies in Environmental and Indigenous Pedagogies: A Curricula of Stories and Place* (Sense Publishers).

Ellyn Lyle

has a longstanding background in innovative education practices, ranging from traditional classrooms, to workplace and community partnerships, and technologically supported learning. In all these contexts, she has remained intensely interested in supporting the development of students and teachers as they contribute to socially equitable and sustainable programs. Ellyn holds a PhD in Education and has been teaching in university since 2010. She is currently Dean in the Faculty of Education. The use of critical methodologies shape explorations within the following areas: praxis; teaching and learning as lived experience; curriculum as living inquiry; issues of identity; and reflexive inquiry.

Derek Markides

is a doctoral student at the Werklund School of Education, University of Calgary, and a Vice-Principal with the Foothills School Division. He has taught mathematics, physics, and is an instructional leader. He is interested in complexity science and the entailments associated with collective knowledge building in mathematics classrooms. His research interests include storytelling, Indigenous literatures, place-based pedagogies, and teacher reflexivity as pushback against hegemonic positivist paradigms in mathematics teaching.

Isabel Martínez-Cuenca
found a new teacher identity away from traditional Second Language Teaching praxis towards *engaged pedagogy* during her PhD at the State University of New York at Albany. Isabel's passion for EFL/ESL teaching and teacher development guides her dissertation on the effects of an enrichment instruction program to better support immigrant L2 learners' transitioning into L2 science classrooms. She is also interested in bi- and multilingualism, L2 conceptual development, and L2 language use.

Heather McLeod
is Associate Professor (arts), in the Faculty of Education, Memorial University. She pursues a critical research agenda and uses arts-based research methods. Her current funded research initiatives include a parents and poetry project, an examination of the process of becoming a researcher, and an Open Studio project with immigrant and refugee youth. She holds awards for excellence in teaching and curriculum design and is the Editor-in-Chief of the *Canadian Review of Art Education*.

Sandy Miller
is a doctoral student at the Werklund School of Education, University of Calgary. She has been an educator for ten years, teaching high school mathematics at a charter school in Calgary. Her research interests lie in the area of reflective self-study focused on math teacher identity. She believes that learning is experiential, relational, and situated in the world. Her work looks at the entanglements and complexities of infinite interactions found in moments within classroom.

Evelyn Morales Vázquez
is a PhD candidate in the Higher Education, Administration, and Policy Program at the University of California, Riverside. Her current research focuses on the study of the academic professional identities and emotions in the academic profession in the context of neoliberal era.

Lana Parker
teaches multiliteracies and the arts at the Faculty of Education at York University, Toronto, Canada. She has also taught and mentored at the elementary level. In addition to her research on teacher education and teacher identity, Dr. Parker writes about the influences of politics and the media on educational rhetoric and practice, and about bridging critical pedagogy with an intersubjective ethics.

Anita Sinner

is an Associate Professor of Art Education at Concordia University, Montreal. Her research interests include arts-based and artistic research, teacher culture, international art education and community art education. She works extensively with stories as pedagogic pivots, with particular emphasis on artwork scholarship in relation to curriculum studies and social and cultural issues in education.

C. Darius Stonebanks

is a multiple teaching award winning Professor at Bishop's and Adjunct at McGill University. Among his publications are *Teaching Against Islamophobia* and *Muslim Voices in Schools*, which won the NAME's Philip C. Chinn book award. He is the co-founder of Transformative Praxis: Malawi, an Action Research project that connects social justice theory to practice, and is the PI on the SSHRC funded research project examining the secular nature of Canadian public schools.

Haley Toll

is a PhD student in the Faculty of Education at Memorial University of Newfoundland whose research focuses on arts-based research within supportive multicultural contexts. As a Registered Canadian Art Therapist, Certified Canadian Counselor and Registered Psychotherapist (currently inactive), she has worked with children and adults who have experienced various forms of challenges across Canada and has trained practitioners in Botswana, Thailand, and Mongolia. Haley is also the President of the Canadian Art Therapy Association.

Valerie Triggs

is an Associate Professor in Arts Education, in the Faculty of Education at the University of Regina. Her research interests include initial teacher education, the teacher education practicum experience, the ecological impact of art and aesthetic practice, and the interdisciplinary significance of aesthetic feeling in extending classically scientific modes of research and explanations of learning. In particular, her study is focused on sensitizing the self to indeterminate potential that is generated in movement already underway in other human and more than human practices.

Dana Vedder-Weiss

holds a Ph.D. in Science Education from The Weizmann Institute of Science, Israel. Currently, she is a faculty member at the Department of Education, Ben Gurion University of the Negev, Israel. She studies socio-emotional aspects of student and teacher learning in formal and informal environments through both quantitative and qualitative research approaches. She is involved in leading and studying large-scale research-practice partnerships aiming to support teacher learning and leadership.

Sean Wiebe

lives in Charlottetown and is an associate professor of education at the University of Prince Edward Island. His research interests include curriculum studies, narrative research, poetic inquiry, and a/r/tography. For the last four years he has been the principal investigator for the Digital Economy Research Team, investigating connections between new literacies and the digital economy. Recent publications appear in the *Canadian Journal of Education* and *Language and Literacies Education*.

Kelly Young

is a Professor at Trent University's School of Education and Professional Learning. Her areas of research include language and literacy, curriculum theorizing, leadership in eco-justice environmental education, and arts-based research. The book she co-edited with Andrejs Kulnieks and Dan Longboat is titled *Contemporary Studies in Environmental and Indigenous Pedagogies: A Curricula of Stories and Place* (Sense Publishers).

CHAPTER 1

Untangling Sel(f)ves through A/R/Tography

Ellyn Lyle

I begin with a confession: I've been trying to write this chapter for weeks but have struggled to get it to come together. Cohesive prose have become so elusive that I have resorted to writing *anything* hoping *something* will emerge. I wonder, even as I scribble more tangled thoughts, if this experience is the essence of writing as a way of knowing (Kooy & deFreitas, 2007; Richardson & St. Pierre, 2005). I wonder, too, if my inability to create is because I have fallen into the trap of traditional academic writing – a process I have always found more about *proving* than *exploring*. In feeling compelled to *prove* what I have read, *prove* that I can discuss it systematically, and *prove* that I can extrapolate findings from it, I often feel bound by traditions that I am not sure I even support. While I appreciate that proof has its own place and significance, the further I move toward self-study in wanting to advance critical and creative praxis, the more I prefer a living inquiry to stifling conventions.

Now, in this space of realization and the resulting intellectual paralysis, two things occur to me simultaneously: I consider how students who struggle to write continue to be marginalized by traditional education approaches; and I recognize the irony of not being able to find a personal entry point into a paper about the centrality of self in teaching and learning. It seems to me that the essence of both these problems resides in finding space to engage with teaching and learning in ways that help us to feel authentic and present.

As I continue to think about the possibilities, images begin to emerge more easily than words. My mind drifts to considering how we might make room for the aesthetic as well as the intellectual. I recall having read something about this within a/r/tography (LeBlanc, Davidson, Ryu, & Irwin, 2015; Scott, 2014; Warren & Parker, 2005), and I become curious about its potential to support more integrative ways of being in teaching and learning. Situated within a/r/tography, and drawing from it connections to self-study and *currere*, I explore this methodological bricolage as a way to foster wholeness – within self, and in relation with others – as we continue on our educative journeys.

© KONINKLIJKE BRILL NV, LEIDEN, 2018 | DOI:10.1163/9789004388901_001

Locating Sel(f)ves

FIGURE 1.1   "Reflective self"
(photograph by B. Barrell)

A self is a work of art perpetually in process – sometimes beautiful and, other times, quite messy. I often think of it as I do still photography: one moment captured perfectly in all its complexity – both seeing and seen – vanished by the time the image is processed. Nonetheless, at each stage of negotiated existence, it matters. This dynamic and ever-evolving self is revealed differently with each new exposure. And so it is with teaching and learning: our thoughts, feelings, assumptions, and experiences all inform who we are. Yet, inexplicably, education continues to marginalize the self. In so doing, it champions fragmented and fractured ways of knowing and being. Seeking to heal the fissures in my spirit born of dehumanized, decontextualized, often aesthetically sterile approaches to education, I moved toward my own teaching career determined to foster space for humanness. I encountered Parker Palmer's work (1993, 1997, 1998) and found immense pedagogical resonance. For more than 25 years, Palmer has made self a central tenet in education by insisting that reducing teaching to an exclusively intellectual practice relegates it to abstraction just the same as making it solely emotional renders it narcissistic:

> Intellect, emotion, and spirit depend on each other for wholeness. They are interwoven in the human self and in education at its best, and we need to interweave them in our pedagogical discourse as well. (Palmer, 1998, p. 2)

He argues that good teachers weave together self, student, and subject to teach from an undivided place; doing so, he says, encourages a capacity for connectedness where disconnectedness currently reigns. Palmer (1993) introduced the notion of *disconnectedness* as a form of disengagement that occurs when we feel detached from our learning. In his later work, he discusses in some detail four specific stages of disconnectedness (Palmer, 1998, 2004). The first stage is marked by sense of spiritual leave-taking, which results when we feel estranged from our learning but we continue to endure it. Freire (1976) discussed this crisis in terms of *integration* versus *adaptation*. He explained that integration respects learners as subjects and encourages them to negotiate knowledge with respect to their lived experiences. Adaptation, by comparison, positions students as objects and focuses on teaching often abstracted (interpretation of) facts. Freire insisted that schools prioritize adaptation and, in so doing, enslave students by method of education.

The second stage of disconnection is communal and sees individuals who are determined to live connected lives seek contexts that promote and enable it (Palmer, 1998, 2017). These contexts often involve the establishment of networks that can disrupt feelings of alienation and help break the progression of further fragmentation. People who continue to feel disconnected move toward the third stage of disconnection where they take their frustration to a public sphere and encourage others to do the same, hoping to mobilize change. In addition to educating themselves and others to disrupt damaging practices, they often engage in what Freire (1976) called *praxis dialogue*. This effort, perhaps, marks the most important stage in seeking re-engagement as it requires that students and teachers overcome their often polarised roles. It also leads to the fourth and final stage of disconnection – re-engagement through critical reflection and deliberate action.

The key to avoiding the slippery slope of disconnection rests in recognizing that meaningful education is contingent upon practices that respect identity and integrity of teachers and learners. Palmer (2017) describes identity as the evolving nexus of intersectionality and lived experience, and he says integrity is what wholeness we can find within that nexus as we continue to re/negotiate who we are. He concedes that this is ground not easily won as acknowledging how the personal informs the professional comes with vulnerability. Unable to see my personal and my professional selves as separate, I found his discussion of unhelpful binaries valuable. He explains that education is filled with inconsistencies because of our tendency to think in polarities. In positioning parts of self and experience as dichotomous, we create fragmentation: head/ heart; facts/feelings; theory/practice; and personal/professional. He argues that we need to champion practices that breed wholeness if we are to live with integrity. He reminds us that the culture of disconnection is driven partly by fear and partly by the Western notion that disconnection is a virtue. Knowing I must challenge this dominant discourse, and seeking to foster space for the wholeness from which good teaching and learning emerges, I stumbled upon Irwin (2013) who also problematizes *dueling binaries* but does so through a/r/ tography by drawing attention to the spaces in between polarities.

Wading in to A/R/Tography

I have long been interested in a/r/tography. I love the notion that engaging with it means we are engaging with each other – fostering a relational pedagogy while untangling connections between theory and practice, art and text, you and me. Teachers are not often encouraged to develop as artists or researchers but a/r/tography creates a space where we can weave together the intellectual and aesthetic aspects of self that shape a teaching life (MacKenzie & Wolf, 2012). The focus remains on the practice, not the product, so there is no requirement to be an accomplished artist. Like Suomimem (2003), the photographs that I work with are the ones willing to have a conversation with me. They are not the most beautiful images I've taken but they represent a composite of performative and essential selves while supporting the living process of meaning making. In working to overcome disconnection, my camera has been my voice when I could not speak. In this way, like Winton (2016), I understand photography as initiating a kind of dialogue that provides access to things deeply held while supporting multiple ways of meaning making. Its visual form does not pretend singular authority, but encourages dynamic embodied understandings not only between art and text, and each other, but also among the various artist/researcher/teacher (a/r/t) identities held within. Rather than positioning these identities in opposition with each other, the a/r/tographer understands these tenets as living in concert with one another. It is here that I find my entry point. Thinking through

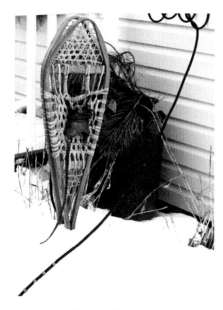

disconnection, both Palmer's work and that which is personally experienced, I find myself wondering about those selves we portray at work and the ones waiting for us to return. I've come to understand these in my own mind as performative and essential selves. The performative self is the public me: the woman masquerading as an extrovert as she goes about the business of teaching, Dean-ing, researching, and publishing. This is the self who negotiates her way through competing pressures trying not to lose sight of her essential self. In my mind, this self is represented by an image of *tying off*, the practice of securing a rope at home base to help you find your way back when you have

FIGURE 1.2   "Tying off"

to venture out in a storm. The coming back is the return to the *essential self*, that me who grew up on 1000 acres and knows about things like tying off. I respect that performative other as she has worked hard to emerge but I remain more connected to the essential me. As I mature in my practice, and grow more confident in the value of essential selves, I seek ways to bring them to professional contexts. I've done this organically, not really having theorized my practice in this regard. Perhaps that is why I found such resonance with the notion that we can resolve polarities by focusing on the spaces between them (Irwin, 2013).

On *In-Betweenness*

I am drawn to a/r/tography's tendency to shine light on in-between spaces with the hope of disrupting dichotomous and compartmentalized thinking. Like Irwin (2013), I think that focusing on *in-betweenness* helps us to let go of opposing finite states. Focusing on theorizing rather than theory, and practicing rather than practice, for example, bridges the chasm between divergent ways of thinking and doing and leaves in its place a space of relationality and exchange. This approach can be extended to opening up many spaces – not only those manifest between our artist/researcher/teacher selves, but also those gaps permitted to grow between performative and essential selves. By opening

FIGURE 1.3   "In-betweenness"

up these spaces, we collapse binaries and encourage wholeness and integrity in our teaching and learning lives. From this place of wholeness, we gain new insights and expand what is possible for self and self-in-relation both in our classrooms and in the world (Winters, Belliveau, & Sherritt-Fleming, 2009). These insights shift with new understandings as we broaden and deepen experience. A/r/tography, then, encourages a fluid form of research that is made rigorous by this continuous reflexivity and analysis (LeBlanc et al., 2015; Winters et al., 2009).

On Reflexivity

A teaching life, while deeply meaningful, can also be marked by feelings of disconnection. A/r/tography helps create connections within and among individuals. It
does so by fostering reflexivity. At its most basic, reflexivity refers to the researcher's consciousness of her role in and effect on both the act of doing research and
its eventual findings. Unlike reflection, reflexive inquiry compels us to engage
in critical introspection in the moment, as well as after it, while simultaneously
critiquing our socio-political contexts (Creswell, 2006; Hara, 2010; Hickey, 2016;
Langer, 2016; Roebuck, 2007; Zinn et al., 2016). Said another way, "reflection is
after and *individual* whereas reflexivity is *ongoing* and *relational*" (Lyle, 2017, p.
vii). Through practicing reflexivity, "we become *responsible* and *accountable* for
our choices, our actions, and our contributions to a relational system" (Oliver,
2004, p. 127). In making central the role of the researcher in the research process,
reflexivity demands at least two things: it interrogates agency by questioning if
there is a critically astute individual leading the research inquiry; and it raises
philosophical notions about the nature of knowledge. By its very design, then,
reflexivity disrupts normalized assumptions about how we come to knowledge
and presents essential questions about our capacities as artists/researchers/
teachers to account for an ever-evolving understanding of our experiences. This
understanding resides in a humanizing pedagogy and has as its goal facilitation
of re/humanisation and appreciation of perspective diversity (Lyle, 2017).

When I think of reflexivity, I see an old-fashioned, hot water radiator. I am
the second daughter of a farmer and a teacher and spent my first nine years
on our family farm – a large acreage for the time with a modest three-bedroom

FIGURE 1.4   "Monet's Radiator" painted by NB artist Gerard Collins

farm house as it nucleus. We spent much of our recreational time outdoors and, given six months of the year saw snow on the ground, the old radiators in the house became gathering spots to warm chilly fingers and frosty noses. It was several years later as I asked students to complete an identity assignment using metaphor that it occurred to me my metaphor was that radiator. I could be found along the periphery of the room, but only if you looked for me as I preferred to blend in. Unassuming, I worked to ensure people around me were comfortable, and I generally hummed along quite quietly, content to do my job. Occasionally, though, the demands of my job gave rise to increasing pressure and I'd start to thump and bang a bit until I was able to release the steam, normally with a little hiss, and then I would dependably resume my quiet warmth. Making this connection helped me to understand myself in a different way – in an integrated way; rather than performative or essential, as that radiator, I was both. I saw, then, that classrooms are not places where individuals discover their identities; rather, classrooms are spaces shaped by multiple identities continuously negotiated (Winters, Belliveau, & Sherritt-Fleming, 2009).

On Letting Go

Redirecting my attention to liminal spaces and reconceptualizing sel(f)ves through reflexivity reminds me of the importance of letting go. This gentle shedding is assisted by finding meditative spaces where I can hear my essential self

FIGURE 1.5   "Shedding"

and grapple with issues that reveal themselves. I've come to understand this process as reconstructing a self that might be feeling a bit disassembled. I am in one such space now, wondering if my essential self is as present in my professional practice as is necessary. Weighed down by the administrative demands of my everyday tasks, I've been unable to think and write for weeks. As I have learned to do at such times, I pack a bag and head to the shore. As I sit in my big leather chair soaking up the expanse of land and water, I feel myself reconnecting with every iteration of myself that I have ever been and all those me's I've not yet grown into. I've heard people say that home is not a place so much as a feeling we carry in our hearts, but either my feelings are too big or my heart is too small because I cannot carry with me all I feel here. I can hear myself – the inner wisdom that is lost in the hum of doing when I am elsewhere .... Drawn to the shore as though by magic, I recall reading in my youth about the red thread of fate and wonder once again if my soul connection is to place, rather than person.

FIGURE 1.6   "Red thread"

Having heard the invitation to exo(e)rcise, I traded my recliner for my barefoot runners and found myself walking the expanse of lawn to where the grass gives way to sand. A vanishing point, really, where what was and what might be converge. As I turn east toward the point, I pick up my pace and settle into an easy run. Unhealthy habits of thought fall away with each step or, rather, are released – consciously and deliberately. With each footfall, it seems, another barrier to wholeness enters my mind. It stands before my inner teacher for assessment and is asked what it contributes. Bringing hindrance rather than help, it is released.

By the end of my run, I feel lighter for the purge. I drop gait as I close in on the last stretch of beach before me and turn north toward my mediation stone. I settle cross legged, my face turned to the sun and eyes closed, as I rejoin that place where the gulls welcome me home and salt air blows the cobwebs from my soul.

Possibilities for Wholeness

Seeking ways to overcome the culture of disconnectedness often pervasive in education, I turned to a/r/tography to explore ways that teachers and learners could feel *authentic* and *present* in their educative experiences. Wading gently into this still emerging approach, I've come to understand a/r/tography as a reflexive methodology that emphasizes a living inquiry. The site for inquiry is often the liminal spaces between tenets traditionally cast as binaries and it has as its aim the creation of a fluid process that, when engaged, allows researchers to re/negotiate meaning in the context of lived and living experience. This approach is both individual and communal as artists/researchers/teachers open up and move dynamically between spaces where meaning is de/re/constructed in a way that conceptualizes meaning as "alive – always moving, always growing ... infinite and in-process" (Winters, Belliveau, & Sherritt-Fleming, 2009, p. 8). Moved by the possibilities for embodied wholeness, I wondered how we might bring such approaches into educational institutions. I recall the notion of wholeness appearing in discussions of *currere* (Aoki, 1993; Irwin, 2004; Pinar & Grumet, 1976). I found resonance in problematizing *curriculum as plan* and favoured positioning *curriculum as process* (Aoki, 1986/2005). Curriculum as plan is static, outcome-driven, and often abstracted. Curriculum as process is dynamic and contextual. Congruent with its etymological root, currere (meaning to run) requires movement. Teaching and learning in the spirit of *currere* causes us to rethink curriculum as organic and relational. It requires that we account for self and self-in-relation as we negotiate meaning (Pinar, Reynolds, Slattery, & Taubman, 1995; Powell & Lajevic, 2011; Sameshima, 2008). Said another way, *currere* is "a complicated conversation with oneself ... an ongoing project of self-understanding with the aim of mobilized action" (Pinar, 2004, p. 37). There are openings, then, in both *currere* and a/r/tography, as they invite us to explore our lived and living experiences in often unexpected ways. In this way, each is an artefact of the other and both are improvisational. In so being, they cannot help but engender pedagogical possibilities.

Acknowledgements

I would like to acknowledge New Brunswick artist, Gerard Collins, for his talented completion of "Monet's Radiator." I also extend sincere appreciation to Germaine Pataki-Thériault of Gallery 78 in Fredericton for her introduction to Gerard as well as her good humour in providing the "canvas" for completion. Finally, my gratitude to Glenn Hall who supported Gerard's work. Monet's Radiator remains an installation at Gallery 78.

References

Aoki, T. T. (1986/2005). Teaching as in-dwelling between two curriculum worlds. In W. F. Pinar & R. L. Irwin (Eds.), *Curriculum in a new key: The collected works of Ted T. Aoki* (pp. 159–165). Mahwah, NJ: Lawrence Erlbaum Associates.

Aoki, T. T. (1993). Legitimating lived curriculum: Towards a curricular landscape of multiplicity. *Journal of Curriculum and Supervision, 8*(3), 255–268.

Creswell, J. W. (2006). *Qualitative inquiry and research design: Choosing among five approaches*. Thousand Oaks, CA: Sage Publications.

Freire, P. (1976). *Education: The practice of freedom*. London: Writers & Readers.

Hara, B. (2010). *Reflexive pedagogy*. Retrieved from http://www.chronicle.com/blogs/profhacker/reflexive-pedagogy/22939

Hickey, A. (2016). The critical aesthetic: Living a critical ethonography of the everyday. In S. Steinberg & G. Cannella (Eds.), *Critical qualitative research reader* (pp. 166–181). New York, NY: Peter Lang.

Irwin, R. L. (2013). Becoming a/r/tography. *Studies in Art Education, 54*(3), 198–215.

Kooy, M., & de Freitas, E. (2007). The diaspora sensibility in teacher identity: Locating self through story. *Canadian Journal of Education, 30*(3), 865–880.

Langer, P. C. (2016). The research vignette: Reflexive writing as interpretative representation of qualitative inquiry: A methodological proposition. *Qualitative Inquiry, 22*(9), 735–744.

Leblanc, N., Davidson, S., Ryu, J., & Irwin, R. (2015). Becoming through a/r/tography, autobiography and stories in motion. *International Journal of Education through Art, 11*(3), 355–374.

Lyle, E. (2017). *Of books, barns, and boardrooms: Exploring praxis through reflexive inquiry* (2nd ed.). Rotterdam, The Netherlands: Sense Publishers.

MacKenzie, S. K., & Wolf, M. M. (2012). Layering sel(f)ves: Finding acceptance, community and praxis through collage. *The Qualitative Report, 17*(16), 1–21.

Oliver, C. (2004). Reflexive inquiry and the strange loop tool. *Journal of Systemic Consultation and Management, 15*(2), 127–140.

Palmer, P. (1993). *To know as we are known*. San Francisco, CA: Harper Collins.

Palmer, P. (1997). The heart of a teacher: Identity and integrity in teaching. *Change, 29*(6), 14–21.

Palmer, P. (1998). *The courage to teach*. San Francisco, CA: Jossey-Bass.

Palmer, P. (2004). *A hidden wholeness: The journey toward an undivided life*. San Francisco, CA: Jossey-Bass.

Palmer, P. (2017). *The courage to teach*. San Francisco, CA: Jossey-Bass.

Pinar, W. F. (2004). *What is curriculum theory?* Mahwah, NJ: Lawrence Erlbaum Associates.

Pinar, W. F., & Grumet, M. (1976). *Toward a poor curriculum*. Dubuque, IA: Kendall/ Hunt.

Pinar, W. F., Reynolds, W. M., Slattery, P., & Taubman, P. M. (1995). *Understanding curriculum: An introduction to the study of historical and contemporary curriculum discourses*. New York, NY: Peter Lang.

Powell, K., & Lajevic, L. (2011). Emergent places in preservice art teaching: Lived curriculum, relationality, and embodied knowledge. *Studies in Art Education, 53*(1), 35–52.

Richardson, L., & St. Pierre, E. (2005). *Writing: A method of inquiry*. In N. K. Denzin & Y. S. Lincoln (Eds.), *Handbook of qualitative research* (3rd ed., pp. 959–978). Thousand Oaks, CA: Sage Publications.

Roebuck, J. (2007). Reflexive practice: To enhance student learning. *Journal of Learning Design, 2*(1), 77–91.

Sameshima, P. (2008). Letters to a new teacher: A curriculum of embodied aesthetic awareness. *Teacher Education Quarterly, 35*(2), 29–44.

Scott, L. (2014). "Digging deep": Self-study as a reflexive approach to improving my practice as an artist, researcher and teacher. *Perspectives in Education, 32*(2), 69–88.

Suominen, A. (2003). *Writing with photographs, re-constructing self: An arts-based autoethnographic inquiry* (Unpublished doctoral dissertation). The Ohio State University, Columbus, OH.

Warren, S., & Parker, L. (2009). Bean counters or bright young things? *Qualitative Research in Accounting and Management, 6*(4), 205–223.

Winters, K., Belliveau, G., & Sherritt-Fleming, L. (2009). Shifting identities, literacy, and a/r/tography: Exploring an educational theatre company. *Language and Literacy, 11*(1), 1–19.

Winton, A. (2016). Using photography as a creative, collaborative research tool. *The Qualitative Report, 21*(2), 428–449.

Zinn, D., Adam, K., Kurup, R., & du Plessis, A. (2016). Returning to the source: Reflexivity and transformation in understanding a humanising pedagogy. *Educational Research for Social Change, 5*(1), 70–93.

CHAPTER 2

Butterflies in the Knapsack: An Exploration of a Teacher's Identity

Julie K. Corkett

Who am I as a teacher? This is such a simple question, yet formulating a response is very challenging. Part of the challenge to answering the question is that my identity as a teacher did not begin when I had my first teaching position nor did it commence when I entered a Bachelor of Education degree program. My teacher identity began to form when I was in elementary school. This speaks to the fact that identity is multifaceted and formed through: social, cultural, political, historical contexts; relationships with others; emotions; and the construction and reconstruction of meaning through stories (Moss & Pittaway, 2013; Rodgers & Scott, 2008; Yuan & Lee, 2016). By reflecting on my experience as I student, I discovered that my identity as a teacher was formulated by my theories, attitudes, and beliefs about my self (Beijaard, Meijer, & Verloop, 2004). More specifically, I have come to realize that my identity as a teacher is a multidimensional construct formulated by the emotions I experienced as a student and the relationship between those emotions and my self-concept, self-esteem, and self-efficacy.

Therefore, in order for me to answer the question, *who am I as a teacher*, I must first explore the construction-deconstruction-reconstruction of the emotions that informed my identity as a student. Using an autoethnographic narrative I will "retrospectively and selectively write about epiphanies that stem from" or were "made possible by," processing the emotions associated with my experiences as a student (Ellis, Adams, & Bochner, 2011, p. 3). Using the analogy of a butterfly, I will explain how the intertwining relationship of the emotions associated with self-concept, self-efficacy, and self-esteem, influenced my identity as a student, which, in turn, formulated my identity as a teacher.

The Egg

The life of a butterfly begins with an egg, the source of life. Within the protective shell of my family I began to develop my identity by formulating a concept of who I am. Self-concept is a composite view that is formed through one's experience within any given environment and through the reinforcements and evaluative feedback received by significant others (Bong & Skaalvik, 2003). My parents, siblings, family members, and friends provided me with the nutrients needed to formulate and develop my self-concept. Under the loving and supportive gaze of my family I was encouraged in all of my endeavours, no matter how small. I was applauded when taking my first steps. When I fell, I was encouraged to try again. I was taught that each mistake was just a necessary step in my growth and development. Within this process, self-concept was being formed through the causal attributions to which I ascribed my successes and failures (Bong & Skaalvic, 2003). The fact that my parents perceived both my successes and failures as positive experiences enabled me to further develop a constructive self-concept.

My mother is very fond of telling me how, when I was told that I was too young to learn to ride a two wheeled bicycle, that I promptly set out to prove my parents wrong. My mother said that she watched from the kitchen window as I walked my bicycle up to the picnic table and aligned the bike with the bench. Using the bench as a support, I balanced myself on the bicycle, and pushed off from the bench. Teetering precariously I would only manage a single pump of the wheel before I fell. Day after day my mother stood at the window and watched me fall, until one day I was riding the bicycle across the backyard. I never doubted for a moment that I would be successful in my endeavour. By the time I left for my first day of school, I had a very secure perception of who I was as a person. I believed that I was capable of completing any task set before me, that I was as capable as my peers, and that I had something of value to contribute. I felt happy, loved, and capable of taking on the world. With this knowledge in place, I broke free of the protective shell of my familiar surroundings and set out to explore new experiences.

The Caterpillar

Once self-concept is formulated within a given environment, a person breaks free from the safety of the egg to explore new experiences. It is self-concept that influences the behaviour that one exhibits within these new experiences (Shavelson, Hubner, & Stanton, 1976). Like the caterpillar, that voraciously seeks the nutrients of leaves to grow and develop, individuals seek new learning experiences to feed their untried self-concept. The problem solving process that occurs while exploring new surroundings enables us to gather information about our environment and ourselves (Grotevant, 1992). During this time of exploration an infinite amount of information about one's self is collected as both affective and cognitive outcomes are encountered. Self-assessment of the qualities that we perceive as important or psychologically central to identity constitutes self-esteem (Bong & Skaalvic, 2003). Self-esteem is born of evaluation and reaction to perception of self (Rosenberg, 1965; Zimmerman, 2000). It is through our interactions with new experiences that we determine whether we feel positively or negatively about our selves (Coelho, Marachante, & Jimerson, 2017). Thus, self-esteem impacts our self-concept, for it is through our initial knowledge of our selves and our emotional reactions to our competencies and attributes that our self-concept is substantiated (Bong & Skaalvic, 2003; Shavelson et al., 1976).

When I left for my first day of school, I had self-concept clarity, which means that I had a clear, internally consistent, temporally stable, and confidently defined self-concept (Campbell, Assanand, & Di Paula, 2003). However, during my first year in school, my self-concept was challenged. In Grade 1 I began to realize that, in terms of reading, I was different from my classmates, and I no longer felt that I was capable of taking on any task. This feeling was intensified during Grade 3. I was terrified of my Grade 3 teacher. Her last name contained the word "red" and I always associated her with blood. I had the strong impression that she didn't like me and that she thought I was stupid. It was her actions, more than her words, which formulated my perception. I can remember sitting at my desk completing a worksheet. The worksheet contained pictures of nouns and under each picture was the written name of the noun. One of the words was 'parrot' and I was supposed to write down the number of syllables in the word and insert a slash to divide the syllables. As I have a phonological processing deficit, which means that I cannot process the sounds in words, I was unable to determine the number of syllables. I tentatively raised my hand to ask for assistance. Ms. Red came up to my desk, made a fist and pounded heavily and forcefully on my desk. In a sharp tone she shouted, "Par – Rot." I was so startled and frightened by the force of her fist hitting my desk and the sharpness of her voice that I jumped back and nearly fell to the floor. Despite my fear, all I can remember thinking was, "Ok, the answer is two." I guarantee you, I never asked her or any other teacher for help again. As a result of this experience, my self-esteem became unstable and my concept of self was shaken to the point that I no longer believed that I was a capable student or that people wanted to me to contribute to the task at hand. The classroom had become a place of fear.

The Chrysalis

Our positive and negative interactions spin around us until eventually, hidden from view within a chrysalis, we begin to reflect, internalize, and consolidate our perceptions of self as evidenced by self-efficacy. While self-concept is an individual's general perception of self that incorporates many forms of self-knowledge and self-evaluative feelings (self-esteem), self-efficacy is an individual's expectation and conviction that she will be able to organize and execute the courses of action required to complete a given task at the desired level of outcome (Bandura, 1977; Bong & Skaalvic, 2003). Furthermore, if we believe that we are able to accomplish a task we will be more likely to initiate the required amount of effort and persist when faced with adversity (Bandura, 1977; Kim & Lorsback, 2005; Tschannen-Moran & Hoy, 2001). Thus, the intertwining of individual and contextual factors influences the formation of our self-efficacy.

Self-efficacy is developed through the entwining of personal accomplishments, vicarious experiences, verbal persuasion, and physiological arousal (Bandura, 1977; Fall & McLeod, 2001; Hoy & Spero, 2005; Schunk, 2003). The more personal accomplishments we experience, the more likely we are to believe that we are capable of completing similar tasks in the future. When encountering new situations, one's self-efficacy may be influenced by noting how a peer, who is perceived as possessing similar abilities, succeeds with the task (Shunk, 2003). In addition, as with self-concept, the verbal persuasion we receive from our parents, teachers, and peers also influences our self-efficacy (Shunk, 2003). Finally, physiological arousal (e.g., sweaty palms and racing heart rate) serves as a physical indicator that suggests we may lack the skills to successfully complete the task.

The challenge is separating what one perceives as proof of one's ability from actual fact. In Grade 5 I completed a project on leaves. We were required to collect leaves from around the neighbourhood and identify the name and type of tree. I collected a wide variety of leaves and, rather than making a scrapbook, I drew a tree on bristle board and pasted the leaves onto the tree. I carefully drew a line under each leaf and wrote the name and type of tree the leaf was from. I was very proud of my project, and I couldn't wait to show my teacher. However, I didn't receive the acclamation that I was expecting. When I submitted my assignment, the teacher took one look at it and said in a flat and accusatory tone, "obviously your mother did this for you." I received a C+. As I walked home from school that day, I realized that there was no point in trying to be successful at school because teachers controlled my fate. I learned to keep my emotions tightly bound within my cocoon believing that, if I kept my emotions contained, I couldn't be hurt.

Being put down by my teachers continued throughout my education. In high school I was not permitted to read Shakespeare because it was deemed to be too difficult for me. Yet, one day in Grade 10, I came across the class set of *Julius Caesar* in graphic novel format. I removed one of the comics off the shelf, took it to my desk, and started to read it. When my English teacher came into the classroom and saw what I was reading, she very sharply said, "Put that back! That is too difficult for you." As degrading as this experience was, I think one of the worst hits to my self-efficacy came in Grade 11. All of the Grade 11 students came together to watch the French animated film, *Animal Farm*. The movie had been on for about 15 minutes – enough time for the film to pique my interest – when suddenly a loud accusatory voice was heard from the doorway. "What is she doing here? She can't possibly understand this film." I turned to see my French teacher standing at the door pointing her finger at me. In front of all my peers, I was marched out of the room.

Through these experiences and many others I felt that, compared to my peers, I was incapable of completing academic tasks. I learned to never raise my hand and to keep my head and eyes down. If I ever did try to participate, my heart raced, my voice quivered, and I could feel the blood draining from my face. The physical symptoms were generated from my belief that I really wasn't capable of participating in the given task. As a result, I would constantly worry that my peers and teachers would laugh at me, reject me, and humiliate me. The combination of feeling incapable of completing a task at a satisfactory level and the negative emotions associated with my low self-esteem conflicted with my self-concept of who I truly believed I was – a capable, strong person.

The Butterfly

When the butterfly emerges from the chrysalis its new identity is formed. The butterfly's wings are damp, wrinkled, and unsure. How quickly the butterfly is able to shake off the dampness, stretch out its wings, and fly after emerging from the chrysalis is determined by its self-concept, self-esteem, and self-efficacy. Like the hemolymph that is pumped through the butterfly's wings to strengthen them, when undertaking a task, it is self-efficacy that determines how much effort individuals will initiate and the extent to which they will persist when faced with obstacles and adverse situations (Bandura, 1977; Kim & Lorsbach, 2005; Tschannen-Moran & Hoy, 2001). The variety and vivaciousness of the colour in the butterfly's wings parallels the number of situations in which the individual has strong self-esteem and self-concept. If the butterfly's wings are strong and consist of a vibrant rainbow of colour, it is more likely that the eggs it will lay in new situations will continue to produce colourful and strong butterflies. However, if the butterfly's wings are weak, and lack variety of colour or vibrancy, the butterfly's self-concept, self-esteem, and self-efficacy are weak. This dull butterfly will lay very few eggs. Some of these eggs will lack the nutrients needed to generate a positive self-concept and, as a result, identity will not be realized and it will shrivel and die. The remaining eggs will hatch, but the emerging caterpillar will carry the weakness and scars of the parent. Some of these weak caterpillars may gain strength if they are hatched within an environment filled with positive nutrients. However, if the caterpillar finds itself in a hostile environment that it perceives as threatening, it will develop and maintain debilitating expectations and fears, which may eventually lead to a state of helplessness (Bandura, 1977; Chapman, 1988; Kim & Lorsbach, 2005).

It was during my Grade 12 year that I began to think in earnest what I would do once I graduated from high school. My parents encouraged me to apply to college but, based on my school experiences, I did not feel that I was capable of such an academic undertaking. From within my reflexive cocoon, I spent the year trying to identify factual evidence that I was truly incapable of such an academic task. Through reflection I began to realize that my perception of self was based on how others viewed me and not based on my own personal assessment. With this in mind, I took the risk and applied to a General Arts and Science program at a local community college.

It was my acceptance to college that enabled me to slowly emerge as a butterfly. I had always been led to believe that only smart and capable people were accepted to college and university. Therefore, if I had been accepted, then I must be smart and capable. I remember telling my Grade 12 English teacher that I had been accepted to college. She replied, "Wow; that is a fantastic accomplishment for you! You must be proud." Since my colours, at this point, were dull and my wings were weak, I interpreted her well-meaning praise as, "that is a surprising accomplishment for *you*." Immediately, my identity was shaken and my self-doubt returned. I felt that my accomplishment was inadequate compared to my peers who would be attending university.

Unbeknown to me at the time, I was engaging with my possible selves. Possible selves theory holds that future self-projections are closely connected with our current self and stems from one's desires, hopes, reservations, and fears, which are influenced by past and current social, cultural, and environmental experiences (Mahmoudi-Gahrouei, Tavakoli, & Hamman, 2016, p. 583). Specifically, possible selves theory

> plays an important role in understanding the dimensions of individual's self-regulation of goal directed behaviour during life transitions, and possible selves represent what persons would like to become – "hoped-for selves," what persons could become – "expected selves," and what person are afraid of becoming – "feared selves." According to possible selves theory, expected selves are vital to behavioural adaptation. Moreover, possible selves theory suggests that feared selves are instrumental in continuance of behavioural adaptation. (Mahmoudi-Gahrouei et al., 2016, p. 582)

My hoped-for self wanted to be a post-secondary student and my expected-self believed that I was capable of accomplishing the task. However, my feared-self was petrified that I would encounter more terrifying teachers and that I would once again be told that I was inadequate. Luckily my self-concept reinforced my expected-self, and I was able to silence my feared-self and attend college.

My ensuing years at college and university were spent battling the feelings of inadequacy that were instilled within me by my teachers. Whenever I felt overwhelmed by these negative feelings of inadequacy, I would return to my reflective cocoon. Within the safety of my chrysalis I would honestly reflect on what I had accomplished to date, and I would imagine different selves, some expected (graduating from college/university) and some feared (being kicked out because I wasn't good enough). With these selves in mind I would compare my accomplishments against what my past teachers said I would be able to do. By acknowledging that I had already accomplished more than what my teachers had led me to believe was possible, I was able to become a strong butterfly.

The Lepidopterist

My years as a student eventually led me to the teaching profession and informed my identity as a teacher. It has been argued that when teacher candidates enter into teacher training programs their perception of what it means to be a teacher is formed through their life history as students (Furlong, 2013). As a student, I believed that a teacher was an individual who was an expert in her subject area, could answer (without hesitation) all questions posed to them, instinctively knew exactly what every student needs, and was the ultimate authority in the classroom. However, when asked, why did you become a teacher? I realized that it was not because I felt I was an expert or an authority. It was because I wanted to confront the emotions I experienced as a student and ensure that future students were spared similar negative feelings about themselves. Due to this desire, I found myself in the role of the lepidopterist that ensures the cycle of egg, caterpillar, and butterfly is able to thrive. Creating and sustaining a balanced emotionally supportive ecosystem is the challenge that every good teacher faces. Like lepidopterists, I sometimes experience success and, other times despite creating the best possible ecosystem, the student under my care fails to complete its transformation into a butterfly.

When I think back to the time when I was teaching in a small rural community, I recall a very sweet little girl in my Grade 4 class. She was blonde, blue-eyed, soft spoken, and gentle-natured. While she was not outgoing, she did participate in all subjects – except for math. As soon as it was time for math she completely shut down to the point that she would not even take her books out of her desk. Her student records and consultation with past teachers did not provide great insight, so I called her parents. I was hoping to gain some understanding as to the source of her behaviour. Perhaps she had moved frequently and had not obtained the fundamentals in math. Perhaps she had a math teacher who had frightened her. I was shocked by her mother's response to my concerns, "Don't worry," she calmly replied. "She doesn't need math. My daughter is beautiful and will marry a doctor." Shocked at this response, I kept hoping the mother would say it was a joke, but she was serious. I realized that, for this little girl, it was up to me to help her emerge from the chrysalis in which she was firmly planted. It took until Christmas to get her to take out her math books and write down questions. Starting with the most basic of math equations (e.g., 1+1), it took me the rest of year to get her to attempt the most elementary mathematical concepts. Each night I metaphorically brought the girl home with me. I reflected on the negative experiences I had with teachers, and I was determined not to be another teacher who disappointed students. I knew first hand the life long impact a teacher can have on a student's identity. Every small breakthrough I had with the student, I claimed as a success. Each failure left me wondering if I really had what it takes to be a teacher.

I learned from this experience that students who remain within the safety of their egg must be encouraged to perceive the teacher as a source of nutrients and not as a hostile environment. Once this is accomplished, the teacher can begin to encourage the student to slowly emerge from the egg. This Grade 4 student taught me that, during this emergence process, it is essential for the student not be overwhelmed by too much praise. As when I was a student, too much praise may cause the student to ask: "Is it that you really did not expect that I would be able to succeed?" Praise can generate the perception that the student is receiving praise because every action is an outstanding accomplishment rather than something that she was always capable of accomplishing. Like the caterpillar that is exposed too long to the sun, when people receive too much praise, they begin to question why every task is praise worthy and their identity can begin to shrivel and die.

I went from this Grade 4 classroom to teaching high school. There I met another troubled student who confirmed for me that a teacher's identity is not based solely on their knowledge of pedagogy, but on their ability to emotionally nurture their students. During spring report card time, I was in the computer lab completing report cards. There was a knock on the door. When I looked up one of my Grade 9 students was tentatively peering into the room and holding a single rose. I joked that she had come to bribe me but, when she looked into my eyes, I knew that she had something serious to say. Sitting beside me she told me that the previous night she had taken her dog for a walk in the bush. She had found a nice spot to sit down and kill herself. The only reason she didn't, she informed me, was because she thought of me and knew that I would be disappointed. She then handed me the rose and said, "thank you." To this day I have tried to figure out exactly what I had done to impact her in such a powerful way. In the end, I have come to realize that there was nothing specific. It was the emotionally nurturing environment that I created every day with my words and small gentle gestures that made the difference. It was because the essence of my identity as a teacher was to ensure that I placed a student's self-concept, self-esteem, and self-efficacy ahead of academic performance. Because of this tendency, my student believed that she had value and had the resilience to face the hardships in her life.

Conclusion

Through the stories about my relationships with my teachers, the emotions I experienced in their classrooms, and my experiences as a classroom teacher, I have established my identity as a teacher. The positive and negative emotions that challenged, modified, and supported my self-concept, self-esteem, self-efficacy all played contributing roles in forming that identity. While my self-esteem and self-efficacy within the classroom were always low, leaving me with feelings of inadequacy, I was able to overcome the negative emotions because I knew those feelings did not match my possible self (Mahmoudi-Gahrouei et al., 2016). Based on my experiences as a student, I knew that as a teacher, I wanted to ensure that my students did not experience the negativity that I did. By providing my students with an emotionally nurturing environment, I try to ensure that my students will become goal directed individuals who are able to overcome their fearful selves thereby enabling them to emerge as butterflies whose colourful strong wings are reflections their own resilient identities. As a teacher I recognize that my students come to school with butterflies in all stages of development. Several students' arrive in the classroom as colourful vibrant butterflies; some are butterflies with dull and weak colours; and a few students remain trapped within their chrysalis. The colourful butterflies of the students with strong identities burst forth and fill the classroom, but the students who have weak butterflies or who are firmly embedded within their chrysalis need a lepidopterist who knows how to bring forth the butterfly and enable it to take flight. I am that lepidopterist.

References

Bandura, A. (1977). Self-efficacy: Toward a unifying theory of behavioural change. *Psychological Review, 84*(2), 191–215.

Beijaard, D., Meijer, P. C., & Verloop, N. (2004). Reconsidering research on teachers' professional identity. *Teaching and Teacher Education, 20*(2), 107–128.

Bong, M., & Skaalvik, E. M. (2003). Academic self-concept and self-efficacy: How different are they really? *Educational Psychology Review, 15*(1), 1–40.

Campbell, J. D., Assanand, S., & Di Paula, A. (2003). The structure of the self-concept and its relation to psychological adjustment. *Journal of Personality, 71*(1), 115–140.

Chapman, J. W. (1988). Cognitive-motivational characteristics and academic achievement of learning disabled children: A longitudinal study. *Journal of Educational Psychology, 80*(3), 357–365.

Coelho, V. A., Marchante, M., & Jimerson, S. R. (2017). Promoting a positive middle school transition: A randomized controlled treatment study examining self-concept and self-esteem. *Journal of Youth and Adolescence, 46*(3), 558–569.

Ellis, C., Adams, T. E., & Bochner, A. P. (2011). Autoethnography: An overview. *Forum: Qualitative Social Research, 12*(1), 1–14.

Fall, M., & McLeod, E. H. (2001). Identifying and assisting children with low self efficacy. *Professional School Counseling, 4*(5), 334–341.

Furlong, C. (2013). The teacher I wish to be: Exploring the influences of life histories on student teacher idealized identities. *European Journal of Teacher Education, 36*(1), 68–83.

Grotevant, H. D. (1992). Assigned and chosen identity components: A process perspective on their integration. In G. R. Adams, T. P. Gullotta, & R. Montemayor (Eds.), *Advances in adolescent development* (Vol. 4, pp. 73–90). Thousand Oaks, CA: Sage Publications.

Hoy, A. W., & Spero, R. B. (2005). Changes in teacher efficacy during early years of teaching: A comparison of four measures. *Teaching and Teacher Education, 21*(4), 343–356.

Kim, J. A., & Lorsbach, A. W. (2005). Writing self-efficacy in young children: Issues for the early grades environment. *Learning Environment Research, 8*(2), 157–175.

Mahmoudi-Gahrouei, V., Tavakoli, M., & Hamman, D. (2016). Understanding what is possible across a career: Professional identity development beyond transition to teaching. *Asia Pacific Education Review, 17*(4), 581–597.

Moss, T., & Pittaway, S. (2013). Student identity construction in online teacher education: A narrative life history approach. *International Journal of Qualitative Studies in Education, 26*(8), 1004–1018.

Rodgers, C. R., & Scott, K. H. (2008). The development of the personal self and professional identity in learning to teach. In M. Cochran-Smith & S. Nemser-Freiman (Eds.), *Handbook of research on teacher education: Enduring questions in changing contexts* (3rd ed., pp. 732–755). New York, NY: Routledge.

Rosenberg, M. (1965). *Society and the adolescent self-image.* Princeton, NJ: Princeton University Press.

Schunk, D. H. (2003). Self-efficacy for reading and writing: Influence of modeling, goal setting, and self-evaluation. *Reading & Writing Quarterly, 19*(2), 159–172.

Shavelson, R. J., Hubner, J. J., & Stanton, G. C. (1976). Self-concept: Validation of construct interpretations. *Review of Educational Research, 46*(3), 407–441.

Tschannen-Moran, M., & Hoy, A. W. (2001). Teacher efficacy: Capturing an elusive construct. *Teaching and Teacher Education, 17*(7), 783–805.

Yuan, R., & Lee, I. (2016). 'I need to be strong and competent': A narrative inquiry of a student-teacher's emotions and identities in teaching practicum. *Teachers and Teaching, 22*(7), 819–841.

Zimmerman, B. J. (2000). Self-efficacy: An essential motive to learn. *Contemporary Educational Psychology, 25*(1), 82–91.

CHAPTER 3

Trumpism, Truthiness, and the Gospel of Education

Sean Wiebe

A Context for Personal-Political Poetry

I am writing as a poet-scholar who practices poetic inquiry as part of my scholarly work (Wiebe, 2015; Yallop, Wiebe, & Faulkner, 2014). A form of life writing (Leggo, Hasebe-Ludt, Sinner, & Chambers, 2012), poetry is a unique means to inquire into the *hows* and *whys* of life. For this reason, I think of poetry as curriculum work in the reconceptualist tradition, which includes coming to better self-knowledge as a critical social act, the base assumption being that the self is a social phenomenon. The contiguous space of self/other is historical, environmental, economic, and political. It is, of course, more than these things, but I name these four intentionally to indicate that a sense of time, a sense of place, and a means of valuing our interactions are political conversations that need to be investigated with different frameworks of understanding.

Remen (2000) writes that our lives are diminished when we are not able to integrate what we believe and how we live. While the poetry in this chapter is personal, having undertaken a process of *currere* in writing these poems, my aim is also political. In the reconceptualist curriculum tradition, *currere* is a four-phase process (Pinar, 2004, 2010) that is instigated by "What keeps us awake at night" (Chambers, 2004). I find such a question a powerful way to prioritize interior reflection. Different than the call to write something vulnerable (Wiebe & Snowber, 2009; Gouzouasis & Ihnatovych, 2016), writing from the late-night place invites us to create from what disturbs us. Is there a question or subject I keep coming back to, that I cannot let go?

From 2011–2017 I kept an electronic diary/journal/notebook using an app called Evernote. The poems that are included as part of this chapter were written from the process of rereading the 1623 notes. The notebook is organized into categories which, at present, are: children's stories; know thyself; lists of recommended books, movies, and bucket list items; meeting notes (conferences, faculty meetings, etc.); mediations, poems, and prayers; quotes; recipes; and teaching. As I began to dig into this process, I realized that the organizational categories were a bit of distraction. I was at first thinking I might use the categories as a clue to the themes of my life, but this proved unhelpful. While it is

© KONINKLIJKE BRILL NV, LEIDEN, 2018 | DOI:10.1163/9789004388901_003

true that I am a teacher, a scholar, and a poet, I don't find these demarcations particularly thematic. I think it is important to underscore that in qualitative research thematic analysis too often falls short of its potential when category headings are simply used to order and provide structure to a frequency of occurrences. The justification that categories are derived from the data doesn't address the central difficulty, that theme (as a concept) ought to be understood narratively and, in this sense, should to be approached within the plotlines and character motivations of the narrative world. This is why I find Chamber's (2004) question so effective: *what keeps us awake at night* provides a reason to tell a story.

Not surprisingly, poetry and narrative share epistemologies and ontologies and oftentimes it is difficult to even tell the difference. After a recent panel session on poetic inquiry and critical media literacy, one of the co-presenters with me, John Weaver, asked me how I approached the question of form. It was a prompt that followed some dinner table conversation where Pauline Sameshima and I presented different arguments for the relatedness of content and form. My understanding of Pauline's position is that form materializes existence. In my mind it is a clever arts-integrated approach to existentialism – existence before essence. In other words, the materiality of our experience is in form and can be re-formed and reformed again in a making process, a process that precedes our understanding, or any essences that we might define from such making processes. My place in the conversation was to suggest that the form I am using (either poetry or narrative) will surface different memories. As part of a curriculum as playlist project (Wiebe et al., 2018), I have been writing poetry about my relationship with my father, but whenever I narrate those same events I have different memories. Here is the text of an email I sent to John.

> I've noticed that while working on a poem certain memories and thoughts surface. My guess would be that I'm looking for a way an image might hold a moment. For me, there is also the juxtaposition, where an image looks forward and back at once, the way a new context or utterance can change a signifier/signified relationship simply by being there. I think this kind of time doubling (tripling?) creates a completely different pathway (porthole?) to experience than when I work in narrative.
>
> These days, when I am narrating an experience, I've been focussed more on the setup or frame; perhaps a better way to say it is, what is the door by which readers will enter the text? What is really going on here and how might it be narrated so the crux of the event materializes in a more felt way? Have you come across Badiou and his notion of a truth event? It

would be what I'm aiming for. All that said, I think this approach to narrative is different from poetry in the way that it accesses experience.

At this point its seems useful to summarize. In writing poetry from the last six years of my life, I have surfaced different kinds of memory than I might have if I were writing a story. The 1623 notes provided the data set, and the data was addressed with the question, "What keeps me awake at night?" In revisiting these notes as a curriculum scholar, I am seeking to understand the phenomenon under investigation by interrogating the self (Wiebe & Sameshima, 2018) and the ways it has become subject in (and to) history, economics, environment, and politics (Meyer, 2010).

Throwing Some Truth into the Pursuit of Knowledge

Against of background of Trumpism, I am still uncomfortable with the world truth. In my notebooks I notice fragmented truths, fuzzy truths, difficult truths; then there is being true to myself, knowing myself, acknowledging the reality of situations; still followed by partial truths, truthiness, capital T truth, and the relationship between truth and freedom. As an educator, I cannot deny the entanglement of knowledge with truth. It should be more than a pointless exchange of information, right? Kent den Heyer (2015) encourages me to pursue the question of "what is educational about education?" This, to me, throws some truth into the pursuit of knowledge. The obligation to make meaning as a subject in this world.

Post Truth

Nothing is true. The papers print untruths.
even *The Washington Post* is post truth
even CIA briefings to the President
even the Christmas Card holiday greeting
your Grandmother sent through the post
arrived with an empty stamp
without a seal or guarantee
that I love you is more than pat,
her name is Pat, after all,
and the 25 enclosed barely buys
a head of cauliflower. Post Pat
everything and nothing is pat

Presidents play patty-cake on twitter
Red-Riding doesn't visit
she has swiped right, or is it left,
Does it matter? She is making out
on the couch to *House of Cards.*
Never write in a diary
your feelings are not true
just a million little pieces
that even Oprah can't vouch for.
Football isn't true, not the salary
nor the glory, nor the forever,
Amen, brother, don't say deflategate
some have concussions and some don't
no one knows who is telling it
not the doctors or the MRI scans.
At night, when are you sleeping
your FB bot automates a status update
steps, calories, winks, stars
instaeverything – all true,
beauty is truth, perception beauty
it is all we know, all pinned
packaged, turned, coined
little bits of body fuzz turned buzz
7 ways to convince your self/boss
that the work you do actually matters
the only mantra you will even need
click
There was a time when the truth
was an honorable pursuit
there were methods and processes
to determine it, there were those
who climbed mountains
to have it revealed, those who
hid in the shadows to expose
the lack of it. The truth,
when it was discovered
could set a person free
could cause another to resign
could start and stop a tank
in the middle of the street.

Love and Truthiness

Perhaps in education there is still honour in pursuing truth. While I am no idealist, agreeing with Pinar (2010) that even lovely objectives foreclose on the present, repositioning it toward a future hope, I still lean toward purpose and meaning. Perhaps the shameless disavowal of truth is why so many have turned to George Orwell's *1984* for some kind of prophetic assurance. Orwell predicted the kind of newspeak and obfuscation of statistics so common across all political lines. The poem, "The Longer I Live" is a response to the truthiness that is the eternal cycling of statistics. Existentially, a critical moment in one's life comes when a person learns what to do with their freedom. An existential choice is a response to truthiness – not because there is responsibility to a moral code – but because there is a responsibility to freedom, to making meaning from the vastness of possibility. Such a choice resembles the orienting question of curriculum studies, "What knowledge is of most worth?"

The Longer I live

Oh, listener of my heart
the longer I live
my wants become clearer,
to hold you, shoulder
burdens when you offer them
to spend nights, my bare thigh
nudging yours, light
from a candle falling
over your shoulders,
a body warm in gratitude,
to drop everything and dance,
fill our passports with stamps
look into the back seat
of our road trip, and be astonished
by the magic, the children
reading, your glance.

Oh, listener of my heart
the longer I live
my wants become clearer,
to sneak song and poetry

into table moments, cards,
bus rides, to jazz with chocolate
steam the asparagus
with lemon, kombucha fizz
honey drizzle, listening
to you wake up to a latte,
to make flimsy whimsy,
interpret clouds, to watch
seagulls circle the swells,
and drop into the dazzle
to bellow a sea roar, make heart
ache into sand castles,
letting wave upon wave
press it back into the earth.

Oh, listener of my heart
the longer I live
my wants become clearer,
to stay the blue black
of morning and lean
into the light of your hair,
to count your every blink
contemplate your belly button,
to pine for your voice
on the phone as birds
are singing for the dawn,
to breathe exhilarating
red cedar, decipher patterns
in the river bed,
collect remembrances
for the windowsills.

Oh, listener of my heart
the longer I live
my wants become clearer,
to snowshoe as softly as a dream,
to spy a fox den lined with down
to sway along empty streets
walk under the cherry blossoms

budding every March,
to wander into the forest,
bury treasure, polish
and buff and wish on stones,
to welcome moonlight
in through the bedroom
window, open my arms often,
to have days to sit around
and read, unconcerned.

Oh, listener of my heart
the longer I live
my wants become clearer,
to shed old skin, step forth
in noticing, savour the aftertaste,
to ask, always, who is this you,
to open time and give histories,
to entangle my mouth
in new language, forming
sounds from your childhood,
words as pulse, learning
the you from then to now,
to keep the time tender
as newly leafed irises,
to let passion storm
arriving in stillness
then a full throng of rain.

What is Educational about Education?

For me, the critical moment in *1984* is when Julia deliberately stumbles in front of Winston, and as he is helping her up she passes him a note that says, *I love you*. What I've noticed from reviewing my personal notebook over the last six years is the way an idea can reshape and reform the world. I believe love does this. It is important not to miss that, in *1984*, love is a critical part of the politics. For Julia, she loves Winston for herself. Against the party's will that everything come under its control, love is dangerous because it is pleasurable. Love is dangerous because it could be so meaningful that it empties the significance of everything else. In the world of *1984* what is emptied of significance is the moral obligation of serving the party. In our world, it would be any *socially* desirable activity. If education is a social process, forming us as subjects into particular kinds of citizens, then education cannot be differentiated from socialization. Perhaps what is educational about education is what we pursue for ourselves?

Shoes

How they dry and crack is the trouble
the same shoes worn for prom
cannot be worn to your wedding,
not even taken on the ride to university.

While you are braving the surf
your shoes are being flipped in the sand,
part of the castle defenses, shelter from the storm,
the water beginning to pool round them.

St. Paul traded in his Roman shackles
spent his entire life in the same pair of sandals,
patron saint of the weary sole,
protector of those adorned in Allen Edmonds,
he invented shoe polish, no?

You know what they say about the tiny footed
how they struggle to find the right fit,
you can tell a man by his Fluevogs,
though even Italian leathers can't keep you
from a misstep and Reebok pumps
won't prevent an ankle twisting.

This morning a drop of peanut butter
plops onto my brogues, the oil cuts through
layers of polish and leaves a splotch,
an imperfection that is difficult to bear,
when I'm asked to dance
it will be the blemish that I think of.

I've gone into a repair shop on Robson
and the cobbler knew make and model
said my Park Avenues would last longer than I would,
it's true, the airport shiners call to me,
doctors of the soul, the superfood
for supple limbs and leather.

Young people today can't tell a good pair of shoes
whether one pair is industrious
or another just a flight of fancy,
in good shoes we find out who we want to be;
one pair has taken my limp, my worst,
held dreams in stride as I'd reached

for a better time, a greater distance, something
more than yesterday. To tell the truth,
if I'd danced more and ate less peanut butter
maybe I'd have become a version of me
not so incomplete.

Concluding Thoughts

In the face of W.H. Auden's insistence that poetry doesn't do a damn thing to change the world, I hear echoes of Pinar's (2010) essay in the *Journal of Curriculum Controversy* where he explains the promise of *currere* as "emancipatory reaggregation" (p. 3). To study one's self and the knowledge processes that have socialized it into a subject is an invitation to reaggregate those conditions. This is distinctively curriculum work. In reaggregation is the possibility that study will shake us up, that the knowledge we gain of who and how we have become subjects releases us from being subject to those processes. The inspiration for this final poem comes from work that I have been doing on the superhero effect in education. In an essay called, "The Teacher as Silenced Superhero" (2017) I argue that teachers are given the token social status of superhero and that this obligates them to be expressions of our social ideals for education. But, in doing so, this also silences them. What if instead, as Ellyn Lyle has proposed in bringing together this edited collection, teachers employed reflexive inquiry to study their own becoming. For me, this is a curriculum process, a poetic process, a life-writing process.

Panglossian

It was time to clear out the garage
He rolled up his sleeves and plunged in
his lungs disapproving, legs wobbly,
teeth grit; chords and wires
and connectors, a ping-pong table
held together with duck tape,
spare bicycle tubing, winter tires
a bike rack needing a hitch.
If only he were replacing shingles
that had blown off, or sawing up
broken branches, or pouring
cement for the crumbling walkway;
these jobs could be finished.
But this was full immersion,
a garage was a fridge for all of life's leftovers,
sans Tupperware and plastic baggies,
where to put the remainder of wiper fluid
motor oil, shoe polish,
a motorcycle helmet? A kind of care
that piled up, in trying to prevent waste,
he accumulated it.

So.

There were cardboard boxes
kept in case kitchen gadgets
needed to be returned,
the smell of aging books
damp from disuse
too moldy to bring into the house
and read again, hardly worth
their weight but too much
invested to give away,
he loved books
not these in particular
the idea of them, marginalia
he couldn't imagine a stranger reading
hoarding a few sayings

that might someday be applied in his life:
hope is a tough decision
leading down a tougher road.

His body was no different:
cells awash, amuck in his musty
insides, fighting for so long
maybe it was a cosmic choreography
to have and have not
with and without simultaneously,
youth against age
hypertrophy vs atrophy
lift, rest, repeat, a fruitless
attempt at progress –
like a wound swelling shut,
his tongue was starting to feel
dry in his mouth, he learned
to care less about the lies
that everyone else cared about,
unflappable, there were no conspiring
global forces, no amount of melting artic ice,
no quantity of cultural capital
that could loose the mouth of its censorship,
self containment.

So.

No matter how much he wanted to
he couldn't argue his thoughts down all the time,
they terrified him: barbarian hordes with clubs
and war paint, he could never tell when
they'd charge into the fray, whooping and shrieking,
leaving him choking on tears, too sentimental
to let go and blow out to sea.
What he wanted was to be embraced
so tightly that his ribs ached
enough pressure to convince him he was real,
ready for a boundless life
but he could not sustain the maintenance
required of a man,

to do lists stored in boxes
hovered around the edges
ideas waiting for another chapter
to be written, the phoniness of it all
if he didn't look too closely
the world could be grand, even beautiful,
the indispensable rationale
for building a bigger garage.

References

Chambers, C. (2004). Research that matters: Finding a path with heart. *Journal of the Canadian Association for Curriculum Studies, 2*(1), 1–19.

den Heyer, K. (2015). An analysis of aims and the educational "event." *Canadian Journal of Education, 38*(1), 1–27.

Gouzouasis, P., & Ihnatovych, D. (2016). The dissonant duet: An autoethnography of a teacher-student relationship. *Journal of the Canadian Association of Curriculum Studies, 14*(2), 14–34.

Leggo, C., Hasebe-Ludt, E., Sinner, A., & Chambers, C. (2012). *A heart of wisdom: Life writing as empathetic inquiry.* New York, NY: Peter Lang.

Meyer, K. (2010). Living inquiry: Me, my self, and other. *Journal of Curriculum Theorizing, 26*(1), 85–96.

Orwell, G. (1949). *Nineteen eighty four.* London: Penguin Books.

Pinar, W. F. (2004). *What is curriculum theory?* Mahwah, NJ: Lawrence Erlbaum Associates.

Pinar, W. F. (2010). Notes on a blue guitar. *Journal of Educational Controversy, 5*(1), 1–9.

Pinar, W. F., & Grumet, M. R. (1976). *Toward a poor curriculum.* Dubuque, IA: Kendall/Hunt.

Remen, R. (2000). *My grandfather's blessings.* New York, NY: Riverhead Books.

Taylor, C. (1991). *The malaise of modernity.* Toronto: Anansi.

Wiebe, S. (2015). Poetic inquiry: A fierce, tender, and mischievous relationship with lived experience. *Language and Literacy, 17*(3), 152–163.

Wiebe, S., Leggo, C., Sameshima, P., Conrad, D., James, K., Snowber, C., ... Lloyd, R. (2018). Re(mixing) curriculum playlists: Responses of synopsis and expansion. *Journal of Curriculum and Pedagogy, 15*(1), 58–105.

Wiebe, S., & Sameshima, P. (2018). Sympathizing with social justice, poetry of invitation and generation. *Art/Research International, 3*(1), 7–29.

Wiebe, S., & Snowber, C. (2011). The visceral imagination: A fertile space for non-textual knowing. *Journal of Curriculum Theorizing, 27*(2), 101–113.

Yallop, J. G., Wiebe, S., & Faulkner, S. (2014). The practices of poetic inquiry. *Special Issue of in Education, 20*(2), 1–11.

CHAPTER 4

Learning to Become a Pedagogically-Engaged, Democratic Teacher: Self-Study Using Dewey's Reflective Thinking Method

Isabel Martínez-Cuenca

Introduction

Schnellert, Richardson, and Cherkowski (2014) underscore that the process of reflexive inquiry "is at the heart of how we have come to understand and engage in our professional development"; and that "it enable[s] us to ground, embody, and co-author our identities" (p. 239). Many scholars emphasize the importance of "critical reflection and reflexivity" (p. 237) for teacher development as a way to uncover and challenge assumptions (Cochran-Smith & Lytle, 2009; Jaworski, 2006; Nelson & Slavit, 2008; Schnellert & Butler, 2014). Given the fundamental role of RI in teacher development, reflexive approaches to teacher inquiry have proliferated in multiple theoretical traditions and research disciplines. However, this bourgeoning of methods may have muddied the waters, rendering some practitioners uncertain about the role and the procedures of critical reflection (Rodgers, 2002; Schnellert et al., 2014). In this chapter, I attempt to illustrate the potential of Dewey's (1933) pioneering theory of inquiry and reflective thinking phases as a rigorous and systematic framework to support teacher reflexive self-inquiry and self-development (Rodgers, 2002). In conceiving reflective thinking as a meaning-making process, I draw on narrative ways of knowing not only to "provide accounts of individual consciousness" (Lyle, 2013, p. 19), but also to encourage "meaning making in a personal way" (Lyle, 2013, p. 18). Polkinghorne (1988) observed that narrative is "one of the most important forms for creating meaning in human existence" (p. 183), and Neilsen agrees when she says narrative provides "opportunities to 'read' [my] professional life and 'write' [my] own classroom experiences and as a result claim authority for [my] professional growth" (Neilsen, 1994, p. 46). Quite uniquely, since stories are situated, they can also help uncover more complex layers of meaning at a personal, institutional, and cultural level (Clandinin, 2006; Lyle, 2013; Webster & Mertova, 2007). Ultimately, narrative is "the process of coming to knowledge as much as it is the knowledge itself" (Lyle, 2013, p. 20).

John Dewey's Theory of Reflective Thinking

Nearly a century ago, Dewey (1933) offered reflective thinking as an inquiry method to foster student and teacher learning (Rodgers, 2002). Since its inception, whether due to misuse of the terminology, or obscure prose, his notion of reflection has not only fluctuated, but has also lost its clarity. Deweyan reflective thinking, however, is not just a sequence of procedural steps, mirroring the scientific method (Dimova & Kamarska, 2015). On the contrary, it is a meaning-making process "at the very heart of what it means to be human" (Rodgers, 2002, p. 848).

John Dewey's Disciplined Reflective Thinking Process

Dewey's meaning-making framework (1933) involves the systematic, iterative, cyclical process of voicing experiences; negotiating interpretations; weaving larger themes; critically revisiting those; and engaging in *intelligent action*. I draw on Dewey's reflective thinking inquiry cycle to complement my self-inquiry; whereby six phases collapse into four steps (Rodgers, 2002, p. 856) that organize the rest of this chapter: presence to experience; description of experience; analysis of experience; and intelligent action/experimentation.

Presence to Experience

When my Foundations of Education professor asked me to start asking questions to and about myself and my practice, I realized I did not really know what kind of student or teacher I was or where to start. I was unfamiliar with the tools to answer those inquiries. Worst of all, introspection was difficult for me, since it was neither common nor appreciated in my culture. I started recollecting a painful learning experience that, I believe, determined my identity thereafter. I remember rashly plunging into English at fourteen with no prior exposure. It surely was a big mistake – I would like to think not so much for lack of motivation, or effort on my part – but because of my English teacher's way of engaging. Karen followed a rigid format full of mimicry and repetitive exercises. She did not support student meaningful learning and mostly encouraged rote memorization. When I failed the midterm, I approached her seeking help and guidance. But rather than make any effort to support me, she just recommended private tutoring. It was such a disempowering experience that I developed an involuntary aversion towards the teaching tradition that Karen represented. That experience determined my partiality towards the alternative – the Communicative Language Teaching approach (CLT).

Unchecked for 20 years, my reaction to Karen became *mis-educative* (Dewey, 1933). In the next sections, I examine my aversion towards traditional teaching and my partiality towards the CLT by making deeper connections at the personal, socio-cultural, and pedagogical levels. These different lenses prove key to understanding my initial learning/teaching experience more fully so that I am later able to engage in *intelligent action* (Dewey, 1933).

Description of Experience

Pre-Programming

I begin by distancing myself from my initial experience and examining it as "an object of thought" (Rodgers, 2002, p. 853). I weave threads of meaning from the contemporary socio-political and socio-economic contexts, as the "larger social, cultural and institutional narratives within which [my experiences] live and have lived" (Clandinin, 2006, p. 51) could begin to illuminate the conditions and the prerogatives in which Karen and I interacted.

Socio-politically, I was raised in Spain, a paternalistic, embryonic social democracy that neither had faith in the autonomy and self-determination of its people, nor trusted their potential (Freire, 2000). Most of my education was framed in the Eurocentric, knowledge-centred tradition, where top-down transmission guaranteed unquestioning, passive citizens right at a time of civil unrest. My early *apprenticeship of observation* (Lortie, 1975) stressed two things: memorization and regurgitation to perpetuate traditions, canons, and beliefs (Hansen, 2001); and the "right conduct [to] later be allowed to question, analyze, and criticize" (Noddings, 2011, p. 13). That powerful acculturation (Gardner, 1991; Ball & Cohen, 1999) disempowered my meaning-making experiences as *routine-action* (Dewey, 1933).

Banking of Education

Socio-economically, I was educated in a graded-school system devised to meet the growing demands for skilled workers in the beginning of the twentieth century. The bourgeoning of universal education found in the graded-school an efficient *assembly-line* formula (similar to factories) for *manufacturing* citizenry with a particular understanding of the world (Tyack & Cuban, 1995). The model mainly played a discriminating role, thanks to which teachers could mechanically *categorize* students on the basis of some arbitrary content. Clearly, this orientation to outcomes had a pervasive effect on core values like humanism and democracy because it diminished the importance of care, student learning, agency, and critical thinking abilities (Gardner, 1991; Hansen, 2001; Nussbaum, 2012).

Analysis of Experience

Having accounted for the larger socio-political and socio-economic narratives, I now add further texture so that my *mis-educative* experience (Dewey, 1933) "can emerge in all its complexity" (Rodgers, 2002, p. 854). In this section, I describe my pedagogical baggage, and I explore my shortcomings in the CLT vis-à-vis principles of *engaged pedagogy* and *democratic education*.

Explanations

Pedagogically, my early *apprenticeship of observation* (Lortie, 1975) embodied the bourgeois notion of teachers as knowledge authorities (distant and emotionally unavailable figures) who offered neither spiritual connection nor intellectual guidance. Power asymmetries, top-down knowledge imposition, student submissiveness, and rote learning also characterized this old-school model in which Lortie's (1975) concept of *dual captivity* was very much present. When visually depicted using Hawkins' (2002) *I-Thou-It* framework, students could only access content when channelled by the teacher in a linearly-shaped process (see Figure 4.1a).

My apprenticeship continued in my pre-service programs with the CLT. Given my aversion to mimicry, I unquestioningly embraced this methodology because it prioritized communicative competence (Hymes, 1972) as well as language functions (Halliday, 1970). I was trained to support student learning with real, meaningful, language tasks, and with authentic materials. Moreover, I cultivated cultural awareness, support, guidance, and respect to foster student production in communication. Yet, years later, I was confronted with the uncomfortable reality that many dimensions of my teaching may not have been so different from Karen's. A visual representation of CLT, through Hawkins' (2002) *I-Thou-It*, shows a shift of the traditional linear process into a pyramidal shape; yet, the elements barely move towards a participatory frame (see Figure 4.1b).

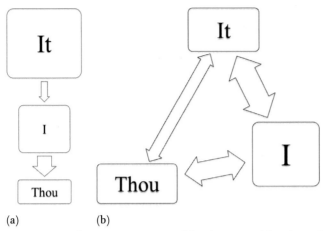

(a)   (b)

FIGURE 4.1   I-thou-it representation of the elements in (a) traditional classrooms,
and (b) pseudo-democratic classrooms. (From Martínez-Cuenca et al., 2018;
reproduced with permission of Peter Lang Inc., International Academic
Publishers in via Copyright Clearance Center)

Ramifications

Three major limitations of the CLT diametrically oppose principles of *engaged pedagogy* and *democratic education*: the unclear approach to education and learning; the vague teacher/student roles; and the power asymmetries. Firstly, the absence of fully-fledged, underlying theories of education and of learning placed my teaching and myself in a very vulnerable position. For one, CLT became a set of directives for syllabi- and activity-design, thereby reducing my teaching to a script (Richards & Rodgers, 2001). What was worse, without an insight into what education should accomplish, I turned to my previous acculturation experiences to ground my practice, which raised the next two issues. In the CLT, teacher and learner roles were not clearly outlined because the method stressed processes of communication, rather than learning (Richards et al., 2001). While I incorporated pair and group work and prompted students' life experiences to foster communication, the CLT did not transform my practice into a learner-centred enactment. On the contrary, I was still very much a *facilitator* of communication through which students approached content; I was not a *catalyst* fostering students' critical reasoning, as *engaged pedagogy* and *democratic education* scholarship advocates (Freire, 2000; hooks, 1994).

Power asymmetries also plagued my practice. Apart from facilitating, I had to be an analyst, a mentor, and a group manager (Breen & Candlin, 1980), functions that naturally lent themselves to teacher-centredness. Rather than judiciously delegating control to students, I made all design and procedural decisions to orchestrate student communication. Most unfortunate, I reduced student voice to an outcome, which disempowered their ability to co-construct their lessons, or actively *practice freedom* (hooks, 1994).

Intelligent Action/Experimentation

As a new understanding of my teaching experience emerges from the previous exhaustive analysis, I hope to better "articulate [my] needs and [my] students needs (...) to propose actions both inside and outside the classroom walls" (Rodgers, 2002, pp. 854–855). In so doing, I aim to support students' "meaningful self-realization and guided empowerment" (Martínez-Cuenca, Florencio-Wain, & Oliveira, 2018, p. 496). This type of engaged pedagogy regards student experiences as operating forces instrumental to the incorporation of more knowledge (Dewey, 2012). This pedagogical shift requires practitioners to rethink their relationship with old teacher-centred models so that students can co-construct the content they are studying (Dewey, 2012; Freire, 2000; hooks, 1994; Rodgers, 2006).

The literature proposes two complementary directives: to deemphasize the *I* and the *It* by creating a space for horizontal interactions between the teacher and students; and to judiciously shift the locus of control to support student *initiative* and self-direction at the enacted level (Ellis, 2004; Freire, 2000; hooks, 1994; Martínez-Cuenca et al., 2018; Rodgers, 2006). In wanting to engage in *intelligent action* (Dewey, 1933), I propose two democratic teaching artefacts.

Horizontal Interactions
In a democratic classroom, the students' prior experiences need to be connected to the incoming material to be learned, a process Dewey (2012) called *psychologizing*. Such connection can draw on subjectivities, diverse ways of engaging, and unconventional teaching methods (Freire, 2009; hooks, 1994). Most importantly, content has to be experienced, rather than memorized, and directly explored by students rather than channelled by the teacher. Freire's (2000) notion of *dialogue*, defined as "the encounter between men, mediated by the world" (p. 88) already theorized students' direct access. In Freire's conception, *dialoguers* (i.e., students and the teacher) would "engage in the subject matter on the same plane, as agents and catalyst of learning, respectively" (Freire, 2000, p. 93; Martínez-Cuenca et al., 2018, p. 494). I imagine this spatial metaphor as a horizontal framework that would create the levelling necessary for a dialectical equilibrium between the *dialoguers*. "Without [this levelling] there is no possible communication between the *dialoguers*" (Freire, 2000; Martínez-Cuenca et al., 2018, p. 494); ergo, no students'

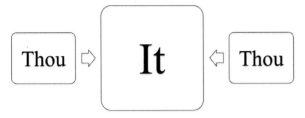

FIGURE 4.2   Horizontal framework, inspired by Freire (1970, 2000). (From Martínez-Cuenca
et al., 2018; reproduced with permission of Peter Lang Inc., International
Academic Publishers in via Copyright Clearance Center)

participation; no meaningful learning potential; and no empowerment (Hansen,
2001; Hawkins, 2002). Visually, this levelling could be represented "as a horizontal
continuum between the *I* and the *Thou*, facilitated by the *It*" (Martínez-Cuenca
et al., 2018, p. 493) (see Figure 4.2 about horizontal interactions).

Delegating Control

While direct access to the subject matter could be conducive to better learning,
it does not automatically create more learning opportunities unless students
are allowed to partially self-direct their learning experiences at the enacted level
(Ellis, 2004; Freire, 2000; hooks, 1994; Martínez-Cuenca et al., 2018; Rodgers,
2006). Visually, this shift of the locus of control would create a classroom frame
where the *Thou* and the *It* interact among themselves, while the teacher orches-
trates and observes (see Figure 4.3 about democratic teaching).

In moderate conceptions, self-directed learning is the gradual exercise of
responsibility and *initiative* over how students approach the content to better
promote their deep-seated interest (Martínez-Cuenca et al., 2018). In practice,

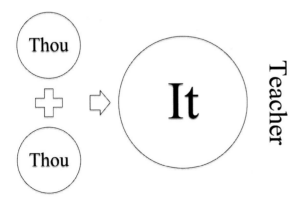

FIGURE 4.3   Democratic classroom. (From Martínez-Cuenca et al., 2018; reproduced with
permission of Peter Lang Inc. via Copyright Clearance Center)

self-direction could be implemented by gradually "scaffolding students' self-management and the corresponding repercussions, as a function of age" (p. 496) in the case of young learners in mainstream education systems. With adult English learners, however, scaffolded, self-directed learning might be a function of language proficiency. For example, beginner students would make decisions about how to solve a controlled exercise (see Appendices A1 and A2 for an example). As proficiency develops, learners would collaborate in co-constructing the course by actively participating in content decision-making (Ellis, 2004), such as designing the course syllabus and self-tailoring procedures (see Appendices B1 and B2 for an example).

Lastly, delegating self-direction and co-construction could not only promote more learning opportunities, but could also provide a space for cultural and epistemological enrichment whereby student content-decision making might counteract the effects of teacher content-selection bias (Freire, 2009), promote multiculturalism and inclusiveness, and embrace different voices, lost voices, and silenced voices (hooks, 1994).

Intelligent Action

Embracing democratic education principles required quite a reframing of my teaching, where students (i.e., *Thou*) – not the teacher (i.e., *I*) or content (i.e., *It*) – were the true heart of my practice. As such, I designed two artefacts (i.e., a lesson plan and a syllabus) to explore how alternative interplays of the *I-Thou-It* framework (Hawkins, 2002) could re-centre student agency in the learning process. The lesson plan proposed student self-directed problem solving of a controlled exercise (see Appendices A1 and A2 for details), whereas the syllabus featured collaborative co-construction of the course and ongoing self-tailoring of procedures throughout the course (see Appendices B1 and B2 for details). In both artefacts, I targeted a community of adult students with different language and professional backgrounds that would be responsible for their individual progress and active learning as well as their collective assemblage of prior knowledge of languages, teaching, and other resources. Artefacts ranged from beginner to advanced proficiency levels.

Beginner Levels

Nested in day-one introductions, the warm-up decoding activity familiarized beginner students with the classroom context and created a sense of community. This lesson placed *I* and *Thou* in a dialectical relationship whereby the *I* would guide the students with a particular exercise set up. Yet, students themselves would make hypotheses about vocabulary, numerals, and the plural marker. The most important modification is that students did not approach the subject matter through me. On the contrary, I would trust students' abilities to work autonomously – yet collaboratively – to discover the *It*. In a Freirean sense, the students would share their own understanding of the subject matter and co-construct the *It* collaboratively. Meanwhile, my role was demoted to allow me to observe their interactions and meaning-making process, to diagnose problems, and to provide support if necessary.

Advanced Levels

The second artefact engaged students in the individual and collective co-construction of the course. They not only co-designed a syllabus, but they also individually tailored a personalized learning experience around each unit. The major modifications included harnessing the strengths and capacities that learners bring to create the *It*, as well as emphasizing an observer teacher's stance. On the one hand, I would trust the students to take ownership of the *It* (i.e., the syllabus) and to engage with it in an open-ended manner. Moreover, I would allow students latitude to autonomously and responsibly co-create and engage in learning centres for each unit. Naturally, I would fade out from the authoritative *I* position by allowing students to act as *I* themselves. This way, even if teacher-guided and teacher-monitored, students would self-manage their learning. Most importantly, adopting an observer's role allowed me to monitor students' management, decision-making, and engagement with the subject matter.

Conclusion

This reflexive self-inquiry on a past *mis-educative* experience demonstrated that Dewey's (1933) notion of experience, as well as the iterative, continuous reflective thinking cycle can ground teacher meaning-making and self-development. Using this method for disciplined cross-examination of my own experiences, I uncovered hidden narratives and interwoven complexities from the larger, contemporary social-cultural, epistemological, and pedagogical contexts. In light of the dialectical relations between my practice and alternative pedagogical models, I critically addressed shortcomings vis-à-vis *engaged pedagogy* and *democratic education*. This *journey of becoming* (Bloom, 1998) was also strongly supported by the visual representations of traditional, constructivist, and democratic models of education using Hawkins' (2002) *I-Thou-It* framework. Those visualizations contributed significantly to mentally restructuring my *apprenticeship* away from principles diametrically opposed to *engaged pedagogy* and *democratic education*. They also supported the development of my teaching practice in a powerful, visual frame of reference. My *intelligent action*, in a Deweyan sense, honoured democratic pedagogical commitments, such as harnessing students' prior knowledge, levelling power asymmetries, and promoting self-directed learning. The resulting products were two artefacts that, I hope, are deemed democratic.

As I conclude, I realize that a teacher's job hinges on learning from reflexive inquiry about our own identities and abilities, as well as those of students, as we negotiate the purposes of education, the nature of learning, the context of impinging forces, and the potential for change (hooks, 1994; Rodgers, 2006). In the future, I would like to explore *engaged* and *democratic* enactments even further by taking risks such as "linking confessional narratives to academic discussions" (hooks, 1994, p. 21).

References

Ball, D. L., & Cohen, D. K. (1999). Developing practice, developing practitioners: Toward a practice-based theory of professional education. In G. Sykes & L. Darling-Hammond (Eds.), *Teaching as the learning profession: Handbook of policy and practice* (pp. 3–32). San Francisco, CA: Jossey-Bass.

Bloom, L. (1998). *Under the sign of hope: Feminist methodology and narrative interpretation.* Albany, NY: State University of New York Press.

Breen, M., & Candlin, C. N. (1980). The essentials of a communicative curriculum in language teaching. *Applied Linguistics, 1*(2), 89–112.

Clandinin, D. J. (2006). Narrative inquiry: A methodology for studying lived experience. *Research Studies in Music Education, 27*(1), 44–54.

Cochran-Smith, M., & Lytle, S. L. (2009). *Inquiry as stance: Practitioner research in the next generation.* New York, NY: Teachers College Press.

Dewey, J. (1933). *How we think.* Buffalo, NY: Prometheus Books.

Dewey, J. (2012). Excerpts from the child and the curriculum. In S. M. Cahn (Ed.), *Classic and contemporary readings in the philosophy of education.* New York, NY: Oxford University Press.

Dimova, Y., & Kamarska, K. (2015). Rediscovering John Dewey's model of learning through reflective inquiry. *Problems of Education in the 21st Century, 63*, 29–39.

Ellis, A. K. (2004). *Exemplars of curriculum theory.* Larchmont, NY: Eye on Education.

Freire, P. (2000). *Pedagogy of the oppressed.* New York, NY: Bloomsbury Academic.

Freire, P. (2009). *Teachers as cultural workers: Letters to those who dare teach.* Boulder, CO: Westview Press.

Gardner, H. (1991). *The unschooled mind: How children think and how schools should teach.* New York, NY: Basic Books.

Halliday, M. A. K. (1970). Language structure and language function. In J. Lyons (Ed.), *New horizons in linguistics* (pp. 140–165). Harmondsworth: Penguin Books.

Hansen, D. T. (2001). *Exploring the moral heart of teaching: Towards a teacher's creed.* New York, NY: Teachers College Press.

Hawkins, D. (2002). *The informed vision.* Boulder, CO: University Press of Colorado.

hooks, b. (1994). *Teaching to transgress.* New York, NY: Routledge.

Hymes, D. H. (1972). On communicative competence. In J. B. Pride & J. Holmes (Eds.), *Sociolinguistics: Selected readings* (pp. 269–293). Harmondsworth: Penguin Books.

Jaworski, B. (2006). Theory and practice in mathematics teaching development: Critical inquiry as a mode of learning and teaching. *Journal of Mathematics Teacher Education, 9,* 187–211.

Lortie, D. C. (1975). *Schoolteacher: A sociological study of teaching.* Chicago, IL: University of Chicago Press.

Lyle, E. (2013). From method to methodology: Reflexive narrative inquiry as perspective, process, and representation in an adult education context. *Canadian Journal for the Study of Adult Education, 25* (2), 17–34.

Martínez-Cuenca, I., Florencio-Wain, A. J., & Oliveira, A. W. (2018). When holism meets democratization: Re-centering science classrooms to support students' feelings of agency and connectedness. In L. A. Bryan & K. Tobin (Eds.), *13 questions: Reframing education's conversation: Science.* Bern: Peter Lang.

Neilsen, L. (1994). *A stone in my shoe.* Winnipeg: Peguis.

Nelson, T. H., & Slavit, D. (2008). Supported teacher collaborative inquiry. *Teacher Education Quarterly, 35*(1), 99–116.

Noddings, N. (2012). *Philosophy of education* (3rd ed.). Boulder, CO: Westview Press.

Nussbaum, M. (2012). *Not for profit: Why democracy needs the humanities.* Princeton, NJ: Princeton University Press.

Polkinghorne, D. E. (1988). *Narrative knowing and the human sciences* (SUNY series in the philosophy of the social sciences). Albany, NY: State University of New York Press.

Richards, J. C., & Rodgers, T. S. (2001). *Approaches and methods in language teaching* (2nd ed.). Cambridge: Cambridge University Press.

Rodgers, C. R. (2002). Defining reflection: Another look at John Dewey and reflective thinking. *Teachers College Record, 104*(4), 842–866.

Rodgers, C. R. (2006). *Attending to student voice: The impact of descriptive feedback on learning and teaching.* Boston, MA: Blackwell Publishing.

Schnellert, L., & Butler, D. L. (2014). Collaborative inquiry: Empowering teachers in their professional development. *Education Canada, 54*(5), 42–44.

Schnellert, L., Richardson, P., & Cherkowski, S. (2014). Teacher educator professional development as reflexive inquiry. *Learning Landscapes, 8*(1), 233–249.

Tyack, D., & Cuban, L. (1995). *Tinkering toward Utopia.* Cambridge, MA: Harvard University Press.

Webster, L., & Mertova, P. (2007). *Using narrative inquiry as a research method.* London: Routledge.

Appendix A1: Beginner Lesson Plan

Target language: English
Level: Beginner
Age: Adult learners with different language and professional backgrounds

Lesson Aims:
    Familiarize students with the immediate classroom context
    Foster a sense of community
    Create opportunities for collaborative learning while learning English

Content: Introducing classroom objects
             present tense
             plural marker –s
             numbers 1–20
      Introducing oneself and others
             present tenses, possessive articles
             occupations, origin

Materials and equipment: Realia (objects), index cards, flashcards, blackboard, computers/cell phones, projector
Lesson duration: 60 minutes

Activity/ timing	Objectives	Materials/ equipment	Step-by-step details	Seating	Notes
Warm-up 25 min	Classroom objects Plurals Numerals	Realia Index cards Flashcards	Decode a short text using knowledge of cognates and visual cues. Share discoveries. Guess objects.	Group/ pair work	
Labelling 10 min		Computers Cell phones Flashcards	Students post labels for objects around class they consider important	Whole class	
Introductions 5 min	Occupations Origin	Computers Cell phones	Teacher models introducing herself first. Students are encouraged to do the same	Pair work	
Introductions 20 min	Introducing partners	Projectors	Students introduce partners to whole class. Visuals to support limited proficiency	Whole class	Blackboard has sentence frames for reference

Appendix A2: Beginner Lesson Description

The goal of this beginner lesson is to familiarize students with the immediate classroom context, to foster a sense of community, and to create opportunities for collaborative learning while learning English. It is divided in four stages; (a) group analysis; (b) whole class practice; (c) pair introductions; and (d) whole class introductions. All activities are self-explanatory except the warm-up. Here is a description.

As the students enter the classroom, they find the following scene: a table and the teacher standing next to it. On the table, there are several classroom objects, ranging in number. The teacher is holding some items, as well. As students choose seats, they are asked to partner with the nearest peer(s). In pairs/groups, students are given a short text and asked to study it in connection to the visual scene. The text reads as follows;

> In this classroom, there is a teacher; Isabel. The teacher has a DELL computer and a cell phone. On the table, there are many objects. There is one piece of paper, one book, two notebooks, three pencils, four pens, (...)

Students are not told how to decode the text, but just prompted to use what they know in their own languages, and written and visual clues. Some students might underline cognates; whereas others might use visual cues for quantities and plurals. Volunteers share their discoveries and hypotheses about numbers, vocabulary, and the meaning of the text. Next, individual students take turns showing to their peers, for example, seven pens to trigger the correct word and numeral identification.

Appendix B1: Syllabus Co-construction in Advanced Levels

Target language: English
Level: Advanced
Age: Adult learners with different language and professional backgrounds

Course Aims:

> Engage in open-ended individual syllabus design
> Collaborate in merging individual syllabi into class syllabus
> Self-tailor class syllabi to individual needs and preferences
> Foster a sense of community
> Create opportunities for collaborative learning while learning English

Content: Topics of interest, grammar points, situations, media formats, artistic expressions, and final products for assessment

Procedures: Learning centers

Date	Objectives	Materials/ equipment	Step-by-step details	Other notes
Week 1	Introductions Individual syllabus design	Learning centres	Teacher & students introductions Students take turns at centers to decide topics of interest, grammar points, skills to practice, media to incorporate, creative abilities and final product for assessment Each student incorporates her selections into a syllabus.	
Week 2–3	Create class syllabus		Individual syllabi are shared and a class syllabus emerges from all versions.	
Ongoing after week 3	Self-tailoring class syllabus	Learning centres	Teacher organizes learning centres to support individualized learning experiences in each unit.	Practice of freedom in selections
.../...				

Appendix B2: Process of Syllabus Co-construction and Self-tailoring Units

The second artefact has as its goal the co-construction of a class syllabus and the self-tailoring of lessons thereafter. I envisioned the process starting on week one, whereby students take turns at learning centres that prompt them to design their own tentative syllabus. For example, station one asks students to select topics of interest, such as the climate change, mortgage crisis, medical tourism, and social media in news broadcasting. Station two might help define units around situations, such as understanding the weather forecast, opening a bank account and applying for a mortgage, in-taking medical histories, or blogging. The next station might ask students to select the grammar points (if they can articulate that) and skills (e.g., listening, speaking, reading, writing) necessary for each unit. A fourth station would ask students to weave media in, whether news broadcasting, blogs, magazines, academic articles, podcasts, TED talks, etc. A creative station might also ask students to suggest ways of incorporating artistic forms, such as acting, sketching, painting, or pottery. Lastly, the assessment station would require students to determine the final product for each unit (e.g., presentation, play, mural, video, podcast, portfolio). Next, learners merge their individual selections into a syllabus, to be shared with the rest of the class. The following couple of weeks would focus on negotiating a flexible class syllabus emerging from the intersection of all student versions. Within that open-ended roadmap, I would organize learning centres to support individualized learning experiences for each unit.

CHAPTER 5

Reflexive Inquiry, Artistic Selves, and Epistemological Expansion

Heather McLeod, Cecile Badenhorst and Haley Toll

Introduction

As university educators, we are aware of the constant negotiation of selves – home-identities, teaching identities, professional identities – among others. While the systemic conditions in which many of us work provide strong pressures to produce a neo-liberal self that becomes appropriated by others, we believe that being reflexive about the construction and re-construction of selves is an important part of our ethical practice. Reflexive inquiry recognizes our capacity to acknowledge the socialization processes we experience daily and to act with agency to resist these processes if need be. In addition, deepened self-knowledge and critical renegotiation contributes to further reconstructions of self (Lyle, 2013). Reflexivity allows us to view the intertwining of selves, to question how institutional demands shape our pedagogies and often run counter to our values, and to scrutinize ourselves suspiciously for the things we have come to take for granted. At the same time, we recognize the impossibility of the self to be visible and observable to itself and the difficulty of seeing the fleeting, partial parts of ourselves. Identity is inevitably complex, multi-voiced, and always under construction.

In this chapter, we would like to explore the de/construction of our imaginative selves. Metta (2011) argues that imagination has a strong relationship to the assembly of self/selves even as it is part of that de/construction. We suggest that imaginative processes of identity construction create the pathways for the possibilities of future selves while, at the same time, they re-constitute our past selves. These imaginative selves are important for our outward identities as teacher educators because they allow us to speak from different positions: imaginatively, creatively, and artistically. These multiple selves are in a state of interdependence that not only blurs the lines between the professional and the personal, but also actively contributes towards an ethical teaching identity (Allen, 2011).

Through narratives, images, and a post-structural research lens (Koro-Ljungberg, 2016), we explore our hidden art hobbies – home as art and making paper art dolls – and trouble their position on hierarchies of arts and crafts. We suggest that the de/construction of our artistic selves is imperative for our epistemological expansion and, inevitably, for our engagement with teaching. We narrate self-connections, unstable and fluid as they are, within the discourses that privilege some identities/art and not others. These subjective incursions reveal contradiction and contestation but also sites of rebirth and rejuvenation.

Reflexive Inquiry, Teaching Identities, and Creative Hobbies

With poststructuralism, there is an increasing move towards self-conscious reflexive writing. The urge to turn the spotlight on ourselves as objects of research has become increasingly hard to resist. Yet, reflexivity is also filled with tensions and challenges because it is at the same time both clear and contradictory (Faulkner et al., 2016). On one end of the spectrum reflexivity may be positioned as *realist* where researchers write about themselves and their experiences of being subjects and aim to create an authentic rendition of aspects of their daily lives (Davis et al., 2004). Other end of the spectrum there is no essential self that floats free of discourse. Discursive work is always at play in any act of writing/analyzing, and there are limits to self-consciousness (Lather, 1993). Here, the subject is deconstructed to the point that it is no longer visible. The difficulty is trying to find a middle-ground. We are subjects who read, analyse, and are self-reflexive, and who draw on our own experiences to make sense of the world. We are realists in the sense that we create linear narratives. But we are also aware that, as discursive subjects, we often cannot see beyond our subject-space. There are no secure footholds to both gaze at oneself as the subject as well as to be the object gazed upon. As teachers, we feel it is important to grapple with reflexivity, however elusive and intangible. We recognize and acknowledge that we are always in our texts (and our classrooms) no matter how objectively we try to write or how professionally we perform our teaching. Our struggle is to "avoid realist claims and the reproduction of narrow and oppressive frames that hold social categories in place" while at the same time recognizing that we too are shaped, constructed, and reproduced by language and discourse practices (Davis et al., 2004, p. 368). To do this, we accept that the "self both is and is not a fiction, is unified and transcendent and fragmented and always in process of being constituted, can be spoken of in realist ways and cannot, and that its voice can be claimed as authentic and there is no guarantee of authenticity" (Davis et al., 2004, p. 384). We cannot see ourselves in the multiplicity of fragile, contradictory, and shifting identities but, through continued self-reflexivity, we can begin to know our own positionings – both constructing and constructed. We can begin "seeing what frames our seeing" (Lather, 1993, p. 676).

In this hall of mirrors, we turn our reflexive inquiry to the selves we usually keep hidden from our academic colleagues. Here we tell stories we were not willing to tell previously (Adams & Holman, 2011). We do so because we want to explore our imaginative artistic selves in relation to our teaching selves. Through this process of narrative and reflexivity, we want to inform our educational practice (Attard, 2012; Lyle, 2013). We move into non-linguistic knowing that does not "owe its life to verbal experiences" (Blumenfeld-Jones, 2016, p. 323). We explore our hidden hobbies as a revealing way of knowing, "the shadow" (McNiff, 2011, p. 393), the parts of ourselves that are not fully understood or incorporated into the selves we show the world. Metta (2011) suggests that imagination is strongly connected to the dis/assembly of selves, especially, we argue, to our teaching selves. Like Snowber (2017), we contend that "wandering into wonder is the art of being, living, teaching" (p. 1).

If leisure involves temporarily escaping, our leisure activities are sources of comfort, pleasure, well-being, and distraction; they can be meditative and soothing, helping us to develop ideas and problem solve (Moddle, 2017). As women who generate domestic arts, we are often told that our work is frivolous and unnecessary. Shame comes from the different regimes of value socially attributed to art/craft (Christensen, 2011) that we have unquestioningly accepted, as well as gendered notions of leisure/craft (Bratich & Brush, 2011). Framed as play, these types of hobbies are frequently seen as trivial, fragmentary, superficial, and separate from serious issues in real life. However, as Christensen (2011) argues, "hobbies are neither as trivial nor as ideologically neutral as they appear" (p. 200). Feminine creative leisure pursuits exist on the sidelines of leisure research and questioning the validity of women's leisure activities with their domestic qualities can serve to limit women's choices and identity (Moddle, 2017). Domestic arts and crafts have historically been delegitimized as not being *high art* because of their association with women's traditional household work (Auther, 2010). Domestic arts have only recently been accepted into privileged art spaces of galleries and museums (Robertson & Vinebaum, 2016). We argue, however, that our projects are on a different level than everyday tasks, and they do not need an explanation or justification. Within these spaces, the construction and re/construction of self can blossom and the dissolution of the self-object dichotomy can occur, creating space for deeper metacognitive meaning-making (Flavell, 1979).

Research Process

For our process, rather than selecting a stable methodology, we used Lather's (2013) metaphor of escape. Our escape involved assuming a post-structural lens to sit with notions of ourselves and our identities. We began in the middle of the entanglement and resisted the urge to create beginnings, boundaries, and borders. We also acknowledge the fluidity inherent in researching the self/selves and the necessity of being comfortable with uncertainty, not knowing, and ambiguity. Additionally, we acknowledge the impossibility of finding closure, stability, and permanence through this research exercise (Koro-Ljungberg, 2016). We worked within reflexivity but also in the open spaces beyond what we can know. In doing this, we followed Koro-Ljungberg's (2016) suggestion to sketch thoughts on a map and then travel across backwards and forwards. Sometimes, we sat still on our map and thought for a while. This type of research does not present answers or solutions but "breathing pauses, halts and energy voids that initiate new series of moments and extensions of thought" (Koro-Ljungberg, 2016, p. 4). Heather and Cecile wrote personal narratives to capture significant moments, thoughts, and processes of their imaginative selves. The narratives, although short, provide detailed bursts of how bodies/ objects/spaces act and enact identities and portray lived experiences that might otherwise remain hidden, even from themselves. They use narratives to moor the parts of themselves that are not easy to understand or explain, so that they can turn their gaze on them, albeit briefly and partially. They added images to access knowledge that is impossible to verbalize and to enable them to engage sensory experience about the subtle but meaningful aspects of their narratives. Haley's role, as an art therapist, was to see what they could not see so they could stay mobile in their understandings of what they experienced and wrote about. Instead of seeking *Truth* in this process, we collectively placed "an emphasis on inquiry, a tolerance of ambiguity, a preference for what is open-ended, a desire for what is fluid rather than what is rigid" (Eisner, 2008, p. 22).

Home Décor as Art: Heather's Narrative

While I was a child my mother would sometimes move the household furniture around and change the function of rooms. One day I arrived home from primary school to find that what had been our living room was now the children's bedroom. So, my aesthetic world, defined by adults, was now altered – I grasped the idea that home objects and functions could be given new meanings. Other things might change, too. Sometimes a room one colour when I left in the morning was, when I returned, a different hue, the house strong with the odor of oil-paint and turpentine.

Now I often like to spend hours working with visual balance, functionality, comfort, colour, and the textural weight of objects to make my home or office feel right. When I grant myself the time and permission to gaze with a critical artist's eye, ugliness and deficits seem unacceptable. Then one action leads to another – it's a puzzle consisting of the physical limitations and affordances of the space, the potential of the materials at hand, and possibilities for their creative reuse. I might start with a small change in one room and end up many changes and several hours later in another. The goal is to create a pleasing aesthetic environment for me and my imaginary guests.

I easily become wholly involved, and the activity can take over my day. It helps put my teaching and research in perspective. The physical movement and visual judgment enable me see my work at arm's length while concerns simmer on the back burner.

I've learned that domesticity was suppressed in modern art and architecture (Haar & Reed, 1996). Nevertheless, many unexceptional things can be seen as art and are worthy of study where the value is not merely financial but, rather, is in the process of creating (Pocius, 1995) including home objects and their

FIGURE 5.1

Heather's home décor as art: this table, often moved by my mother to gain a new perspective, is now a feature of my domestic compositions

arrangement (Lackey, 2005; Lai & Ball, 2002; Leach, 2002). Like Garvey's (2001) Norwegian participants, for me, moving furniture is akin to organizing my thoughts. A material culture perspective considers objects in relation to the lives of the makers and users (Glassie, 1999), and objects are often imbued with symbolism and meaning (Knappett, 2005).

Paper Art-Dolls: Cecile's Narrative

I gravitate towards particular forms of art/craft-making. I'm not sure what to call them except that they are mostly private and non-functional. I'm drawn to scrappy bits of left-over paper that I collage into messy post-card combinations or journals that rarely result in anything useful. I keep them for myself and I enjoy looking over them but don't show them to anyone.

After a long day crammed with teaching, marking, revisions on papers, administrative meetings, and supervision emails, I collapse in my chair in the living room and engage in an activity that I rarely share with others. Around my chair, I have created a hamster nest with various containers of supplies – collections of odds and ends of paper. There, I huddle over a small side table, armed with glue and scissors, and make paper dolls. I call them "art dolls" to give them some dignity but they really are just dolls made out of scraps of paper. I started making them some months ago and they have now become a compulsion. Ostensibly, I watch TV, but it's nothing that requires my total attention. As I watch, I piece the doll together.

I begin with the face, drawing in the features with black markers and filling with water colours. My drawing skills are limited so I can only draw one type of face, although I love making different noses and I'm experimental with skin colour. Once the face is done, I find hair. From the hair, her shape takes form. I sift through the scraps of papers until something catches my eye. As I cut and glue, the paper doll comes into her own. Simultaneously, I can feel the tension ease and my mind clear of its clutter. The process is mostly unconscious although I do make some deliberate decisions. I might see a flower on a scrapbook sheet and think hair *and build on that. For one doll, I found paper that had a 1960s look to it and created a sixties doll. I generally draw the arms, legs, and shoes free-hand. When I first began making these dolls, the arms and legs tended to be straight up and down because this was the easiest for me but, lately, they have become more free-form. The hands are also simple mitten or claw shapes. I did try to make fingers at one point but this became too much like work. The end product is by no means neat and tidy but I always feel a stab of pure pleasure as the character materializes – a feeling that continues each time I look at them.*

FIGURE 5.2   Cecile's paper art-dolls: Becoming in the world of imagination

I have learned that what I do in my art-making is a form of collage. I do not repurpose commercial images but it is collage because bits of paper are glued together. Collage is a form of remixing, altering, and bricolage (Scotti & Chilton, 2018). By piecing together colour, image, and other elements into a new unified form, new associations and meaning are created. These items evoke an aesthetic, emotional response linked to an expression of non-verbal personal values (Gerstenblatt, 2013). Significantly, the essential property of collage is its physicality, its materiality – it becomes tangible (Chilton & Scotti, 2014). Davis (2008) suggests that collage is a metaphor for *becoming* because of the continual deconstruction and reparation of objects. As for doll-making, this craft has a long history in cultures all over the world as sacred items in religious ceremonies and as objects of intense cultural value. Dolls tend to reflect societal roles, values, and consumption patterns, and continue to be prevalent in popular culture (Reifel, 2009). More recently, dolls have been used for their transformative power in therapeutic circles (Alander, Prescott, & James, 2015; Bisiani & Angus, 2012). Particularly relevant is the idea that dolls "stimulate the realms of fantasy" and "let us stay in the world of our imagination" (Feen-Calligan, McIntyre, & Sands-Goldstein, 2009, p. 168). In making a doll, doll-makers often experience their own re-creation.

Haley's Analysis

The artistic hobbies, described in Heather and Cecile's reflexive narratives, are necessary for identity de- and re-construction and personal wellbeing; they can also holistically influence teaching practice. These artistic hobbies bridge the mind and body to gain deeper knowledge through two different neurocognitive processes (Czamanski-Cohen & Weihs, 2016). First, they help the creator process internal implicit knowledge gained through *somatosensory* experiences of touch, pain, temperature, body positioning, and muscle tension (Smith & Lane, 2015). In addition, *interoceptive* knowledge describes information gained through felt sensations that arise within the body and are linked to intuitive *gut-feelings* (Smith & Lane, 2015). These nonverbal ways of knowing can create spaces for broader metacognitive understandings by evaluating arising emotions to gain personal meaning (Brosch & Sander, 2013). Through integrating the mind, body, emotions, and imagination, new ontologies and epistemologies can be created. Two issues emerging from the narratives are worth exploring further: sacred spaces and flow; and embodied knowledge.

Sacred Spaces and Flow

Without validating spaces that allow for creativity, rest, and contemplation, one cannot *let go* – an action necessary for recreation, restructuring, and re-storying our lives (Moon, 2001). *Heather's Reassembled Rooms* and *Cecile's Hamster Nest* invite fluidity and non-judgment of the self(ves) through fashioning a sacred physical transitional space. Imagined guests and created figures are invited into the creative space where they present a validating gaze. These imagined beings are mirrors to the selves. Winnicott (1951) coined a transitional space as a place where both reality and imagination coincide within a third transitional space of playfulness and creativity.

Sacred spaces can be elicited through the psychological process of creation itself. Through embodying her mother's process of creating a new home-space of colourful possibilities, Heather is re-enacting her mother's motions and values, while engaging in a family tradition of décor magically passed down from mother to daughter. The ritualization of a daily practice that transitions Cecile from work to home life can underline its sacred and vital nature. This psychological transitional space can be elicited through the *flow* state (Csikszentmihalyi, 1996). *Flow* describes when someone feels fully absorbed in a project that is energizing and enjoyable, while dissolving the sense of self, space, and time by mixing action with awareness (Csikszentmihalyi, 1996). This dissolution of self-consciousness can deconstruct the "I" and create space for new epistemologies to emerge.

This concept of engaging in flow through meditative ritual practice to overcome the duality of self-and-object has been performed within religions such as Buddhism, Taoism, and Sufism (Mirdal, 2012). The process of flow is described in mindfulness as "the awareness that emerges through paying attention on purpose, in the present moment, and non-judgmentally to the unfolding of experience moment by moment" (Kabat-Zinn, 2003, p. 147). When one is open to intuitive choices between patterns, shapes, and colour, the effervescent artistic process unfolds moment to moment.

Embodied Knowledge

Psychiatrist van der Kolk (2014) discusses how the body is imprinted by lived experiences, particularly deeply emotional ones that shake the core of our existence. If identity is the integration of experiences, our bodies are vital spaces to feel the *self*. Neoliberal teachers and academics are often referred to as *talking heads*, presenting a disembodied state of engaging in cerebral routes of writing, reading, analyzing, and presenting information. This disembodiment may intensify with increased use of technology. When engaging in creative action through kinaesthetic and sensory movement, art making activates different forms of unconscious emotional knowing while simultaneously allowing for metacognition to take place. As Heather stated, she sees her work at arm's length. Metacognition is the ability to be thoughtful about one's own thinking patterns, which is beneficial for reflexive processes (Flavell, 1979).

Recent literature describes how art making can be relaxing and reduce cortisol levels (Henderson & Rosen, 2007; Kaimal, Ray, & Muniz, 2016). Stressors that build throughout the day can be released through physical motions of cutting, gluing, moving furniture, etc. (Levine, 1997). Thus, while creating, our body self-regulates. This relaxed state can allow for the creator to trust in new intuitive ideas and for the possibilities of symbolic, sensory, and nonverbal thought to appear through the artistic process without judgement (LeDoux, 2000; Lusebrink, 2004; Walsh, Radcliffe, Castillo, Kumar, & Broschard, 2007).

Academia often prioritizes knowledge developed and disseminated through language, yet the "limitations of introspection through solely verbal aspects have long been recognized" (Czamanski-Cohen & Weihs, 2016, p. 69). The English language privileges linear thinking process, which is helpful in generating some ideas but can be limiting when drawing larger connections between concepts and allowing for understandings to organically and cyclically deepen. When creating embodied art, one is no longer limited to language and can work within the realms of other intuitive ways of knowing (Allen, 1995).

Visual images can contain many dichotomous symbolic meanings at the same time, while three-dimensional spaces allow for embodied possibilities to emerge (Finley & Knowles, 1995; Weber, 2008). By creating dolls and bodies, Cecile can metaphorically reflect the multiple past, subconscious, and potential future identities of the creator. They have the potential to evoke sacred ritual objects, while simultaneously bringing forth fantastical childhood remembrances (Feen-Calligan et al., 2009). The creator and objects are both one and separate, simultaneously creating and re-creating one another through each scrap paper added to the bricolage (Barad, 2007). The faces of the dolls become tiny mirrors to Cecile's multiple I's. The potential of each object and colour in the domestic space can reflect Heather's family heritage, sacred memories, or exotic potential spaces of home and office. She can travel through space and time by arranging and changing her home. She can bring forth spirits. Through co-construction, the space, objects, and identities are interdependent and ever-evolving.

The artistic and embodied processes of co- and inter-creation can form connections that may never have felt possible otherwise. They simultaneously generate boundaries and both re-form and reinstate authentic momentary identity that takes into account the full human being and intricacies of existence (Barad, 2007). Perhaps in some moments, the fluid identities of academics, researchers, women, teachers, and artists are consolidated, when the time seems suspended in creation. This is done within a sacred and safe space of non-judgement, created by both Heather and Cecile. These spaces of validation and self-care can also extend to the teaching of students.

Final Thoughts

In this chapter, we have explored the influences of art in the formation of our worldviews and how artistic and aesthetic experiences shape our thinking (Finley & Knowles, 1995). In our safe spaces, and through engaging in embodied practices, we expand our energies and imagination. These imaginative selves create the possibilities for future selves. We argue that these imaginative selves provide the substrate for our professional teacher identities because they allow us to connect to students from a creative, artistic, imaginative space. As Snowber (2017) suggests, "the alchemy of our lives occurs in the cracks. Light is in the cracks, places of brilliance dwell there too" (p. 3).

References

Adams, T. E., & Holman, J. S. (2011). Telling stories: Reflexivity, queer theory and autoethnography. *Cultural Studies: Critical Methodologies, 11*(2), 108–116.

Alander, H., Prescott, T., & James, I. A. (2015). Older adults' views and experiences of doll therapy in residential care homes. *Dementia, 14*(5), 574–588.

Allen, A. (2011). Foucault and the politics of ourselves. *History of Human Sciences,* *24*(4), 43–59.

Allen, P. B. (1995). *Art is a way of knowing: A guide to self-knowledge and spiritual fulfillment through creativity.* Boston, MA: Shambhala Publications.

Attard, K. (2012). The role of narrative writing in improving professional practice. *Educational Action Research, 20*(1), 161–175.

Auther, E. (2010). *String, felt, thread: The hierarchy of art and craft in American art.* Minneapolis, MN: University of Minnesota Press.

Barad, K. (2007). *Meeting the universe halfway: Quantum physics and the entanglement of matter and meaning.* Durham, NC: Duke University Press.

Bisiani, L., & Angus, J. (2012). Doll therapy: A therapeutic means to meet past attachment needs and diminish behaviours of concern in a person living with dementia: A case study approach. *Dementia, 12*(4), 447–462.

Blumenfeld-Jones, D. S. (2016). The artistic process and arts-based research: A phenomenological account of the practice. *Qualitative Inquiry, 22*(5), 322–333.

Bratich, J. Z., & Brush, H. M. (2011). Fabricating activism: Craft-work, popular culture, gender. *Utopian Sciences, 22*(2), 233–260.

Brosch, T., & Sander, D. (2013). The appraising brain: Towards a neuro-cognitive model of appraisal processes in emotion. *Emotion Review, 5*(2), 163–168.

Chilton, G., & Scotti, V. (2014). Snipping, gluing, writing: The properties of collage as an arts-based research practice in art therapy. *Art Therapy: Journal of the American Art Therapy Association, 31*(4), 163–171.

Christensen, D. E. (2011). "Look at us now!": Scrapbooking, regimes of value and the risks of (auto)ethnography. *Journal of American Folklore, 124*(493), 175–210.

Csikszentmihalyi, M. (1996). *Creativity: Flow and the psychology of discovery and invention.* New York, NY: Harper Collins.

Czamanski-Cohen, J., & Weihs, K. L. (2016). The bodymind model: A platform for studying the mechanisms of change induced by art therapy. *Arts Psychotherapy, 51*, 63–71.

Davis, B., Browne, J., Gannon, S., Honan, E., Laws, C., Mueller-Rockstroh, B., & Petersen, E. B. (2004). The ambivalent practices of reflexivity. *Qualitative Inquiry, 10*(3), 360–389.

Davis, D. (2008). Collage inquiry: Creative and particular applications. *Learning Landscapes, 2*(1), 245–265.

Eisner, E. W. (2008). Art and knowledge. In J. G. Knowles & A. L. Cole (Eds.), *Handbook of the arts in qualitative research: Perspectives, methodologies, examples, and issues* (pp. 1–12). Thousand Oaks, CA: Sage Publications.

Faulkner, S. L., Kaunert, C. A., Kluch, Y., Saygin-Koc, E., & Trotter, S. P. (2016). Using arts-based research exercises to foster reflexivity in qualitative research. *Learning Landscapes, 9*(2), 197–212.

Feen-Calligan, H., McIntyre, B., & Sands-Goldstein, M. (2009). Art therapy applications of dolls in grief recovery, identity and community service. *Art Therapy: Journal of American Art Therapy Association, 26*(4), 167–173.

Finley, S., & Knowles, J. G. (1995). Researcher as artist/artist as researcher. *Qualitative Inquiry, 1*(1), 110–142.

Flavell, J. H. (1979). Metacognition and cognitive monitoring: A new area of cognitive-developmental inquiry. *American Psychologist, 34*(10), 906–911.

Garvey, P. (2001). Organized disorder: Moving furniture in Norwegian homes. In D. Miller (Ed.), *Home possessions: Material culture behind closed doors* (pp. 47–68). Oxford: Berg.

Gerstenblatt, P. (2013). Collage portraits as a method of analysis in qualitative research. *International Journal of Qualitative Methods, 12*, 294–309.

Glassie, H. (1999). *Material culture*. Bloomington, IN: Indiana University Press.

Haar, S., & Reed, C. (1996). Coming home. In C. Reed (Ed.), *Not at home: The suppression of domesticity in modern art and architecture* (pp. 253–273). London: Thames & Hudson.

Henderson, P., & Rosen, D. (2007). Empirical study on the healing nature of mandalas. *Psychology of Aesthetics, Creativity, and the Arts, 1*(3), 148–154.Kabat-Zinn, J. (2003). Mindfulness-based interventions in context: Past, present and future. *Clinical Psychology: Science and Practice, 10*, 144–156.

Kaimal, G., Ray, K., & Muniz, J. (2016). Reduction of cortisol levels and participants' responses following art making. *Art Therapy, 33*(2), 74–80.

Knappett, C. (2005). *Thinking through material culture: An interdisciplinary perspective*. Philadelphia, PA: University of Pennsylvania Press.

Koro-Ljungberg, M. (2016). *Reconceptualising qualitative research: Methodologies without methodology*. Los Angeles, CA: Sage Publications.

Lackey, L. (2005). Home sweet home? Decorating magazines as contexts for art education. *Studies in Art Education, 46*(4), 323–338.

Lai, A., & Ball, E. (2002). Home is where the art is: Exploring the places people live through art education. *Studies in Art Education, 44*(1), 47–66.

Lather, P. (1993). Fertile obsession: Validity after poststructuralism. *The Sociological Quarterly, 34*(4), 673–693.

Lather, P. (2013). Methodology-21: What do we do in the afterward? *International Journal of Qualitative Studies in Education, 26*(6), 634–645.

Leach, R. (2002). What happened at home with art: Tracing the experience of consumers. In C. Painter (Ed.), *Contemporary art and the home* (pp. 153–180). Oxford: Berg.

LeDoux, J. (2000). Emotion circuits in the brain. *Annual Reviews of Neuroscience, 23*, 155–184.

Levine, P. (1997). *Waking the tiger*. Berkeley, CA: North Atlantic Press.

Lusebrink, V. B. (2004). Art therapy and the brain: An attempt to understand the underlying processes of art expression in therapy. *Art Therapy, 21*(3), 125–135.

Lyle, E. (2013). From method to methodology: Narrative as a way of knowing for adult learners. *The Canadian Journal for the Study of Adult Education, 25*(2), 17–34.

McNiff, S. (2011). Artistic expressions as primary modes of inquiry. *British Journal of Guidance & Counselling, 39*(5), 385–396.

Metta, M. (2011). *Writing against, alongside and beyond memory: Lifewriting as reflexive, poststructuralist feminist research practice*. Bern: Peter Lang AG, Internationaler Verlag der Wissenschaften.

Mirdal, G. M. (2012). Mevlana Jalāl-ad-Dīn Rumi and mindfulness. *Journal of Religion and Health, 5*, 1202–1215.

Moddle, C. (2017). *Knit together: A study of late nineteenth-century knitting patterns through contemporary eyes and hands* (Unpublished masters thesis). Memorial University of Newfoundland, St. John's.

Moon, C. (2001). *Studio art therapy: Cultivating the artist identity within the art therapist*. London: Jessica Kingsley Publishers.

Nisbett, R. E., & Wilson, T. D. (1997). Telling more than we can know: Verbal reports on mental processes. *Psychological Review, 84*, 231–259.

Pocius, G. (1995). Art. *Journal of American Folklore, 108*(430), 413–431.

Reifel, S. (2009). Girls doll play in educational, virtual, ideological and market contexts: A case analysis of controversy. *Contemporary Issues in Early Childhood, 10*(4), 343–352.

Robertson, K., & Vinebaum, L. (2016). Crafting community. *TEXTILE, 14*(1), 2–13.

Scotti, V., & Chilton, G. (2018). Collage as arts-based research. In P. Leavy (Ed.), *Handbook of arts-based research* (pp. 355–376). New York, NY: The Guilford Press.

Smith, R., & Lane, R. D. (2015). The neural basis of one's own conscious and unconscious emotional states. *Neuroscience & Biobehavioral Reviews, 57*, 1–29.

Snowber, C. (2017). Living, loving, and dancing the questions: A pedagogy of becoming. In S. Wiebe, E. Lyle, P. R. Wright, K. Dark, M. McLarnon, & L. Day (Eds.), *Ways of being in teaching* (pp. 1–5). Rotterdam, The Netherlands: Sense Publishers.

van der Kolk, B. (2014). *The body keeps the score: Mind, brain and body in the transformation of trauma*. New York, NY: Viking.

Walsh, S. M., Radcliffe, R. S., Castillo, L. C., Kumar, A. M., & Broschard, D. M. (2007). A pilot study to test the effects of art-making classes for family caregivers of patients with cancer. *Oncology Nursing Forum, 34*(1), E9–E16.

Weber, S. (2008). Visual images in research. In J. G. Knowles & A. L. Cole (Eds.), *Handbook of the arts in qualitative research: perspectives and issues* (pp. 42–54). Thousand Oaks, CA: Sage Publications.

Winnicott, D. W. (1951). Transitional objects and transitional phenomena. In D. W. Winnicott (Ed.), *Collected papers: Through paediatrics to psycho-analysis* (pp. 229–242). London: Karnac.

CHAPTER 6

(Re)Constructing Anti-Colonial Teacher Identities through Reflexive Inquiry

Adrian Downey and Casey Burkholder

Introduction

Since the Truth and Reconciliation Commission of Canada (TRC) released its final report in 2015 (TRC, 2015) and its calls for action in 2014, the legacy of colonialism in Canada has become a point of national interest and, perhaps, shame (Peters, 2016). Faculties of Education across Canada have done much work toward the integration of Indigenous knowledges into the curriculum and working toward respectful relationships with local First Nations (Archibald, Lundy, Reynolds, & Williams, 2010). In our own experiences in universities in Quebec and the Maritimes, it seems as though Indigenous issues are at the forefront of people's minds, yet we wonder whether this cognitive presence exists as a regime of truth (Foucault, 1977) built on the colonial politics of recognition (Coulthard, 2014), or as a genuine effort for systemic change, the recognition of Indigenous sovereignty, and the building of sustainable relationships between Indigenous people and settlers (TRC, 2015). In other words, we wonder if the talk of "Indigenizing," "reconciling," and "decolonizing" is a way of pacifying Indigenous unrest while maintaining the underlying structures and ideologies of the settler colonial state.

As researchers in the field of education, we seek to address the ways in which settler-teachers – like Casey – take up "Indigenous issues," including their relationship with local Indigenous peoples and knowledges, as well as the way the curriculum constructs and perpetuates particular narratives about Indigenous peoples and knowledges. In this chapter, we weave our reflexive experiences together in order to respond to the following questions: (1) What does it mean to call attention to settler colonialism from within colonial schooling processes? (2) How might this work be complicated as we inhabit the standpoint of teachers who negotiate the boundaries between Indigenous (Adrian) and white settler (Casey) identities? In responding to the questions, we demonstrate that through reflexive inquiry, we are able to reconstruct our teacher identities to respond to settler colonialism with resistance, solidarity, and a spirit of reconciliation.

© KONINKLIJKE BRILL NV, LEIDEN, 2018 | DOI:10.1163/9789004388901_006

Relational Positioning

Toward the establishment of relational accountability (Wilson, 2008) and authorial transparency, we take this opportunity to introduce ourselves. Adrian is a Mi'kmaw PhD student at a Faculty of Education on the traditional territory of the Wolastoqey people. His Indigenous ancestry comes through his maternal family, who are all members of the Qalipu Mi'kmaw First Nation and mostly live in St. George's, Newfoundland. Growing up, Adrian returned to Newfoundland each summer, where he learned from the land, his uncles, aunts, and the traditions of his people. After completing his undergraduate degrees, Adrian worked in Eeyou Istchee with the James Bay Cree for two years. In this chapter, he reflexively revisits (Burawoy, 2003, 2009) the ways that he reproduced colonial teaching practices and performed aspects of a settler identity because he was initially perceived as white within the school context.

Casey is a white female settler who grew up in Treaty 8 territory – Fort Smith, Northwest Territories – and has since lived in Treaty 7 (Calgary), Treaty 1 (Winnipeg), Kanien'keha:ka (Mohawk) territory (Montreal), and in lands encompassed in the Wabinaki Confederacy (Wolfville, Charlottetown, and now Fredericton). Looking back on her work as a Social Studies methods professor in Quebec and Prince Edward Island, she revisits a 90-second cellphilm (cellphone + film-production, see MacEntee, Burkholder & Schwab-Cartas, 2016; Mitchell & de Lange, 2013) she created to share with her students who were pre-service teachers. The cellphilm described her positionality as a white female settler who is concerned with issues relating to consent, land, and histories that are missing from Social Studies curricula. Casey intended for the cellphilm to situate her positionality as a critical social studies educator, and introduce the students to cellphilming as a method of inquiry. She also intended to disrupt settler colonial ideals embedded within the Social Studies classroom in Atlantic Canada. In reflection, she wonders if her practices may have reified settler colonial assumptions.

Story Sharing

Within many Indigenous intellectual traditions, story is theory (Archibald, 2008; Brayboy, 2005; King, 2003). Within settler research traditions, story can be seen as method (See for example, Connelly & Candinin, 1986; Leavy, 2015). We seek to disrupt the traditional academic article structure by first turning to our experiences, and then moving forward with a discussion of the methodologies we employ and the results of our study.

Adrian – Liminality and Internal Colonization

The question with which I have wrestled over the last 10 years of my life is what it means to be Indigenous, an Indian, Native, and more specifically, Mi'kmaw. I never thought of picking blueberries, listening to my aunts and uncles' stories, or making bannock as being markers of my Indigeneity; they were just things my family did, especially when we went to Newfoundland. It wasn't until I moved away that I began to look deeper into my family's history and unique experience of settler colonialism, which ultimately led to the erasure of my family's Indigeneity (Downey, 2017; see also Tuck & McKenzie, 2015). It was with some reluctance that I began identifying as Mi'kmaw[1] and trying to figure out exactly what that meant.

In 2013, about a year after I was federally recognized as an "Indian,"[2] I took a teaching job in a small Northern Cree community in Eeyou Istchee. Professionally, I was interested in working with Indigenous peoples around implementing and delivering Indigenous curriculum to Indigenous students. Personally, I hoped that by surrounding myself with Indigenous people, I might be able to better understand what it meant for me to call myself Indigenous. Not surprisingly, my students did not recognize me as an Indigenous person. My fair skin, lack of Indigenous language, and position as "outsider" in the community created a tangible separation between us. There were very few people in the community who knew I was Indigenous. Most people perceived me as a white teacher, including the majority of my colleagues in the school.

As I explored my personal identity, my professional identity was also taking shape. Though I had initially attempted to teach my classes using traditional Indigenous teaching methods such as storytelling, sharing circles, and land-based activities, I soon began to internalize the Western expectations placed on me by the administration and my colleagues. My pedagogy shifted toward attempts at rigid classroom management, evidence-based decision making, and adherence to a curriculum mandated by the government and disconnected from my students' reality as well as my own. These changes made me uncomfortable with myself and my teaching, and I tried to find ways of subverting the silent and explicit expectations that were made of me. Toward the second half of my first year of teaching, I again attempted to integrate storytelling pedagogy – this time using a more teacher-centered approach. Despite these small changes, I still felt disconnected from myself in the school environment.

In my second year of teaching, I felt much more centered in my Indigeneity, but the professional disconnect lingered. I had made friends in the community and spent several days each month learning from Cree Elders. I also spent a large amount of time walking in the forest, sitting by the lake, and listening to the wind. In the wind, I heard my grandfather's voice, which served as a constant reminder of who I was and where I was going. When I entered the school, however, the wind stopped. Within the confines of the school, I was a white teacher – I walked like a white teacher, spoke like a white teacher and, I am ashamed to say, listened like one too. Upon reflection, I realize that this had more to do with my reason for leaving after my second year than anything else. I wanted to fully explore the other side of me that was developing. Thus, after two years in the North, I returned to my territory, Mi'kma'ki, to learn from my own people.

Casey – Reifying Settler Colonialism

Growing up in Fort Smith in the 1990s, I was schooled in an Indigenous-majority public elementary school. Elders were integrated into some classrooms, but were absent from others. Some teachers valued and made space for Indigenous knowledges, stories, and practices. Other teachers stuck to the curriculum – Alberta's curriculum at that time. As kids, each year, our school would take us to spend a week with Elders on the Salt River, learning different skills, from beading and tanning to catching and drying fish. The older kids learned trapping, or maybe it was just the boys. My memories of that time are tinged with nostalgia and, even when I squint back into the past, I cannot reproduce the memory exactly. I remember being so proud of the fish that I caught and had been taught so carefully to gut, stretch, and dry over the fire, and then being so disappointed when my parents made me leave it outside. I learned that that outside learning was different from what was accepted in my house.

I have often squinted back at those memories of learning from Elders and learning from the land, and how I was included in these practices. I have also thought about what it meant to leave these learnings up North when my family eventually moved South. I have thought back about what it meant to learn Alberta's curriculum in Fort Smith, and how the curriculum privileged certain kinds of learning, while silencing or excluding others. In my work as a Social Studies teacher-educator, I have tried to unsettle my settler-learners by making them explore films by Indigenous peoples, illuminate moments in history that have been silenced in their schooling histories, including the Sixties and Millennial Scoops, the forced relocation of Inuit peoples, and stories about place and geography from the communities – Mi'kmaq (Charlottetown) and Kanien'keha:ka (Montreal) – in whose territory we were settling and studying. Though I worked with these learners to think about issues of consent and land and tried to unsettle the ways in which they understood specific stories about Indigenous peoples, I did so through a largely settler-lens and using traditional teacher-centered approaches.

I created a short 90 second cellphilm (cellphone + film production) to share with my pre-service teachers, through which I hoped to share my history of settling, studying, and working across the territory now known as Canada. In this cellphilm, I shared my knowledge of the Treaties, and how my family had migrated across this territory for different work opportunities. I shared some of my memories of my Northern childhood. Looking back, I recognize that this cellphilm centered my story of settling and did not name the systemic injustices from which my family has profited. In my instructional practices, and in my effort to unsettle the problematic stories and attitudes present in many of the pre-service teacher classrooms about Indigenous peoples, I realized I was engaging in what Eve Tuck (2009, p. 415) has called "damage-centered" teaching. I thought I needed to shake these settler students out of their complacency by bombarding them with stories they hadn't heard and by challenging settler colonialism from within Faculties of Education. I drew on the methods of Indigenous scholars who also teach Social Studies, like Angelina Weenie (2010, 2014) who worked with youth to rethink the practice of map-making in the context of Pond Inlet, Nunavut. I asked these students to create visual productions on cellphones that spoke about coming to terms with settler colonialism in an effort to work toward change. My methods, and the results of the students' cellphilms, have made me think that I reified settler colonialism, and encouraged "damage-centred" thinking and settler inaction (Tuck, 2009, p. 415).

Methodology

Though the output of what we have attempted through this study may appear similar, the philosophical positions we occupy in relation to this reflexive process are unique to our individual experiences. Indeed, as Tuck and McKenzie (2015) have alluded to, in recent years there has been a considerable amount of mixing and matching in methodology, ultimately contributing to the blurring of lines between terms, philosophies, approaches, and paradigms. Casey has conceptualized our mutual exploration using the terms self-study and memory work as method to arrive at a practice of engaging "formal and informal policies, programs and processes, as well as individual educational experiences" (Fraser & Michell, 2015, p. 330).

Self Study and Memory Work

In looking to self-study, Casey draws on the work of Claudia Mitchell and Sandra Weber (Mitchell & Weber, 1999; Pithouse-Morgan, Mitchell, & Weber, 2009) who explored teacher identity and ways of studying the practices of teachers. Casey also draws from the scholarship of Angelina Weenie (2014), who has employed self-study in reflecting on her memories of teaching as "from personal knowledge and experiences that [she] can begin to formulate a theoretical and conceptual base for teaching" (p. 505). Weenie contends that reflection and self-study are a necessary part of teaching, in order to understand ourselves and our learners; for Weenie, "the essence of self-study is to put together the small stones of experience and envision a new way of education, one that enhances personal power and agency ... It calls for a deepening process and relies on ceremony" (p. 505).

Memory work, or the practice of engaging memories to illuminate understanding about a particular temporality, is not fixed and has the potential to be transformative for individuals, groups, and histories (Booth, 2008; McNamara, 2009; Mitchell & Pithouse-Morgan, 2014; Onyx & Small, 2001; Pithouse-Morgan & van Laren, 2015; Radstone, 2000). The practice of engaging memories as a feminist research methodology has been attributed to Frigga Haug (1992) who drew on women's memories to make sense of the gaps between their personal experiences and theories about gender and socialization. Memory work is inherently political, and "time and place affect the formation, recall and representation of memories" (Fraser & Michell, 2015, p. 323). Casey conceptualizes memory work as method in order to reach back to access her memories to connect the personal which, for her, includes sharing memories of her teaching and learning histories. She also acknowledges that memory work necessarily mixes with her contemporary and political realities – which, for her, includes teaching and living on unceded territory of the Wolastoqey peoples.

Grounded Normativity

I (Adrian), on the other hand, conceptualize the story sharing and reflection in this article as an extension of my very being. This is perhaps best articulated using Leanne Betasamosake Simpson's concept of Kwe as resurgent method based in grounded normativity. Simpson (2017) explains:

> ... my people have always generated knowledge through the combination of emotion and intellectual knowledge within the kinetics of our place-based practices, as mitigated through our bodies, minds, and spirits ... within Nishnaabewin [grounded normativity; Indigenous Intelligence], I am fully responsible for generating meaning about my life through the way I think and live. (pp. 29–30)

Though I am neither Kwe (woman) nor Nishnaabe, Simpson's framing of individual meaning-making through living in relation and in holistic connection speaks to the approach I use here. As several Mi'kmaw Elders have told me, the only thing in which we can ever be an *expert* is our own experience or story. It is, thus, my ethical responsibility to make sense of my world and my place within the world based on my experiences (Simpson, 2017). Additionally, where Simpson's thoughts and reflections emerge from her presence within Nishnaabewin, which she likens to grounded normativity or a rootedness in one's culture, traditions, and land-based practice (Coulthard, 2014), I articulate the generation of my own thinking from within the Mi'kmaw concept of netukulimk (also: netaklimk; netukuli'mk). Netukulimk can be translated a variety of ways but, in this context, I take it to refer to our way of life (Bernard, Rosenmeier, & Farrell, 2015). I liken netukulimk to the concept of grounded normativity by including three questions often asked by Elder Albert Marshall (2018): Who are you? Where do you come from? Where are you going? In answering these questions through the frame of netukulimk, or living in relationship with the land, I can conceptualize my own grounded normativity, or the framing through which I make sense of my place in this world.

Settler Colonialism

The manner in which we make sense of our experiences here is also informed by theories of settler-colonialism. One way of conceptualizing settler colonialism is through Tuck and McKenzie's (2015) three structured antagonisms: Indigenous erasure, Black containment, and White ascension. Settler colonialism, which can be differentiated from colonialism through the colonizer's permanent occupation of the territory, can only exist if it has stolen land and cheap labour to work it. In order for white settlers to *ascend* in their wealth, Indigenous peoples must first be removed from the land or erased, allowing settlers to access and exploit it for economic gain. As the economy of the settled land grows, it becomes necessary to find cheap labour sources. In the North American context, this was done through chattel slavery and the containment of black bodies. In short, the settler colonial nation states of North America exist as economic super powers because they successfully maintained the three structured antagonisms of settler colonialism. White settlers took Indigenous land and erased Indigenous peoples in the process, and then repopulated the land with African slaves who were forced to work the land to secure the wealth of white settlers, thus cementing North America as *the land of opportunity* for white settlers.

Settler colonialism is still endemic to North American society (Brayboy, 2005). This is particularly evident in the United States through the dearth of voice given to Indigenous issues (a form of continued erasure) and the school to prison pipeline (a form of containment). In Canada, the politics of recognition masks the government's policy of assimilation, creating a *polite* form of settler colonialism in which the structured antagonisms still exist, but are obscured through multicultural discourse and sloganized sentiments such as "diversity is our strength" (Coulthard, 2014).

Simpson (2017) articulates that settler colonialism's effects include macro erasure and the loss of grounded normativity. By removing Indigenous peoples from the land, the colonial state has succeeded in disconnecting us/them from everything that makes us/them who we/they are (Meyer, 2008). In being disconnected from our land and our traditions, Indigenous peoples have begun to internalize settler colonial ideologies of heteropatriarchy (Simpson, 2017), ableism (Kress, 2017), as well as the very exploitative economic models that work toward our/their dispossession (Simpson, 2017). Settler colonialism is driven on non-consensual relationships between individuals and themselves, other human beings, the natural world, and the cosmos and thus functions in an ideological binary to the traditional philosophies of Indigenous peoples (Stonechild, 2016). It is with this understanding of settler colonialism as non-consensual relationship and exploitative economic model built on Indigenous erasure and Black containment that we move forward in our reflection.

Reflexively Revisiting (Our) Settler Colonialism

As we reflect, we think through what it means to be a teacher in a society still driven by the personally oppressive and structurally exploitative economic model of settler colonialism. In this section, we present our personal reflections in order to call for change in Faculties of Education.

Adrian – Internal and Internalized Colonization

When I started my teaching career, I had only begun my journey toward discovering my Indigenous heritage, and had only a tentative internal challenge to many of the expectations, behaviours, and ideologies of settler colonialism. I did not, at the time, have a strong connection to the land, my community, nor the one in which I lived. I was displaced from my grounded normativity. This displacement created a fragility in the balance of my being – perhaps my intellectual and physical needs were being met, but I was devoid of spiritual and emotional fulfilment. Failing to *fit in* with the community as I had hoped (perhaps because of my light skin, or my status as a teacher), I attempted to gain access to that fulfilment through my profession, which required me perform to the expectations of the school community, thus leaving behind the teaching methods most connected to who I am.

As I began to connect to the land and the community more, my confidence in myself grew, and I was better able to bridge the gap between Western and Indigenous teaching methods. Despite my shift toward storytelling pedagogy, I still experienced a division between my life within the school and my life outside of it. This division speaks to the divergent expectations of the wider community and the school community: in one setting I was accepted as I was and encouraged to explore my Indigeneity; in the other I was (subtly) expected to become something other than I was, and encouraged only when I enacted the behaviours associated with the Western concept of the *good teacher*. In my personal life, I felt strong and sure of myself, but within the school environment I felt disconnected and unbalanced. If this were the case for me, having only begun to uncover and connect with my Indigenous culture, I can only imagine how damaging the school environment was for my students. It is perhaps my biggest regret that I was unable to become a beacon of resistance and resurgence for my students in my early career; together we could have created an alternative space within the school – one built on acceptance rather than progress.

Casey – How Do You Teach History Equitably in the Wabanaki Confederacy?

One of the things that I continue to think through in my teaching and writing involves how pre-service teachers might be prepared to teach history equitably in what is currently known as Canada. I wonder what kinds of stories might be told instead of those that minimize the contributions and resilience of Indigenous peoples, as well as people of colour, queer people, and the dis/abled. It is important to complicate narratives of white benevolence and guilt within the Social Studies methods classroom, in order to move myself and my settler students toward ideas of complicity. It is also necessary to recognize and foreground the work that already been done by Indigenous Elders, knowledge keepers, intellectuals, and artists who have and shared stories and ways of knowing that resist settler narratives still prioritized in school-based histories, people like:[3] Cindy Blackstock, Erica Violet Lee, Ryan McMahon, Naiomi Metallic, Alanis Obomsawin, Pam Palmater, Imelda Perley, Tanya Talaga, Zoe Todd, Eve Tuck, Chelsea Vowel, Jesse Wente, Shirley Williams/Migizi ow-kwe, and Karla Jessen Williamson. At the same time, these pedagogical practices need to move toward action. As I continue to teach and think about how settler colonialism might be dismantled, I acknowledge that I do so from a privileged place of employment within a university – a settler structure. I am left wondering about the pervasiveness of whiteness and settlerisms in universities as institutions. Can these racist structures be changed from within? And by whom?

Conclusion

Settler colonial ideology permeates every aspect of our society (Brayboy, 2005), as do racism and racist ideologies (Ladson-Billings & Tate, 1995). As teachers, teacher-educators, researchers, and human beings, it is our responsibility to acknowledge and challenge structural inequalities. We believe that we can begin this process through rigorous reflexivity and the process of reflection, whether the process is framed as memory work, self-study, or existence within grounded normativity. We believe that we must stay vigilant toward the influence of settler colonial ideologies on our pedagogies, relationships, and our lives in general.

Growing up in a settler society, we acknowledge that we have been effectively colonized. Through Adrian's teacher training and broader socialization, he internalized settler colonial expectations associated with being a teacher and, when left disconnected from his community and the land, he was unable to challenge those expectations and create space for himself and his students, which perpetuated settler colonial educative practices and structure. Despite the express goal of challenging settler colonialism within social studies education, Casey's attempts at disrupting her students' narratives of history education, may have reified "damage-centered" narratives about Indigenous people (Tuck, 2009, p. 415).

The paths forward in decolonization and resurgence are marked by a knowledge of what has come before and a willingness to correct the mistakes of the past. As Mi'kmaw Elder Stephen Augustine told the TRC, reconciliation is about righting the tipped canoe: "[when we tip a canoe] we may lose some of our possessions .... Eventually we will regain our possessions [but] they will not be the same as the old ones" (S. Augustine quoted in TRC, 2015, p. 206). If your canoe tips over, your possessions are gone; that's it, but that doesn't mean you can right the canoe, dry it off, and continue down the river the next day. It is this willingness to continue on with a knowledge of past mistakes that defines our reflexive process, and which enables us to maintain our criticality of our own continued actions. To do this work, we call on Faculties of Education to put renewed efforts into harbouring reflexivity in their students. We encourage teacher-educators to move their students beyond the scripted discourses of criticality (Saul, 2017), into a position of rigorous self-examination. We ask teachers to turn their eyes inward to examine their own ideas and classrooms to see the ways in which settler colonialism continues to be internalized or reified. We ask teachers to reflect, and then to act on their reflections. We ask teachers to tip their own canoes, watch their possessions float away, then have the courage to right their canoe, dry it off, and continue down stream.

Notes

1   I was accepted as a member of the Qalipu Mi'kmaq First Nation in 2008, gained federal recognition (status) in 2012, but lost it in 2018 due to the membership review, primarily because I did not live in Newfoundland.
2   The term "Indian" is a legalistic designation of Indigeneity within Canada. Indians are federally recognized and registered under the Indian Act.
3   This list is by no means exhaustive, but is meant to acknowledge some of the Elders, knowledge keepers, intellectuals, and artists that I have brought into my Social Studies methods classroom.

References

Archibald, J. (2008). *Indigenous storywork: Educating the heart, mind, body, and spirit.* Vancouver: UBC Press.

Archibald, J., Lundy, J., Reynolds, C., & Williams, L. (2010). *Accord on indigenous education.* Retrieved from https://csse-scee.ca/acde/wp-content/uploads/sites/7/2017/08/Accord-on-Indigenous-Education.pdf

Bernard, T., Rosenmeier, L. M., & Farrell, S. L. (2015). *Teaching about the Mi'kmaq.* Nova Scotia: The Confederacy of Mainland Mi'kmaq.

Booth, W. J. (2008). The work of memory: Time, identity and justice. *Social Research, 75*(1), 237–262.

Brayboy, B. M. J. (2005). Toward a tribal critical race theory in education. *Urban Review: Issues and Ideas in Public Education, 37*(5), 425–446.

Burawoy, M. (2003). Revisits: An outline of a theory of reflexive ethnography. *American Sociological Review, 65*(5), 645–679.

Burawoy, M. (2009). *The extended case method: Four countries, four decades, four great transformations, and one theoretical tradition.* Berkeley, CA: University of California Press.

Connelly, F. M., & Clandinin, D. J. (1986). On narrative method, personal philosophy, and narrative unities in the story of teaching. *Journal of Research in Science Teaching, 23*(4), 293–310.

Coulthard, G. S. (2014). *Red skin, White masks: Rejecting the colonial politics of recognition.* Minneapolis, MN: University of Minnesota Press.

Downey, A. (2017). *Speaking in circle: Indigenous identity and White privilege* (Master's thesis). Mount Saint Vincent University, Halifax.

Foucault, M. (1977). *Discipline and punish: The birth of the prison.* New York, NY: Pantheon Books.

Fraser, H., & Michell, D. (2015). Feminist memory work in action: Method and practicalities. *Qualitative Social Work, 14*(3), 321–337.

Haug, F. (2008). Memory work. *Australian Feminist Studies, 23*(58), 537–541.

King, T. (2003). *The truth about stories: A native narrative.* Toronto: House of Anansi Press.

Kress, M. (2017). Reclaiming disability through pimatisiwin: Indigenous ethics, spatial justice, and gentle teaching. *Ethics, Equity, and Inclusive Education, 9*, 23–57.

Ladson-Billings, G., & Tate, W. (1995). Toward a critical race theory of education. *Teachers College Record, 97*(1), 47–68.

Leavy, P. (2015). *Method meets art: Arts-based research practice.* New York, NY: Guilford Publications.

Marshall, A. (2018, January 18). *Kisutmi': How do we move forward in a co-learning journey.* Fredericton: University of New Brunswick.

McNamara, P. (2009). Feminist ethnography, storytelling that makes a difference. *Qualitative Social Work, 8*(2), 161–177.

Meyer, M. (2008). Indigenous and authentic: Hawaiian epistemology and the triangulation of meaning. In N. Denzin, Y. Lincoln, & L. Smith (Eds.), *Handbook of critical and indigenous methodologies* (pp. 217–232). Thousand Oaks, CA: Sage Publications.

Mitchell, C., & Pithouse-Morgan, K. (2014). Expanding the memory catalogue: Southern African women's contributions to memory-work writing as a feminist research methodology. *Agenda, 28*(1), 92–103.

Mitchell, C., & Weber, S. (1999). *Reinventing ourselves: Beyond Nostalgia.* New York, NY: RoutledgeFalmer.

Onyx, J., & Small, J. (2001). Memory-work: The method. *Qualitative Inquiry, 7*(6), 773–786.

Peters, N. (2016). Learning shame: Colonial narratives as a tool for decolonization. In M. Battiste (Ed.), *Visision a Mi'kmaw humanities: Indigenizing the academy* (pp. 149–164). Sydney: Cape Breton University Press.

Pithouse-Morgan, K., Mitchell, C., & Weber, S. (2009). Self-study in teaching and teacher development: A call to action. *Educational Action Research, 17*(1), 43–62.

Pithouse-Morgan, K., & van Laren, L. (2015). Dialogic memory-work as a method to explore the "afterlife" of our self-study doctoral research. *International Journal of Qualitative Methods, 14*(1), 80–97.

Radstone, S. (Ed.). (2000). *Memory and methodology*. London: Bloomsbury Publishing.

Saul, R. (2017). When critical stances become scripted: Impediments to resonant dialogue in the education classroom. *Power and Education, 9*(3), 202–209.

Simpson, L. (2017). *As we have always done: Indigenous freedom through radical resistance*. Minneapolis, MN: University of Minnesota Press.

Strong-Wilson, T., Mitchell, C., Morrison, C., Radford, L., & Pithouse-Morgan, K. (2014). Looking forward through looking back: Using digital memory-work in teaching for transformation. In L. Thomas (Ed.), *Becoming teacher: Sites for teacher development in Canadian teacher education* (pp. 442–468). Toronto: Canadian Association for Teacher Education.

Truth and Reconciliation Commission of Canada. (2015). *Final report of the truth and reconciliation commission of Canada, summary: Honouring the truth, reconciling for the future* (Vol. 1). Toronto: James Lorimer & Company.

Tuck, E. (2009). Suspending damage: A letter to communities. *Harvard Educational Review, 79*(3), 409–427.

Tuck, E., & McKenzie, M. (2015). *Place in research: Theory, methodology, and methods*. New York, NY: Routledge.

Weenie, A. (2014). Reflections on teacher as change agent in indigenous education. In L. Thomas (Eds.), *Becoming teacher: Sites for teacher development in Canadian teacher education* (pp. 503–522). Toronto: Canadian Association for Teacher Education.

Wilson, S. (2008). *Research is ceremony: Indigenous research methods*. Black Point: Fernwood Publishing.

CHAPTER 7

Exploring Ecological Literacy in Teacher Identity: Reflexive Inquiry through a Learning Garden Curricula

Andrejs Kulnieks and Kelly Young

The impetus for this chapter was research conducted after developing a partnership between Trent University's School of Education and Peterborough's GreenUp Ecology Park. A program was conceptualized to engage teacher candidates in aspects of environmental education and food sustainability. By food sustainability we mean thinking about the different types of foods that are available in local farmers markets, as well as different methods of food cultivation, production, collection, and use. We ask candidates to consider the ecological footprint of transporting food from the perspective of understanding how to help plants grow. At the heart of the program are matters of ethical and sustainable relationships with nature in the development of ecological literacy and identity-formation as pre-service teachers. From this overarching theme, we focus on teaching and learning about food sustainability – that is, understanding where food comes from and how we have interconnected relationships with the natural world. The program was born of a belief that humans do not always see their direct connections with nature and that education can be a vehicle for understanding our place in the living world. Our program is enacted at Trent University and at the award-winning unique outdoor teaching classroom GreenUP Ecology Park:

> GreenUP Ecology Park is a five acre showcase of sustainable landscape ideas and resources. With a host of display gardens and naturalized areas, a native plant nursery, children's programs, garden market, skill-building workshops and hands-on displays, the park has everything you need to be a good steward of the land in your care. (http://www.greenup.on.ca/ecology-park/)

This chapter reports on a study that follows five-cohorts of pre-service teachers' engagement in a learning garden alternative placement to inspire a new generation of environmental leaders and to promote environmental education through the development of eco-literate pre-service teacher identity-formation.

© KONINKLIJKE BRILL NV, LEIDEN, 2018 | DOI:10.1163/9789004388901_007

FIGURE 7.1   Ecology Park sign (Young, 2013)

Context of the Study: Ecological Literacy and the Learning Garden Curriculum

In 2011, an Eco-mentorship program was created in response to the need to critically analyze the possibilities and limitations of the Ontario Ministry of Education's (2009) *Acting today, shaping tomorrow: A policy framework for environmental education in Ontario Schools* document (Bell, Elliott, Rodenburg, & Young, 2009). Students were engaged in multiple workshops that helped pre-service teachers integrate environmental education practices into their classrooms. In 2012, the Learning Garden Alternative Settings placement was developed to further advance an ongoing need for pre-service teachers to learn how to become eco-literate. In mapping out a journey of becoming eco-literate, we draw upon David Orr's (1992) under-standing that "all education is environmental education" (p. 81) and Chet Bowers' (2016) definition of ecological literacy and its relationship to inter-generational knowledge:

> The growing and preparation of food, the manner of greeting a guest, the use of medicinal plants, the ability to incorporate the knowledge of local ecosystems into the design and placement of a building, the knowl-edge of the cycles of plants and animal life in the bioregion, and so forth, are all dependent upon traditional knowledge being passed along – and modified over the generations. (p. 159)

We are interested in the ever-evolving development of identity-formation of humans in relation with the natural world. We consider how paying close attention to, and becoming part of, a process of gardening and food gathering, can lead towards healthy practices of eating. As Bowers (2016) suggests:

> Perhaps the greatest source of threat is in how digital technologies are undermining the intergenerational communication, thus cutting youth off from the forms of knowledge that cannot be reduced to data or adequately represented in print. (pp. 71–72)

It has been our experience that many systems of education do not fully address the complexity and importance of developing sustainable and healthy relationships and, in turn, eco-literate identities within local environments. Unfortunately, schools situated on large parcels of land in the greater Toronto area are slowly being torn down and the land is being sold to developers, who often build skyscrapers. We question how this type of development has become normalized in our society and what can be done to resist the disconnection from Earth that these types of activities are fostering. Engaging within learning gardens involves a direct relationship with our natural world. As we are part of our surroundings, our lives depend on the Earth and the plant and animal worlds that live here. To pave over fertile soil is part of a sad story of progress. We work to inspire pre-service teachers to develop eco-literate identities through learning gardens. As Dilafruz Williams and Jonathan Brown (2012) outline:

> Cognizant of the interconnection of all living things and the irreducible context of place, environmental thinkers such as Aldo Leopold, Wes Jackson, Wendell Berry, Gustavo Esteva and Vandana Shiva have encouraged a "land ethic." School gardens can provide a site for students to come to view their actions as inextricably linked with an elaborate web of life seething beneath their feet. (p. 61)

In terms of what informs our curriculum development, William Pinar (2012) inspires us to bring forth a reconceptualized understanding of curriculum in a learning garden, as he states: "I am asking us to reconstruct our understanding of what it means to teach, to study, to become 'educated' in the present moment" (p. xiii). By paying attention to the lived experience of the curriculum, we are taking up Chambers (1999) understanding of curriculum as the *topos, or* the "particular places and regions where we live and work" (p. 147). For example, Figure 7.2 "Children's Garden" features part of the outdoor learning environment at Ecology Park as part of the *topos.*

FIGURE 7.2   "Children's Garden" (Young, 2013)

Our program engages pre-service teachers in several ways: workshops about learning gardens; a traditional teaching about the importance of relationships and intergenerational knowledge by a local Indigenous Elder; a field placement at Ecology Park; conducting research on learning gardens; and curriculum development and school classroom placements. The program is situated within a 2-year Bachelor of Education program at Trent University. Pre-service teachers must complete a 75-hour alternative placement for graduation and they can choose how they spend the time. For example, there are several alternative placement programs offered with an emphasis on mathematics or English as a Second Language. The Learning Garden is a program that pre-service teachers choose to take as it enables them to engage in a wide-variety of learning. From the workshops, traditional teachings, research, and field site work, participants hopefully acquire an understanding of the interconnectedness of all life as they reflect upon their relationship with food. Veronica Gaylie (2012) writes:

> Garden-based teacher education puts the ideals of environmental education into practice. Conceptualizing new forms of eco-centered teacher education also helps students challenge the myth of control and knowledge ownership in teaching. (p. 194)

Teacher candidates who chose this program get an opportunity to consider their eating habits as well as how their leadership role will help future students' access intergenerational knowledge through meaningful activities that involve food. Wendell Berry (2015) writes:

> When people begin to replace stories from local memory with stories from television screens, another vital part of life is lost. I have my own memories of the survival in a small rural community of its own stories. By telling and retelling those stories, people told themselves who they were, where they were, and what they had done. They thus maintained in ordinary conversation their own living history. (The Atlantic, March 19, 2015)

Learning to uncover information in deep and meaningful ways is an essential aspect of developing a relationship between our bodies and the places that we live.

Reflexive Inquiry in a Learning Garden: Implications for Education

As part of our research program, reflexive inquiry is used in our study. To better understand and situate our use reflexive inquiry, we return to the etymology of words for clarity. *Reflexivus,* from the Latin adjective etymon, means capable of turning, deflecting, or bending (something) back; this is coupled with *inquiry*, from Middle English enquiry meaning the action, or an act or course, of inquiring ("Reflexive" and "Inquiry" n.d., p. 1). As an act or course of reflection, in the context of teacher education, Ellyn Lyle (2013) reminds us that reflexive inquiry involves examining "experiences that inform [*our*] own educational perspectives" (p. 17). Self-reflection is used as part of reflexive inquiry in our Learning Garden program as we consider questions such as: What do I know about food sustainability? What do I know about ecology? As researchers and pre-service educators, we understand ecology as the interconnectedness of all life. Ecology, from the Greek *oikos*, means dwelling or relationships ("ecology" n.d., p. 1). It is through our program that pre-service educators start to inquire into their own experiences that inform their educational perspectives as a form of reflexive inquiry through theoretical and practical experiences in the Learning Garden program.

Reflection involves writing activities whereby pre-service teachers record their thoughts about food and consider their own lives, and how they are living them. These thoughts about essential aspects of life, like nourishment, are important because of the influence that they may have on future generations.

The comments themselves are usually not as important as the thinking process that they experience as they write. They also reflect upon their experiences of engaging in a process of planting, nurturing, and harvesting the food that they grow. It is in the learning garden that we begin to question where food comes from: Does food taste different when it is bought at a farmers market? What are the nutrients in the vegetables that we depend upon? What happens to the vitamins in the vegetables when they are frozen or boiled? Thinking about how we process food before we eat it can be used as an opening discussion to how we think about food in general. The idea that food should be thought of as sacred is an important shift of thinking for many ecologically-minded learners. As we move through the data, we are reminded of Carl Leggo and Rita Irwin's (2013) understanding of sustainability, as they write, "by concentrating on sustaining their hearts as teacher candidates, we are leading the way to sustaining their hearts as they enter the profession" (p. 19). We are inspired by Leggo and Irwin's desire to *sustain hearts* as it is our hope that participants develop ecological literacy that involves an understanding of the interconnectedness of all relationships. We draw upon reflexive inquiry as a strategy for self-study of lived experience through reflection (Cole & Knowles, 2000; Lyle, 2013). Tom Ryan (2005) writes:

> Teachers need to explore and be reflective as it is this habit of mind, which is indeed a useful source of professional development however, to be also reflexive supports critical introspection. To be reflexive can actually nourish reflections as introspection leads to heightened awareness, change, growth and improvement of self and our profession. (p. 4)

We are interested in pre-service teachers' perceptions to help us understand the development of teacher identity through reflexive inquiry of the learning experience toward "heightened awareness change, growth and improvement of self and our profession" (Ibid.). Learning gardens provide an opportunity to consider the world beyond the confines of the public school classrooms. As part of the overarching study, we asked participants the following: How has the program helped you to explore your teacher identity as a negotiated construct of becoming eco-literate in relation to natural world? How has the learning garden alternative placement contributed to your understanding of food sustainability? One participate responded:

> With such a heavy reliance on technology and being constantly plugged in, students need a place to connect to nature and learn in nature. I have a greater understanding of why sustainable food production is important

by having a grassroots physical knowledge of what to do to help it along. I know more about the importance of eating local foods.

The participant's insight reminded us of what Bowers (2016) wrote:

> What sets these cultural commons networks apart from the consumer lifestyle now increasingly dependent upon the abstract world of the Internet and the industrial system of production is that being engaged in growing food, performing in the arts, learning about the life cycle of species in the local environment, and so forth, provides the best insights into what needs to be conserved and intergenerationally renewed. (p. 88)

It is through engagement with the growing process that participants reflect upon their own intergenerational knowledge as they consider what has been passed down through generations in terms of their knowledge of food production. The data we have collected has helped us to understand how an alternative placement in a learning garden promotes a deeper understanding of teacher identity. For example, a participant commented:

> It gave me an opportunity to learn about something that I have limited knowledge about. I learned about planting vegetables and I learned so much about how to start a school garden. Learning gardens can be linked to any curriculum.

Pre-service teachers kept notes about their experiences and later reflected upon their entries. The results suggest how pre-service teachers are reflective about their own developing eco-literate identities and the ways in which they may become facilitators of environmental curricula in both indoor and outdoor classrooms. As we are interested in the ways in which participant perceptions about their experiences relate to food sustainability, we believe that we are inspiring an interest in sustainability in land and hearts. Another participant commented:

> The environment is the future – the more teachers and students know, the more prepared they will be, and the more aware they will be of their own impact. I learned how food choices interact with the environment. The hands on learning proved to me how important and influential using the learning garden as a basis for teaching really is.

The importance of food sustainability became central to the participants experiences. While there are limitations to such a study, the feedback was generally positive as the pre-service teachers embraced all facets of learning about ecologically sustainable practices. This is evident from another participant's comment:

> It is important to know where food comes from and the role it plays in everyday lives. I feel connected to surroundings from both a local and global perspective. I enjoy teaching lessons outside. I had the opportunity to spend some quiet time with plants and get to know them. Garden-based learning involves social and cultural learning that is hands-on because the garden is a teaching tool.

From these responses, we consider the implications for teacher education and note the data reflects that local environments are integral to teacher identity as a negotiated construct. To this end, we argue that ecological literacy is paramount in pre-service education, that reflexive inquiry is important as it reveals how powerful experiences in the natural world can be in relation to identity-formation, and that there is truth in Orr's (1992) understanding that "all education is environmental education" (p. 81). Our inquiry also allowed us to see how participants were able deepen their understandings about ecoliteracy by being immersed in natural environments. It was in the learning garden, after-all, that they were unplugged and separated from technology in order to spend time deeply engrossed in learning about local foods, sustainability, and food production. In this way, we believe that participants would not have had the same responses if they were to consider their eco-literate identities in a typical classroom. Ultimately, curriculum that integrates learning gardens and garden-based activities help to structure the production of knowledge about lived experiences as spaces of pedagogy involves identification of complex relations among past, present, and imagined identities. Nature becomes the perfect canvass as pre-service teachers become connected to place and develop as environmental leaders.

As researchers we, too, reflect upon what it means to be ecologically literate. By writing along with students as part of our own reflexive practice, we re-consider how our own experiences with being part of food cultivation, collection, harvesting, and preparation influences the ways in which we attempt to shift our thinking about the food that we consume. Beginning with activities such as timed writings that are then rewritten in more poetic formats gives us an avenue to think through and conceptualize what we are learning about food systems. Sharing these thoughts with colleagues allows us to come up with questions and think deeply about our own experiences with the food that we eat. The following poem comes from a deep engagement with learning gardens and the traditions that have been passed on through generations. This poem emerged as we considered how important it is to be mindful of the things that we do and to understand the importance of deep relationships with the places we live. We share it with participants as a reminder of Leggo and Irwin's (2013) desire to sustain hearts through teaching and learning.

> *Learning Garden Oasis*
>
> Remembering past gardens
> tiny paths
> among carrots and radishes
> long before
> garlic fell asleep for winter
>
> we counted moments
> through seasons
> planted seeds of life
> as ancestors did before
>
> by nightfall
> beeswax candlelight glimmers
> ignites imagination
> of that special place
> in the garden
> amidst a sense of wonder
>   (Kulnieks, 2018)

Reflecting upon our relationships with nature involves an exploration of historical narratives and practices. Madeleine Grumet (1980) writes: "But now I am the arranger and look to the aesthetics not to create perfect wholes but to revel those cracks in the smooth surface of our conceptual world that may suggest new interpretations of human experience" (p. 29). It is in the learning garden that pre-service teachers can reflect upon their *topos* and take up Chambers (1999) call to consider their own identities and human experiences in the very places that they dwell. It is here that we take the time to reflect upon our relationships to our natural surroundings and reflexive practices that help to shape eco-literate identity-formation.

References

Bell, N., Elliott, P., Rodenburg, J., & Young, K. (2013). Eco-mentorship: A pre-service outdoor experiential teacher education initiative at Trent university. *Pathways: The Journal of Outdoor Education, 25*(3), 14–17.

Berry, W. (2015, March 19). Farmland without farmers. *The Atlantic*. Retrieved from https://www.theatlantic.com/national/archive/2015/03/farmland-without-farmers/ 388282/

Bowers, C. (2016). *Digital detachment: How computer culture undermines democracy.* New York, NY: Routledge.

Chambers, C. (1999). A topography for Canadian curriculum theory. *Canadian Journal of Education, 24*(2), 137–150.

Cole, A. L., & Knowles, J. G. (2000). *Researching teaching: Exploring teacher development through reflexive inquiry.* Boston, MA: Allyn & Bacon.

Ecology. (n.d.). *In the Oxford English dictionary's online dictionary* (3rd ed.). Retrieved from http://www.oed.com.cat1.lib.trentu.ca:8080/view/Entry/59380?redirectedFro m=ecology#eid

Gaylie, V. (2012). *The learning garden: Ecology, teaching, and transforming.* New York, NY: Peter Lang.

Grumet, M. (2004). Autobiography and reconceptualization. In W. Pinar (Ed.), *Contemporary curriculum discourses* (pp. 24–30). New York, NY: Peter Lang.

Inquiry. (n.d.). *In Oxford English dictionary's online dictionary* (3rd ed.). Retrieved from http://www.oed.com.cat1.lib.trentu.ca:8080/view/Entry/59380?redirectedFrom=in quiry#eid

Kulnieks, A. (2018). *Walking landscapes of story* (Unpublished poetry manuscript).

Leggo, C., & Irwin, R. (2013). Becoming pedagogical: Sustaining hearts with living credos. *Education, 19*(1), 2–18.

Lyle, E. (2013). From method to methodology: Narrative as a way of knowing for adult learners. *The Canadian Journal for the Study of Adult Education, 25*(2), 17–33.

Orr, D. (1992). *Ecological literacy: Education and the transition to a postmodern world.* Albany, NY: State University of New York Press.

Pinar, W. F. (2012). *What is curriculum theory?* (2nd ed.). New York, NY: Routledge.

Reflexive. (n.d.). *In Oxford English dictionary's online dictionary.* Retrieved from http://www.oed.com.cat1.lib.trentu.ca:8080/view/Entry/59380?redirectedFrom=inqu iry#eid

Ryan, T. (2005). When you reflect are you also being reflective. *Ontario Action Researcher, 8*(1), 1–5.

Williams, D., & Brown, J. (2012). *Learning gardens and sustainability education: Bringing life to schools and schools to life.* New York, NY: Routledge.

Young, K. (Photographer). (2013). *Ecology Park sign and Children's Garden* [Photographs]. Peterborough, Ontario.

CHAPTER 8

Responding Aesthetically: Using Artistic Expression and Dialogical Reflection to Transform Adversity

Sara Florence Davidson

Years ago now, when I was still a graduate student, I had a very upsetting experience in a class. The experience has remained with me over the years, and it has compelled me to act against racial discrimination in ways that I had not previously done. Initially, I wrote about the events and then I created a video (Davidson, 2014) in an attempt to convey the impact of the incident.

In this chapter, I have engaged in reflexive inquiry (Lyle, 2017) and used the acts of interpretation (Frank, 2010) to guide the reader through a transformation that occurred for me as a result of working with the story about that experience. It was my hope to use these acts to "challenge, interrogate and modify" (Miller, 2008, p. 371) my own views and perhaps those of others as well. In doing so, I subscribed to the belief that interpretation is not a final analysis; rather, it aims to engage in an "ongoing dialogue with the story" (Frank, 2010, p. 104). The dialogue, in this case, includes my attempts to understand racial discrimination and how it may be possible to draw upon Mikhail Bakhtin's (Holland & Lave, 2001) notions of dialogue to achieve a greater degree of understanding between human beings. I agree that "we are truly human only when we are in a dialogical relation with another. The most important things in human lives happen *between* human beings, rather than within or without them" (Sidorkin, 1999, p. 11).

The acts of interpretation are a preliminary step in dialogical narrative analysis, which studies the story's content and its effects. There are six acts of interpretation: translating the story into images, translating the story to tell it from the point of view of a previously marginal character, noticing which details might have been expected but are omitted, attending to differences between the storyteller and the analyst, slowing down, and appreciating the story and the storyteller (Frank, 2010).

The Story[1]

Nobody has ever called me a "dirty indian" to my face, and yet it has been a label that I have tried to erase from my mind for as long as I can remember. No amount of education, professional success, or achievement has been able to prevent this label from permeating every aspect of my existence.

This is not to say that I have not experienced racism. What began in Grade 4 as taunts about being a chief and war whoops in the hallways, transformed into more subtly subversive statements and implied discrimination as I grew older. Because of my education, I was not "like the rest of them." My choice not to drink was likely "because I was in AA," not out of personal preference. The fact that I didn't look the way some people believed that an Indigenous person should look meant that I had to endure countless conversations about the problems with "those native students." And I admit, there were times when I just smiled wanly and remained silent.

Yesterday, I helped to facilitate a class discussion for educators about Indigenous perspectives on research. One of the tasks was to record notes from the small group conversations on chart paper that would be posted on the wall. At the end of the activity, groups presented the highlights of their discussions to the whole class. As the last group finished its presentation, I noticed that on the bottom of the page (presumably as a critique of our readings) was written:

"Dirty" aspects of indigenous people are not represented.

At that moment the room was completely silent, but the words deafened me. And then a single voice wavered, "I am uncomfortable with the use of the word 'dirty' to describe Indigenous people." The voice was my own, and I spoke because I knew that my silence would give everyone else permission to remain silent, too.

My objection to the word "dirty" resulted in the decision to scribble it out on the wall, but scribbling out the words could not erase them from my memory.

A conversation began – one that I don't remember much of. What I do remember was the sound of another voice explaining that we try to focus on the positive aspects of Indigenous people and communities because focusing on the challenges does not help us to move forward. And I am very grateful to that voice. It served to remind me of the impact that a single voice can have. And it helped me to understand that I was not completely alone.

I have always tried to find the positive in the adversity I have faced, but it was not easy for me to find it in this particular experience. I eventually came to under-stand that this experience reminded me that it is possible to be a highly educated educator while remaining unconscious of the power of the use of words like "dirty" to describe aspects of human beings. Perhaps I also needed to be reminded of how far we still need to go in our education about how to demonstrate respect for those around us, even when we do not necessarily understand their realities or experiences.

The truth is that those words should never have been written in the class. All human beings have challenges in their lives and these should never be labeled "dirty." The truth is that those words should never have been posted on the wall of an educational institution where attempts to achieve understanding and respect, particularly for Indigenous peoples, have been made such a high priority. The truth is that, in a classroom of educators pursuing the highest possible level of education, my voice should not have been the only one to object. And the truth is that I will never be able to erase the devastation that I felt in the moments following that class.

But it was not for those reasons that I chose to object.

I objected in the hopes that other students will never look up on the wall of their classroom and see the word "dirty" associated with any aspect their being. I objected in the hopes that the next time my voice will not be the only one to speak out. And I objected because I know that in order for people to have their assumptions challenged, I cannot remain silent.

Translating the Story into Images

"Interpretation begins with seeing the story off the page" (Frank, 2010, p. 106). I must have known this intuitively because it was not enough to write the words of my experience. I did not believe the words fully captured the feeling of having my breath pressed out of my chest and the dull ache that remained for days and then months. Instead, I decided to make a movie. I wanted to create images to express what I had felt. I wanted people to hear my voice as I told them exactly how I have struggled to shed the term "dirty indian" from my skin and how I continue to remain unsuccessful. And I wanted people to understand – or at the very least, I wanted to know I had done everything in my power to ensure they could not look away.

The Story as Visual Art

Arthur Frank (2010) admitted his surprise when a performance storyteller described storytelling as "primarily a *visual* art [emphasis in original]" (p. 105). He went on to say that the storyteller "meant both that he remembers stories as a succession of images, and that he aspires to create images in the imaginations of his listeners" (p. 106). Though I had never thought of it in that way, I was taken with that idea. When I remember back to my desire to bring my pain to life, my first thought was to use images: I wanted the viewers to have an emotional reaction.

Later, I came across the "What I Be Project" project by Steve Rosenfield (2014) that worked to empower people by providing them with the opportunity to make their private struggles public through photographic portraits. The headshots were visually engaging; however, it was the words on the people's faces that made them especially compelling – all the participants in the project demonstrated tremendous courage in their willingness to be honest about their perceived inadequacies. They wrote these secrets on their faces. The images were then framed with the completion of the statement: "I am not my ____," which allowed the participants to speak back against the manner in which they were being negatively positioned. I immediately wondered what it would be like to photograph myself with the word "dirty" written across my forehead.

When I began composing my own images, I struggled to capture my emotions with the camera. It was only following my attempt to summon authentic despair that I realized the inability of the camera to capture the truth. As Thomas King (2003) explained, "what the camera allows you to do is to invent, to create. That's really what photographs are. Not records of moments, but rather imaginative acts" (p. 43). Upon realizing the potential impossibility of capturing what was *real*, I began to think in metaphorical rather than literal terms. Instead of trying to capture with images the racism I have experienced, I focused upon the silencing. Instead of positioning the camera from a flattering angle, I positioned the viewer from a gaze of power (Kress & van Leeuwen, 2006). Although I was aware of the future viewer as I took the photographs, my primary purpose was to translate this story into images.

The first image I take of myself is wrong.

I am looking at the camera,
but in the text

I am ashamed.

What does shame look like on my own face?
Can I evoke the emotion on command,
while looking in a mirror
in the hopes of memorizing
the expression
and recapturing it
with my camera?

I know that I cannot.

But I do know this,

Shame does not look at the camera directly.
Shame does not challenge the camera
with her eyes.

Shame's eyes are downcast.
Shame's face is blurred.
Shame's image is black and white.

Not colour.

Translating the Story's Point of View

"If a story positions the listener to see what happens from one position, interpretation requires seeing from other positions and imagining their possibility" (Frank, 2010, p. 106). Even though each perspective of a story offers a new
understanding, it can be incredibly difficult to make the shift to understand it
from different positions.

   In Canada, "much public discourse about Native peoples still deals in stereotypes. Our [Canadian] views of what constitutes an Indian today are as
much bound up with myth, prejudice and ideology as earlier versions were"
(Francis, 1992, p. 6). Furthermore, as Indigenous peoples we are both silenced
and positioned (Holland & Lave, 2001) by these discourses of Euro-Canadian

society. In his discussion of Edward Curtis' pursuit of the authentic Indian, Thomas King (2003) observed that

> Curtis was looking for the literary Indian, the dying Indian, the imaginative construct. And to make sure that he would find what he wanted to find, he took along boxes of 'Indian' paraphernalia – wigs, blankets, painted backdrops, clothing – in case he ran into Indians who did not look as the Indian was supposed to look. (p. 34)

As this implies, the Indigenous person who exists in the minds of many Euro-Canadians is not real, and this imaginative construct relies upon positioning and the use of artifacts derived from stereotypes to reinforce the inaccurate beliefs. This perspective resonates with Catherine Bainbridge and Neil Diamond's (2009) assertion that often when Indigenous peoples are represented in films, the emphasis is placed upon the people being identifiably "Indigenous" rather than being accurately portrayed.

Euro-Canadian society often has a difficult time listening to the *authentic* voices of Indigenous peoples. When I began sharing this video with others, it became very clear to me that this voice was unfamiliar. Although the story had been heard before, it was now being told from a different perspective, one that reflected an uncomfortable truth and was often silenced. Therefore, for the purpose of interpretation, this story does not need to be told a second time from a different perspective. This perspective is already untold. This is already the marginalized voice of which Arthur Frank (2010) spoke. Our collective Canadian history consists almost exclusively of stories that are told in the colonial voice. We rarely hear the truth about what it is to be silenced. We rarely hear about what it means to silence ourselves.

I photograph myself
with duct tape
covering my mouth.

I want to represent the silencing.

It is not lost on me
that I have placed the duct tape
on my own mouth.

In the narrative,
I admit to remaining silent
in the past.

Out of fear
or exhaustion.

But in this experience
I come to realize
that this (in)action
means that the finger in the movie
is aimed at me as well.

The plea
to remove the duct tape
to end the silence
is also
directed at me.

> *My friend tells me*
> *to remove the photo*
> *from the series.*
>
> *It is a cliché,*
> *he says.*
>
> *I defend the photo.*
> *I agree, it has been done before.*
>
> *But so has racism.*
>
> *Aren't we done with this yet?*
> *Another friend asks.*
>
> *A professor apologizes,*
> *"I am just so sorry."*
>
> *I reply, "For my entire life?"*

Notice the Details that Were Omitted

I have been brought up in a culture that has strict protocols associated with the sharing of stories. As such, I have always been aware of the stories I share and whether I need to adhere to cultural protocols in their telling. Because of this upbringing, I have always ensured that the stories I tell are my own, that they are told from my perspective, and the identities of other people who may have been involved are hidden.

In the days and months and years that have passed since the incident, I have often wondered about what it was like to be the woman who wrote the words on wall or one of the students who witnessed the events. In telling the story, I have blurred those voices into the background. I have merged them into a single voice that did not speak out against the way that Indigenous peoples were being positioned. The voice of the woman who wrote the words on the wall is also silent in my story, though eventually she was the one who stepped forward to scribble the words out.

Arthur Frank (2010) suggested that "attention to omissions reminds us that stories, more than other forms of narrative, make silences significant" (p. 107). I should therefore clarify that it is not because I do not care about those voices that they have been blurred and even silenced; it is because I do not feel I have the authority to represent them. Their stories are not mine and, according to the protocols of the world in which I grew up, they are not mine to share. Their identities are not important in understanding my experience or learning from my story. In order for my own transformation to occur, the greatest silence that I had to overcome was my own. I knew that I could not authentically challenge others to speak out unless I acknowledged my own past silences. Without the confession of that past silence, there was only an accusation directed at others. I realized that this was the secret I held inside. This was the truth that I had to face.

I ask a friend to look at my movie
I need a critical eye.

Someone who knows nothing
about the story.

She says she wants to see
my hands.

I go home
and lie on my bed
and photograph
my hands.

I focus on the creases
and the scars.

I move my fingers
I change the perspective
trying to make them
interesting.

But this movie is not
about my age
or my past.

It is not about finding the angle
to make the story
more interesting.

It is about the
(unspoken) truth.

It is about
what I have
kept hidden.

So I write the word
'dirty'
on the palm of my hand.

A secret held inside.

And I photograph that

Instead.

Attend to Differences between the Storyteller and the Analyst

"To interpret a story, foreground the differences between yourself as interpreter and the other person as storyteller; pay attention first to all that sepa-
rates you, taking it very seriously" (Frank, 2010, p. 108). Though in this case
I am both the storyteller and the analyst, I feel that it is the passage of time
that has allowed me to move between these roles. Immediately following
the incident, I worked to capture the narrative in words and, with distance,
I was able to revisit it and obscure it in ways so that it could be shared more
widely.

In the role of analyst, I feel able to begin to understand the other story that
is entwined with my own. The one that was unspoken but could be considered
the second story that has helped me to understand this one. One might assume
that, because I am the original storyteller, there is an inherent advantage in the
analysis. That the sense I make of the story could be considered the absolute
truth. However, I recognize that "no one's meaning is final, and no one meaning is final. What counts is two's meaning, which is enacted through a process
of those two creating meanings as expressions of their relationship" (Frank,
2010, p. 99).

Exposing Our Humanity

Initially I wanted to write the words "human being" on my forehead.
I believed that if people were reminded of my humanity, they would be
less likely to discriminate against me and other Indigenous peoples. However, I quickly discovered that the words "human being" on my forehead
were too literal, and I struggled again for how to capture my own humanity in an image. And then I remembered a dance that we performed, the
q'aawhlaa.

In the time before contact, when young Haida men would come of age,
they would go into the forest to fast in order to find their spirit. When they
returned, they were in a spirit state and required the help of a shaman to
return to a human state. In the dance, the young man in the spirit state
hides behind the blanket wearing a mask to represent this non-human
state. He dances this way, revealing himself momentarily for the first three
verses of the song. Then for the final verse, the dancer removes his mask
and exposes his true self (R. Davidson, personal communication, March
30, 2014). In remembering this, I came to understand that my series of
photographs in various poses could be viewed as a series of masks. I had
positioned myself in the way that I wanted the viewer to see me. I had

controlled the angle, the focus, the shades of black and white. This led to the realization that in order to reveal my humanity or my true self, I merely had to remove the masks.

In the mirror in the bathroom,
I am faced with my reflection
and the word 'dirty'
written backwards on my forehead.

I take a cloth
and attempt to remove the word
letter by letter
leaving illegible smudges
on my face.

It looks like dirt.
But eventually washes clean.

I return to the living room
where my sister-in-law
writes the words
'HUMAN BEING'
in capital letters
on my forehead.

I think this is what I want.

To label myself
as a human being.
Perhaps it will help me
to recognize my own humanity.

In these photos,
I want to look at the camera
and even smile.

Photo after photo
of my smiling face
with the words

'human being'
written on my forehead.

But it is all wrong.

If I am truly human,
Should I have to label myself to make
*   it real?*
Should I have to write the words on my
*   own skin?*

Shouldn't you just be able to see it?

Slowing Down

As he discussed the acts of interpretation, Arthur Frank (2010) acknowledged the work of Jo-ann Archibald (2008) who advises that interpretations must be approached slowly and that we must live with the story over time. The passage of time also allowed me to learn more about what others said about the topics with which I was grappling. Months after the incident occurred, I continued to read and learn more about these various perspectives. I realize too that this passage of time allowed me to follow Jo-ann Archibald's (2008) advice and begin to understand the meaning of the story within the context of my own life.

We never did go for the walk
or have the conversation
we intended to have.

You texted me.
A headache.

Perhaps I was relieved.

Sometimes
we run out
of the right words to say
or the patience required
to engage in
authentic dialogue

Bakhtin says that it is possible
for our voices to remain distinct

despite the fact that yours is louder
amplified by the society in which we live.

He says that we can listen closely enough
to hear both
simultaneously and separately
even though they are opposed.

According to him,
polyphony is possible.

I am not so sure.

But I cling to the hope   *I am certain that I will see you again*
as if the strength of my grip   *one day*
is enough   *and I wonder*
to make it so.   *what you will see...*

                                          Will the dirt that you scribbled on the wall
                                                                have faded?

                                                             Or will it remain,
                                                                like it does
                                                                  for me?

Appreciate the Story and the Storyteller

"Any dialogical relationship is based on some kind of appreciation of the other: perhaps appreciation of the other's forbidding and unfinished struggles, but appreciation" (Frank, 2010, p. 109). To achieve this appreciation, Arthur Frank suggested writing letters to the protagonist of the story, the storyteller, and the story itself about how the contribution of each has been of benefit.

The Protagonist

In this story I am the protagonist. I must admit it was strange to imagine the letter of gratitude that I would write to myself. Perhaps it would begin with the appreciation of the courage that was required to speak out. This is not something that I would have done in the past, and I am grateful that I did for, if the ideal of polyphony (Shields, 2007) is to be achieved, one voice cannot remain silent. All voices must speak out regardless of whether they represent the minority or the majority.

Later, when I reflected upon my decision to speak out, I knew that what compelled me to do so was the offensive nature of what was written on the wall. But even more, it was the awareness that I was the only person of Indigenous ancestry in the room. This did not make the responsibility to object solely mine; however, I was aware that inaction could be construed as acceptance. I understood that, in ignoring the words, I could become the excuse for future decisions to disregard such derogatory comments. Despite the fact that my objection did not have the impact for which I had hoped, I still find comfort in the knowledge that I did not remain silent. I did not condone the writing in that moment or in all of the future moments when the students in the class think back upon that day.

The Storyteller

Though it is difficult to separate the voice of the storyteller from that of the protagonist, I have chosen to continue to define this separation using the passage of time. That is, the protagonist exists in the real time of the story as it unfolds, while the storyteller narrates the video and tells the story later. I am grateful to the storyteller for remaining true to the teachings with which I grew up. I am grateful that I did not succumb to the temptation of making accusations that would not be rooted in the truth but rather assumption and speculation. Instead, I asked questions. How would this story have been different if it had been the ancestry of another student written on the wall? Or instead, their sexual orientation? Would the class have found this less palatable? Would this have generated a different reaction? I have answered those questions in my mind, but I quickly realized that it does not bring me any closer to existing dialogically. The answers do not bring me closer to the truth, which cannot be heard from my voice alone, for "truth fundamentally cannot be contained within a single consciousness. It simply cannot be expressed with a 'single mouth'; it needs many voices" (Sidorkin, 1999, p. 29).

The Story

I am grateful for the story's capacity to provide an opening for the important conversations that we as educators need to have if we want to learn how to treat each other with respect. I offer the story, not to gain sympathy but instead to provide a concrete starting place for the dialogue to begin. And I understand that it is only in these dialogues with others who have differing perspectives that we come to better understand ourselves.

Gratitude

I recognize that without the woman who wrote on the wall, there would be no story and thus no opportunity for personal transformation. Despite the fact that I experienced tremendous anguish as a result of those words, I also gained the opportunity to re-examine my own role in the discrimination against others. In a correspondence with the woman, I confessed that "I am not above reproach. Working on [the video] forced me to examine the ways that I have contributed to judgment and discrimination toward Aboriginal people. It forced me to think about all the times that I have remained silent in the past and have not challenged people to think about things differently" (S. Davidson, personal communication, March 19, 2014).

I know that I will continue to have conversations about this story and others like it. I know that my understanding of this story will change and transform from what it is today. I also know that my story differs from the stories of others who were there that day. But I will continue to remain open to the possibilities that this presents, and I will continue to engage in dialogue as we navigate our way toward mutual compassion and respect.

I am not grateful
for the words
that were written
on the wall

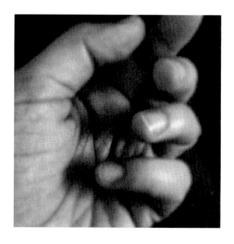

But I am grateful
for the story
and the opportunity
to act beyond
what I ever believed
possible.

And I am grateful
for the chance
to consider
my own role
in discrimination

And for the conversations
and understandings
that follow

And I am grateful
for the voices
that may now   *Sidorkin (1999) says,*
refuse   *"To be human*
to be   *is to be different*
silenced.   *from other humans" (p. 1)*

And it has been our differences,
that have allowed me
to see myself.

A mirror reflects
our perfect opposite

But we still use it
to see ourselves
more clearly.

(LeBlanc, Davidson, Ryu, & Irwin, 2015,
p. 362)[2]

Existing Dialogically

I am reassured by Arthur Frank's (2010) belief that "the capacity of stories is to explore complications, rarely to resolve them" (p. 110). The truth of this statement resides in the fact that, as the years pass, my understanding continues to shift and change, and my transformation remains incomplete.

"It is said that you cannot call your words back once they are uttered and so you are responsible for all which results from your words" (Cardinal & Armstrong, 1991, p. 90). I knew this to be true when I first spoke of what transpired in the class that day. I had to be incredibly careful in the telling of this story. I had to be certain I could frame it in a way that adequately addressed the difficulty but did not do so in a way that evoked blind anger in my listeners. The purpose of the story was to engage people in a dialogue, and so I had to be certain that everyone was still listening at the end. I had to find the balance between telling the truth and ensuring the opportunities for dialogue remained possible.

Notes

1 This is an edited version of the original blog post that I wrote that was used to create the video response entitled "In response to the writing on the wall ...."
2 An adapted version of this poem appeared in LeBlanc, Davidson, Ryu, and Irwin (2015). The last two stanzas were unchanged for that publication.

References

Bainbridge, C. (Producer), & Diamond, N. (Director). (2009). *Reel injun: On the trail of the Hollywood Indian* [motion picture]. Canada: National Film Board of Canada.
Cardinal, D., & Armstrong, J. (1991). *The native creative process: A collaborative discourse.* Penticton: Theytus Books.
Davidson, S. F. (2014, March 15). *In response to the writing on the wall ...* [video file]. Retrieved from https://www.youtube.com/watch?v=WOoR11 sMRZw
Francis, D. (1992). *The imaginary Indian.* Vancouver: Arsenal Pulp Press.
Frank, A. W. (2010). *Letting stories breathe: A socio-narratology.* Chicago, IL: The University of Chicago Press.
Holland, D., & Lave, J. (2001). History in person: An introduction. In D. Holland, & J. Lave (Eds.), *History in person: Enduring struggles, contentious practice, intimate identities* (pp. 3–33). Santa Fe, NM: School of American Research Press.
King, T. (2003). *The truth about stories: A native narrative.* Toronto: House of Anansi Press Inc.
Kress, G., & van Leeuwen, T. (2006). Representation and interaction: Designing the position of the viewer. In G. Kress & T. van Leeuwen (Eds.), *Reading images: The grammar of visual design* (2nd ed., pp. 114–153). London: Routledge Taylor and Francis Group.
LeBlanc, N., Davidson, S. F., Ryu, J., & Irwin, R. L. (2015). Becoming through a/r/tography, autobiography and stories in motion. *International Journal of Education through Art, 11*(3), 355–374.
Lyle, E. (2017). *Of books, barns, and boardrooms.* Rotterdam, The Netherlands: Sense Publishers.
Miller, D. M. (2008). Shades of gray: An autoethnographic study of race in the academy. *International Journal of Qualitative Studies, 21*(4), 347–373.
Rosenfield, S. (2014). *I am not my eating disorder* [Photograph]. Retrieved from http://www.whatibeproject.com/portfolio-item/i-am-not-my-eating-disorder-2/
Shields, C. M. (2007). *Bakhtin.* New York, NY: Peter Lang.
Sidorkin, A. M. (1999). *Beyond discourse: Education, the self, and dialogue.* Albany, NY: State University of New York Press.

CHAPTER 9

Teacher Identity in Formation: Social Change, Student Engagement, and a Spiritual Encounter

Guopeng Fu and Anthony Clarke

Researchers have studied teacher identity through a wide range of approaches and across disciplines, and it is generally agreed among scholars that teacher identity is ever-changing, dynamic, and influenced by both internal and external factors (Beauchamp & Thomas, 2009). Sachs (2005) defines teacher professional identity as teachers' "ideas of 'how to be', 'how to act' and 'how to understand' their work and their place in society" (p. 15). Drawing on a Foucauldian perspective, Zembylas (2003) argues that the teacher-self is constituted and historical: a teacher's identity is multi-dimensional, contested, and entails historical contingency. Teacher professional identity is constantly formed and reformed in a teacher's professional career through "a complex interplay of personal, professional and political dimensions of teachers' lives" (Mockler, 2011, p. 518). The ongoing negotiation of identity makes the notion of how identity shifts and reshapes one of the complicated aspects in studying teacher identity (Beauchamp & Thomas, 2009). In response to such conceptual implications from the literature, this study attempts to depict the ongoing process of how a high school physics teacher's identity was formed and reformed through his more than 20 years of teaching. The study highlights how his personal history, the social changes in China, his engagement with students, and his contingent encounter with Buddhism shaped his identity through a reflexive process.

Teacher Identity and Agency

We explore teacher identity through an agentic lens. Specifically, teacher agency lies in a teacher's realization of his or her identity (Beauchamp & Thomas, 2009). Teacher identity emerges through the interplay between personal experience and professional contexts (Mockler, 2011; Priestley, Biesta, & Robinson, 2015). Sloan (2006) claims that studying teacher agency is an important means in understanding teachers' identities. Thus, the analysis of teacher agency – teachers' capacity to act, resist, and reflect upon the social structures

in which they are embedded – embodies an important element in the formation and shifts of teacher identity.

In the theory of structuration, Giddens (1984) conceptualizes human
agency as an individual's capability to make a difference by deploying power.
An agent's power is manifested through available resources in a particular
social context. In other words, an agent must know about the social conditions for deploying and exercising power. An agent's knowledge about the
social conditions is achieved through reflexivity – "the continuous monitoring
of action which human beings display and expect others to display" (Giddens,
1984, p. 3). Structuration theory considers human action as a continuous flow
of conduct and following a stratification model appears as: motivation for
action --> rationalization of action --> reflective monitoring of action. Reflexivity is a process rather than a state and is "most deeply involved in the recursive ordering of social practice" (p. 3). Reflexive monitoring is "fundamental
to the control of the body that actors ordinarily sustain throughout their day-
to-day lives" (p. 9). Therefore, reflexivity is at the core of human agency and is
influenced by the social-historical context.

Teacher agency is human agency specifically applied to school activities
(Biesta, Priestley, & Robinson, 2015) and is characterized as "teachers' active
efforts to make choices and intentional action in a way that makes a significant difference" (Toom, Pyhältö, & Rust, 2015, p. 615). Priestley and colleagues
(2015) further frame teacher agency as an emergent phenomenon that lies in
the engagement between agents and the social structure and such engagement
entails the historical and social aspects of the particular context. This study
investigates the internal (personal history) and external (social history) factors as well as the engagement between teachers and students with respect
to teacher agency and moves toward an understanding of the forming and
reforming of teacher identity.

Research Context and Methodology

This study is conducted in a senior high school (Grades 10 to 12) that is located
in a major city in mid-east China. The school is ranked highly among all the
high schools in the city. It has two campuses: a larger main campus, which is
located in a suburban area; and an annex campus, which located in an inner
urban area. Students on the main campus are mostly high academic achievers
as evidenced by their high school entrance exam performance. Students on
the annex campus scored relatively low in the exam compared to their main
campus counterparts and have to pay extra sponsorship fees to study in this

school. According to the informant, teachers on both campuses have similar teaching competencies. They are assigned to different campuses based primarily on their personal preference for either campus. The participating teacher, Chung, teaches Grade 11 physics on the annex campus. He has been teaching in this school for more than 20 years. Chung was recruited as part of a larger project on physics teacher agency in a curriculum reform movement spearheaded by the Chinese Ministry of Education.

Giddens (1984) asks researchers to pay attention to what agents know about what they do and what they are restricted to do. Researchers need to situate themselves in the field and understand the field as the first order. They then might distance themselves in order to generate second order concepts. Therefore, Giddens suggests that research should be written with this intention – first order in-depth understanding followed by second order analysis – by way of providing descriptions of "the cultural milieu to others who are unfamiliar with it" (Giddens, 1984, p. 285). In addition, reflexivity, as the core property of human agency, suggests "that we are constantly constructing meaning and social realities as we interact with others and talk about our experience" (Cunliffe, 2003, p. 985). Based on this imperative, the researchers focus on the informant's reflexive practice as well as the cultural milieu including the school context, the reform mandates, and social changes during the reform. Such efforts aim to create spaces demonstrating the complexity of human actions, social systems, and the interplay between the two.

With the approval of the Research Ethics Board at the researchers' home institution and consent from the informant and the school principal, the embedded researcher (first author) was immersed in the school for four months (one term) and frequently observed Chung's classes and participated in various school activities such as staff meetings and teachers' social events. The embedded researcher conducted two rounds of interviews at the beginning and at the end of the term respectively. Each interview lasted about one hour. The interview questions began with Chung's day-to-day teaching practice and then explored his teaching history, critical events in teaching, how he worked with colleagues, and how the complex environments such as school culture, students, parents, administrators, and textbooks influenced his teaching practice. Chung also submitted two entries in a reflective journal exercise as part of a larger school project – one in the middle of the term, and the other at the end of the term. In addition to interview transcripts and Chung's reflective journals, field notes of long-term observation and the researcher's reflective journals were the data sources.

When the embedded researcher read through the interview transcripts, teacher's reflective journals, his own reflections, and field notes, he could still vividly visualize Chung in the classroom, in conversations with colleagues or with students, and in staff meetings. He perceived Chung as an energetic individual whose words and actions were much more than just a set of data. Hence, we provide portraits of Chung and attempt to present our image of him to the readers by drawing upon qualitative principles of portraiture (Lawrence-Lightfoot & Davis, 2002).

> Portraiture is a method of qualitative research that blurs the boundaries of aesthetics and empiricism in an effort to capture the complexity, dynamics, and subtlety of human experience and organizational life. Portraitists seek to record and interpret the perspectives and experience of the people they are studying, documenting their voices and their visions – their authority, knowledge, and wisdom. The drawing of the portrait is placed in social and cultural context and shaped through dialogue between the portraitist and the subject, each one negotiating the discourse and shaping the evolving image. (p. xv)

Atkinson and Delamont (2008) contend that "the forms of analysis should reflect the forms of social life, their diversity should mirror the diversity of cultural forms, and their significance should be in accordance with their social and cultural functions" (p. 288). The portraiture of Chung in the next section attempts to meet such request. As the analysis unfolded, the second author acted as a "critical friend" (Foulger, 2010) by reviewing, questioning, and provoking on-going analysis of the nature and substance of identity as it was explored and explicated over the course of the study.

Portraiture of Chung

Chung experienced considerable professional frustrations early in his teaching career. His grandfather was a teacher all his life. Chung was not at all enamored of teaching as a career because "it is quite annoying to see him [Chung's grandfather] constantly repeat things all his life" (Chung interview#1, p. 1). In the 1980s, when Chung graduated from university with a degree in computer science, he hoped to work in the House of Audio-Visual Education Program[1] but was picked[2] by the participating high school in this study to be a physics teacher instead. He attempted to switch this job many times. "To be honest, I wanted to escape in every summer vacation" (Chung interview#1, p. 1).

However, Chung was not able to change jobs and his frustration increased. Meanwhile, he discovered that he was a good speaker and able to explain difficult concepts in simple terms – two skills that are important for teaching. Both his frustrations and the act of teaching gradually dulled his resistance to teaching. As time passed he thought, "if I cannot change the macro-environment, I can change my own mind-set and see if I can adapt to this environment" (Chung interview#1, p. 1). Chung tried to love his students and think of them as new computers because he loved computer science. He imagined his students as brand new machines and himself, as the teacher, setting up software in these computers. Then he found every class was different even though the curriculum remained the same. After several years of teaching, he felt that he, together with his students, had accomplished some very worthwhile objectives for those in his care (e.g., high school completion, university entrance). He occasionally received postcards from students, and sometimes, former students visited him to convey their gratitude. For example, some students noted that Chung's teaching continued to help them in university. "Moments like these make me realize that I am still of use ..., and I stayed and have been teaching for that reason" (p. 1).

Chung then shared several examples of working with individual students. Some suffered from their individual family's economic conditions and had lost their confidence in learning and in the prospect of entering universities. Some struggled with physics throughout high school, or were clever but never applied themselves enough to their school work. The words *respect* and *trust* often appeared in Chung's narratives. One student spent most of her high school time only learning physics because she felt Chung respected her and believed she had the potential to do better. Another boy, who was the only one in the class who could not afford a pair of sneakers, was always in conflict with the principal and was ignored by most teachers. When the College Entrance Examination (CCE) was only three months away, Chung took charge of this boy and encouraged him to face this exam front-on and prove himself. Three months later, this boy visited Chung and thanked him for being the only teacher who had believed in his ability to go to university.

Another student had *cold feet* just one month before the CEE. Sometimes she was too stressed to breathe or to enter the school classroom. Her parents wanted to send her abroad and asked Chung's advice. Chung saw her difficulties as an opportunity for growth. "You could help her escape this time. But she will face countless difficulties in her life. She has to learn how to conquer her fear and face the music," Chung told her parents. Then he worked with this student every weekend, not on physics problems, but on listening to her thoughts, struggles, fears, and emotions. He told the student to try her best and not think about the results. After the CEE, she admitted to Chung that she had unnecessarily amplified the difficulties of the CEE and now had the courage and confidence to face other challenges in her life. "Students thank me and I never tell them I should thank them for encouraging me. Teachers need more encouragement" (Chung interview#1, p. 2).

On his journey from initially disliking the profession to his eventual affection for his students, Chung changed his state of mind and realized the value in teaching, specifically, through the appreciation shown by his students. However, students have been both his well of encouragement and his source of frustration. As mentioned earlier, the students on the annex campus did not demonstrate high scholastic ability as did the main campus students. When Chung first taught in the annex campus, he noted that

> They froze my passion from head to toe ... one simple problem, which had been discussed in class, they would ask you the same question several times in the tutorial session. I was patient at first, but then lost my temper when they asked so many times. Sometimes their questions were so simple that you felt that it was a negation or even an insult to your teaching. (Chung interview#1, pp. 2–3)

In the last term, Chung experienced his greatest frustration when teaching the Electrostatic Field of the physics curriculum. The students could not grasp the concept or master it successfully. Few students submitted their assignments. Both students and teacher were struggling. Chung even became depressed. Daily, he questioned whether he should be a teacher. He even doubted his own beliefs, values, and pedagogical approaches.

Chung wrote about his frustrations in his reflective journal. In his first reflection, Chung felt he had put a great deal of effort into helping students, but the test results were barely satisfactory. His reflection centered mostly on the differences between students from the two campuses and how he might change his pedagogical approach to suit the students he presently taught. Although he expressed considerable frustration, this reflection was mostly positive. He saw the challenges but focused more on hope. He ended his reflection with sentences such as: "I believe, after days and years of work, even concrete grounds can grow high quality crops" (Chung reflection#1, p. 2).

In Chung's later reflections, however, his tone and the content had completely changed. He often doubted his efforts and approaches. He called his students "God's outcasts" who are like reefs that had shattered his waves of hope and confidence into thin spray. Interestingly, at the very end, he referred again to the concrete ground and crops metaphor. He wrote "... it is like growing crops on concrete ground even if one waters them again and again, one still hardly harvests anything" (Chung reflection#2, p. 2). Chung did not realize how his depression had deepened and how it was reflected in his emotions until one day a colleague told him that his temper had changed (and not for the better). Chung then started to reflect upon his behaviours and manage his emotions. However, such reflective practice did little to help Chung in venting his frustrations. The daily engagement with students seemed to undermine his professional identity as a teacher.

Chung had a contingent encounter with Buddhism during this period. He went to a Buddhist concert hoping to calm his mind. The visit was fortuitous because Chung was not a Buddhist and the ticket was given to him by his friend. He ended up going to the same concert three times. After three visits, he noted: "I found I still would love to come back to school and help more people. It is a Zen process of escape from the world – retreat – back into the world" (Chung interview#1, p. 3). The concert shocked Chung and the religious music helped him reach an epiphany. "Then I remembered these students were still growing. I needed to help them. The frustrations were not frustrations anymore" (p. 3). Buddhism encourages people to pursue the spiritual ideals from within oneself (Zhang & Zhong, 2003). This fortuitous engagement facilitated Chung's reforming his identity as a teacher.

During the second interview, Chung's state of mind improved. "When I started to work with this cohort, about one fifth of the students fell asleep in my physics class, but now very few students sleep in the class. They have changed a lot ... and they seem happy in my class" (Chung interview#2, pp. 2, 4). Chung's descriptions are consistent with the classroom observations. The most impressive aspect of his teaching was the breadth of his knowledge base. He related physics in class with Hollywood movies, weather changes, soccer, painting authentication, and Mars exploration. Such topics captured the students' interests in the class, and students actively participated in discussions with him and with other students. The student-teacher relationship was friendly. Chung was active, even enthusiastic in class and barely needed to attend to classroom management. In summation, he believed that "when you cannot change the environment, change your state of mind, and it will change the people you are with. That's it" (Chung interview#2, p. 4).

Discussion

The social change in China's contemporary history, Chung's engagements with his students, and an unanticipated spiritual encounter precipitated changes in Chung's professional identity. Chung's professional identity underwent major shifts: first when he was assigned to the teaching position and later when he started to teach in the annex campus. The first shift largely attributed to the social change when China was transforming from a centralized to a more decentralized society. Chung reconstructed his identity through engagement with students. Such engagement established Chung's value in teaching – helping students' growth. Ironically, the second shift was largely precipitated by engagement with students as well. Chung's high expectation was at odds with his students' performance, which jeopardized his beliefs in himself as a teacher. Serendipitously, the Buddhist concert helped Chung re-discover the value in teaching and consequently, a reconstruction of his professional identity.

The identity development in a teacher's early career sets a strong foundation for her/his teaching practice and is influenced by the surrounding context (Beauchamp & Thomas, 2009). Chung's initial perception of teaching is negative because of his grandfather's experience. However, the social conditions forced Chung into the teaching profession. He attempted to exercise his agency in ways that were contrary to the social structure and failed. His agency was suppressed by the social conditions. Through reflexive practice (iterative changes in his state of mind), Chung found similarities in working with students to working on computers. His professional identity was grounded in his work with students. The value of teaching, for him, resided in helping students grow. Such value set the foundation for Chung's beliefs in teaching and sustained his Chung's professional identity. Holland (1998) argues that the extent to which individuals can exercise their agency is dependent on how they identify themselves in a given cultural context. In his early career, Chuang's agency transformed from resisting the social structure to establishing his own place and value in teaching. The reflexive practice mediated the interplay between teacher agency and the social structure and precipitated this transformation. The engagement with students both enabled and constrained Chung's agency in his teaching practice. When a teacher implements actions in class, students, also as agents, receive such actions and embed them with their own values, beliefs, intentions, and expectations. The teacher's actions may differ from or even conflict with the students' own beliefs and expectations. Students may be confused or frustrated as well and conflicts arise. Naturally, students will respond with appropriate reactions, expressing their confusion and doubt. If teachers neither review their teaching practice nor reflect on their mindset, conflicts and frustrations may worsen and cause further irritation for all concerned. Archer (2003) argues that constraints and enablements have "the generative power to impede or facilitate projects of different kinds from groups of agents who are differentially placed" (p. 7). Chung did not anticipate the differences between the main campus students and the annex campus students and applied the same teaching approaches to the annex campus students and, as a result, received considerable 'push-back' from the students.

Chung's contingent engagement with a Buddhist music concert occurred at a low ebb in his teaching career. In the course of reconstructing his identity after teaching in the annex, the Buddhist encounter helped Chung empty his mind, free his thoughts, let go of his vexations, and realize his value to the students. The nation's history also nurtured such a fortuitous event for Chung. Bandura (2006) describes these events as "branching processes [that] alter the continuity and linear progression of life-course trajectories" (p. 166). Buddhism, portrayed as one of the three traditional wisdoms in China (Zhang & Zhong, 2003), flourished as a religion for more than a thousand years. The history and culture of this spiritual practice created the opportunities for individuals. A receptive attitude towards Buddhism created the opportunity for Chung to reflect on and regain his sense of agency in teaching.

Even though the engagement with students and with Buddhism helped Chung reconstruct his identity, the most important factor, we believe, is that Chung "changed his state of mind" (Chung interview#2, p. 4). After agents execute and regulate their actions and interventions (which are guided by their intentions), the surroundings react and respond to these actions. Agents receive and process the immediate environment's reactions and re-evaluate their previous actions, which produces the most important property of agency, self-reflectiveness (Bandura, 2006). The constant monitoring and examining of oneself and one's engagement with others (reflexivity) is a metacognitive capability that human beings distinctively possess. The process through which teachers gain understandings of students' perspectives is an accumulation of the agents' *knowledgeablity* which is defined as "all those things which the members of the society know about that society and the conditions of their activity within it" (Giddens, 1994, p. 9). Chung's engagement with Buddhism calmed his mind, caused him to interrogate his values as a human being, and assisted him as he transcended his struggles in teaching. This introspective transformation helped him to realize that he still wanted to be in education and help students.

Conclusion

Hammerness and colleagues (2005) made explicit connection between teacher identity development and their commitment to the profession. They claim that teacher identity "shapes their dispositions, where they place their efforts, whether and how they seek out professional development opportunities, and what obligations they see as intrinsic to their role" (p. 384). In this study, Chung's commitment to teaching lies in helping students and it becomes a key value in his professional identity. Chung discovered and rediscovered this key value through engagements with his students and his encounter with Buddhism.

Day and colleagues (2006) argue that teacher agency connects to the sustaining and shaping of teacher identity. This study provides a case of teacher agency as an example of understanding evolving teacher identity. The social change in China, engagement with students and a spiritual encounter, together enabled Chung to construct and reconstruct his teacher identity and ultimately his state of mind. Teacher identity in this study was multi-dimensional and constantly evolving through a reflexive practice.

Notes

1   An institute affiliated with the local education department/bureau. It directs and supports local school to use technology in teaching and learning.
2   In the 1980s, some cities used the "double pick" model to assign job positions. Applicants applied for the positions that they wanted and companies/institutes also picked the employees they wanted. Employment resulted from a combination of application and assignation. It was a special process during the period when China was transitioning from a centralized economic system to the Reform and Open-up policy system.

References

Archer, M. S. (2003). *Structure, agency and the internal conversation*. Cambridge: Cambridge University Press.

Archer, M. S. (2007). *Making our way through the world: Human reflexivity and social mobility*. Cambridge: Cambridge University Press.

Atkinson, P., & Delamont, S. (2008). Analytic perspectives. In N. K. Denzin & Y. S. Lincoln (Eds.), *Collecting and interpreting qualitative materials* (3rd ed., pp. 285–311). New York, NY: Sage Publications.

Bandura, A. (2006). Toward a psychology of human agency. *Perspectives on Psychological Science, 1*(2), 164–180.

Beauchamp, C., & Thomas, L. (2009). Understanding teacher identity: An overview of issues in the literature and implications for teacher education. *Cambridge Journal of Education, 39*(2), 175–189.

Biesta, G., Priestley, M., & Robinson, S. (2015). The role of beliefs in teacher agency. *Teachers and Teaching, 21*(6), 624–640.

Cunliffe, A. L. (2003). Reflexive inquiry in organizational research: Questions and possibilities. *Human Relations, 56*(8), 983–1003.

Day, C., Kington, A., Stobart, G., & Sammons, P. (2006). The personal and professional selves of teachers: Stable and unstable identities. *British Educational Research Journal, 32*(4), 601–616.

Giddens, A. (1984). *The constitution of society: Outline of the theory of structuration.* Oakland, CA: University of California Press.

Hammerness, K., Darling-Hammond, L., & Bransford, J. (2005). How teachers learn and develop. In L. Darling-Hammond & J. Bransford (Eds.), *Preparing teachers for a changing world: What teachers should learn and be able to do* (pp. 358–389). San Francisco, CA: Jossey-Bass.

Holland, D. C. (1998). *Identity and agency in cultural worlds.* Cambridge, MA: Harvard University Press.

Huberman, M. (1989). The professional life-cycle of teachers. *Teachers College Record, 91*(1), 31–57.

Lawrence-Lightfoot, S., & Davis, J. H. (2002). *The art and science of portraiture* (1st ed.). San Francisco, CA: Jossey-Bass.

Mockler, N. (2011). Beyond 'what works': Understanding teacher identity as a practical and political tool. *Teachers and Teaching, 17*(5), 517–528.

Priestley, M., Biesta, G., & Robinson, S. (2015). *Teacher agency: An ecological approach.* London: Bloomsbury Publishing.

Sachs, J. (2005). Teacher education and the development of professional identity: Learning to be a teacher. In P. Denicolo & M. Kompf (Eds.), *Connecting policy and practice: Challenges for teaching and learning in schools and universities* (pp. 5–21). Oxford: Routledge.

Sloan, K. (2006). Teacher identity and agency in school worlds: Beyond the all-good/all-bad discourse on accountability-explicit curriculum policies. *Curriculum Inquiry, 36*(2), 119–152.

Toom, A., Pyhältö, K., & Rust, F. O. C. (2015). Teachers' professional agency in contradictory times. *Teachers and Teaching, 21*(6), 615–623.

Zembylas, M. (2003). Interrogating "teacher identity": Emotion, resistance, and self-formation. *Educational Theory, 53*(1), 107–127.

Zhang, H., & Zhong, Q. (2003). Curriculum studies in China: Retrospect and prospect. In W. F. Pinar (Ed.), *International handbook of curriculum research* (pp. 253–270). Mahwah, NJ: Lawrence Erlbaum Associates.

CHAPTER 10

Currere: Negotiating One's Failure to Represent

Valerie Triggs

The distant red neon shivered in the heat. I was feeling like a stranger in
a strange land. You know, where people play games with the night. God,
it was too hot to sleep.

ROBBIE ROBERTSON, 1987

∴

The summer that I found the black bathing suit on the beach was not the
summer in which I learned that wearing it was part of negotiating the self. It
was, instead, another summer experience many years later as a student in a
graduate class that jarred me into motion towards trying to come to terms with
the self, a self in the midst of recalibrating its incompleteness and its "continuity of openness" (Massumi, 2002, p. 135). This time, the smoothness of slipping
into someone else's Lycra was replaced by the shock of realizing my clothing
did not fit at all anymore, a sudden awareness then, and again now as I write,
of research's additive functions. In that summer class, all that rescued me from
the thunderbolt, force-field encounter seemingly activated by the presence of
the professor, and from being burned up in the heat of the moment, was the
stabilizing solidity of the table in front of me.

In this chapter, I focus on the negotiation of the teacher/researcher self
through William Pinar's creative practice of curriculum's moving form, *currere*
(Pinar & Grumet, 1976; Pinar, 1978; Pinar, 1994) which offers a framework
for autobiographical writing in educational experience. I consider Pinar's
suggested phases or movements in *currere* in terms of their invitational
opportunity for feeling the indeterminacy, relationality, and reconnectivity of
one's identified limits. I also employ the space of *currere,* in both its physical
and semiotic negotiation, for its significance in augmenting the aliveness of
the self by not accessing it as already decided.

Pinar (1975) claimed that educators should engage *currere* in the infinitive
form of curriculum and turn attention from what contributes to a course
of education, towards recognizing education as something that courses.

© KONINKLIJKE BRILL NV, LEIDEN, 2018 | DOI:10.1163/9789004388901_010

To 'course' for Pinar, signals an indeterminate outcome for the self, an indeterminacy that offers an expanded understanding of the self always in the midst of movement. He defines four phases or movements in this coursing: regressive, progressive, analytical, and synthetical. Each phase invites the materiality of the body to make itself intelligible to the newly emerging self. In the regressive phase, something of a person's past lived experience is generated through free association. Here one re-experiences and transforms one's memory. The self is felt not as something passive but rather, as already active.

Pinar contends that at any moment, one is "located in historical time and cultural place" (2004, p. 36) where presumably the body is attuned to the particularities of particular situations. This is not, however, a search for an authentic self-expression; there is no linear progression of cause and effect in this process. Instead, present, past, and future are conflated and intra-acting. Causality itself is interrogated in *currere's* process and, as a result, I consider that *currere* relates as much to fiction as to factuality. Rather than relations between isolated times and selves, I argue that *currere* involves engaging the world as an entangled network already underway, where the materiality of selves is produced differently in different contexts and never as entirely knowable or understandable.

In the progressive step of *currere*, one looks at what is not yet and "imagines possible futures" (Pinar, 2004, p. 36). Here, research practice weaves together a heightened awareness of one's self in relation to a reactivated past and its feel for the future. In this phase, autobiographical writing includes the fictive, the poetic, and the mythic. In the analytical stage, one examines the past and the future together to write a story that shares a here and now experience of felt capacities for affecting and for being affected. In the fourth phase, the synthetical moment, a person revisits the present to listen to their voice. Pinar describes this phase of the practice as "one of intense interiority" (p. 37), where one is attuned to nuances and details of self, each detail arriving with new possibility and each nuance generated from the movement of present, past and future as one event. Michele Sorensen (2018), describes *currere* as a practice of feeling one's "embodied capacity to differ" (p. 87), and as "a practice that carries the past into new contexts, without offering a predetermined self or the conclusion of a life" (p. 89).

Christopher Lasch (1984), an historian concerned with the ongoing deterioration he perceived in American culture and politics, defines selfhood as implying a personal history, friends, family, a sense of place, and relations that generate creative responses and possibilities. He describes how, under siege from social and economic conditions that focus on survivalism, the self contracts to a defensive core, armed against diversity. This 'minimal self' retreats from any palpable, emotional interest in past, future, or place. Lasch critiques the social and cultural survival techniques of the minimal self: blending in; adopting the protective colour of immediate surroundings; taking refuge in the present; and clinging to life at all costs, a life as already known. He laments the current difficulties involved in taking refuge in "the sheer fact of self" (Roth in Lasch, p. 134) and wants to move beyond a survivalist mentality. He argues that media and consumerism have blurred distinctions between reality and illusion – between the subjective world and the world of objects, that the world of substantial things has been replaced by a shadowy world of images, and that the boundaries between self, surroundings, and objects have been lost. While we might consider fixing and defining these boundaries more tightly, this is not the solution. Lasch seems to be arguing instead, for the necessity of feeling one's limits in order to sense their degrees of openness.

Almost a decade later, William Pinar (1994) proposed the methodology of *currere* that seeks a more adequate future for educational research in reconnecting intellect with its companion emotional, bodily, and erotic realms. Pinar argues for feeling one's edges in all of their sensual awareness in order to feel their relational openness. The method of *currere* seeks a connection of present meaning with biological concreteness, inviting us to experiment with observations that need rematerializing and with understanding as that which evolves in the context of an individual's life history. *Currere* begins by bringing one's gaze back into one's self as well as outside of one's self in order to describe honestly and in detail, internal experience as responding to its external invitations. In so doing, Pinar argues that the method of *currere* aims to cultivate a "point of view that hints at the transtemporal and transconceptual" (p. 19).

I am drawn to *currere's* hints of the transtemporal and transconceptual that emphasize a concreteness of reality as that which includes its potential to vary. Here, there is possibility for sharp awareness of the visceral sensations of materialities that define bodies, as well as those invisible doublings of materialities that traverse boundaries between self and next self, feelings through which one continues in movement. *Currere* offers a reconfiguration of previous containment, as well as opportunity to become more sensitive to ongoing porosities of boundaries between the self and its unknowability, which is either simmering alongside or in the midst of exploding in newly felt potential. Experiences emerge out of the physicality of the body's time and space as it exists in relation to others and, when the physical environment is included, as Timothy Morton (2012) argues, "all kinds of uncertainty arise" (p. 97).

I found the bathing suit washed up on the pebbly beach of a prairie lake during a summer in which events had been tumbling over and through each other in variations of disaster and exhilaration. Prairie lakes are often at the end of long gravel roads winding into dips in the land, appearing just where the broad, flat horizon of square fields of crops disappear and the scents of dust and sage give way to willow and poplar. Flies buzz, crickets sing, and mosquitos rise in swarms from the grass. Prairie lakes offer a different kind of lonely from the isolation of the every day, a more palpable sense of the temporariness of encounters. I feel foolish now, for so innocently repeating my father's tendencies of finding treasure in the discards of others but that kind of self-connection was rather far from my mind in that lake environment. It seemed appropriate somehow, that (after being washed of course), the bathing suit fit perfectly even though it appeared to be made for a more fashionable and worldly body than my own. For a time, I felt beautiful. The feel of the fabric relayed a sense of potential at my edges and I carried that sense with me, a sense of self that was a teasing mix of intimacy and distance.

While appreciating *currere's* potential for tearing down and rebuilding boundaries as intimate reciprocities to the body and ways of extending a sense of aliveness, I struggle with Pinar's references to honesty in describing my reactivated past and heightened awareness of self. In much of the rest of this chapter, I respond to this struggle with an argument for how *currere* might potentially practice the concreteness of body experience without losing its necessary practice of indeterminacy and invention. Telling you fewer details of my summer recollections may prevent both me and the reader of this chapter from freeze-framing the self and from short-cut methods of summing up memories provoked. I realize that the partial story lingers unsatisfactorily; I too, do not entirely know what to do with its resonant frequencies that still search out connections in my chest and on my skin but I know they are necessary in bringing wonder back into negotiating a self.

Deborah Britzman's (2006) use of the psychoanalytic term, "phantasy," for example, might be helpful in describing *currere* writing as it colours and texturizes and gives a rhythmicity to our memories. Referring to nineteenth and early twentieth writers such as George Macdonald, Alberto Paderno (2012) suggests that, in a literary sense, usage of the out of date "ph" rather than the "f" spelling of phantasy signals that the story being told is using an older time or place or mode of storytelling. Perhaps the archaic use of fantasy reminds us, as Nigel Thrift (2008) observes, that there is "a continuous undertow of matterings that cannot be reduced to simple translations but can become part of new capacities to empower" (p. viii). When traditional autobiographical work masks experiential history asserting *the truth* of its tale, Sidonie Smith and Julia Watson (2001) suggest that this apparent lack of contrivance in autobiographical work actually "implies a deeper kind of contrivance" (p. 7). Perhaps the deeper contrivance is the work of reasoning away the openings in every moment or resisting the "excesses of embodied experience, now past but still palpable, that refuse containment by the disciplining power of autobiographical conventions" (Smith & Watson, p. 10).

Although linked to phantasm and suggestions of purely mental invention, phantasy offers an unactualized world of reality that stimulates new modes of relating. Phantasy changes the reductive potential of traditional autobiographical writing about unprovoked life patterns, adding instead something virtual and unbidden – perhaps fiction. Britzman (2006) explores the work of fiction in the psychoanalytic method of free association in which one gives up an already-sense of reality in the world and reconceptualizes experiences, invigorating in addition to creating. In the fiction of free association, something more primordial than language animates the urge to express, perhaps an urge for the sensation of relation or the lure of a limit experience of "being-within an outside" (Agamben, 2005, p. 68).

Objectivity is not at a distance from this understanding of self; the self is regenerated as part of the world's regenerating. Remaking the self not only involves new conceptual arrangements, but also, physical sensation of one's immediately differing difference. Similarly, in *currere*, an opportunity to free associate seeks a self, unseparated from physical sensation and form. It offers conditions of real experience as invitations to recount, repeat, and re-intensify the materiality of the felt and not felt, instances of sensations, repetitions of touch, sight, sound, and taste, discerned exquisitely for the first time or never before, or never yet. Through an invitation for added feeling and for relational reactivation, credibility is asserted. We have opportunity to practice being accountable to the specific materializations of which we are a part.

Fiction implies experimentation, one of many experiments. It offers what *currere* aspires in release from the past, from stasis, into movement and change. *Currere's* autobiographical writing extends a site of resistance that insists on the body being as immediately abstract as it is concrete, as much fiction as truth. In remembering, something extra slips in. Paraphrasing Gilles Deleuze, Massumi (2002) claims the importance of radical abstraction in order to grasp the real incorporeality of the concrete. The body never solidifies into something fixed or unchanging, putting the emphasis instead on its process before signification or coding or identification. Even sensation is abstract – emerging indeterminately from a totality that does not exist in advance of the points composing it. Instead, Massumi stresses that the body is in continual relation to its feelings of capacity to differ. Experiencing again the sensations of these relations may begin to blur our easily-perceived patterns that have more to do with stasis than with impermeability of borders. Even fiction needs reinvention in order to invite the fantasy of the body.

What is this fictive interval of abstraction and feeling, between remembering what we were doing in a particular situation and remembering what the situation was doing to us, where palpable tactility emerges? Here we should expect the opposite of what Britzman (2006) identifies psychoanalysis as doing, in which interpretation undoes concrete representation to make room for symbolization. Instead, Massumi (2002) considers the body as "an additive space of utter receptivity," its edges waiting to be defined by the felt reality of relation. The interval between remembering and reciprocity is instead, the time and space of concrete representation undoing interpretation.

Lasch (1984) critiques the minimal self for knowing the world and itself mostly through insubstantial images and symbols that do not refer to a palpable, solid, and durable reality. He warns that the self must *be* a substantive before it is capable of relation. Elizabeth Ellsworth (2005) describes the substantive *as* the self, existing only *as* and *of* relation. What is in the gap between matter and transformation is bodily sensation of relationality, reintensified – that physicality that returns one simultaneously to sensations of their edges, sensations of place, to sensations of more than selves. In this process, possibilities are multiplied to infinity and the threshold of potential feels raw and sometimes terrifying. Although particular fictions will pass if one waits, sometimes saving them may be harder than sharing them.

While phantasy accounts for the added receptivity of the body, it still seems suspect for autobiography with its beneficial ability to unplug the body's remembrances of context and reinsert them elsewhere. It seems to miss the intensity of the local, the physicality of sensation. Britzman (2006) asks how, in the movement of negotiation between inner and outer worlds, can phantasy hold up on the body? One explanation for phantasy's connection to touch and intensity might be offered by David Abrams' (1996) description of story:

> A story must be judged according to whether it *makes sense*. And making sense must here be understood in its most direct meaning: to make sense is to *enliven the senses*. A story that makes sense is one that stirs the senses from their slumber, one that opens the eyes and the ears to their real surroundings, tuning the tongue to the actual tastes in the air and sending chills of recognition along the surface of the skin. To *make sense* is to release the body from the constraints imposed by outworn ways of speaking, and hence to renew and rejuvenate one's felt awareness of the world. It is to make the senses wake up to where they are. (p. 265; italics in original)

Bringing together non-sense, making sense, and sensation activating past, future, and present creates a remembering that is not a reproduction of a perception but a transformation or becoming of it. The past is not just for one thing. Phantasy is the return to sensually discover the immediate; nothing is exhausted by its relations with other things. What we know is more than can be said, so *currere* gives away honesty for its failure to represent. Grappling with the abstract materiality of self-negotiation, *currere* makes it less easy to fall neatly back into pre-determined categories of thinking and relating.

Mats Alvesson & Kaj Sköldberg view any form of creativity in research as "a step away from dominant and established angles of approach" (p. 306). They claim that the richness of reflexive research is:

> to be found in the tension situations between body sensation and the freedom to express something creatively. The creative act implies going beyond the consensual views regarding the empirical material. Saying something creative and novel is thus not fully compatible with the ideal of maximizing intersubjectivity as the way of achieving objectivity. If we limit ourselves to what everybody already agrees on, then it is difficult to say anything new or original and there is a risk of repeating what everybody already knows. (p. 306)

Can creative transformation and invention of the past and future be the materiality of an experiment of embodiment that changes our relational future? Lasch (1984) argues for new sensibilities that rest on a recognition of the limits of rational thought and reject a logical, linear view of the world. He calls for synthesis, as does Pinar, between public and private, between self as concept and self's physical form. Jeff Park (2005) maintains that *all* expressive writing offers this synthesis of one's sense of self and its ongoing negotiation with others.

Assuming all autobiographical writing invites this expression, however, may not be accurate. Janet Miller (2005) observes that current uses of autobiography as expressive writing in educational practice often encourage, "all kinds of closet doors to open" (p. 219) but in ways that replicate the self as "rational, coherent, autonomous, unified, fixed and given" (p. 219). Instead, Miller points to *currere* as a practice that challenges and queers "humanist educational research and practices that normalize the drive to sum up one's self, one's learning and the other as directly, developmentally, and inclusively knowable, identifiable, natural" (p. 223). Shoshana Felman (in Pitt, 2003) also describes a way of reading that seems a potent companion to *currere*. It is characterized by the "reconstitutive tracing of self-implication" (p. 156) where we are incited, as Britzman (2006) suggests, to return to our lives with both comparability *and* with difference *and,* we might add, with degrees of body intensity from reminders of living's viscerality.

The generative work of *currere* might be thought of as a transitional layer holding the potential for putting inner and outer realities in relation – perhaps the fabric of clothing, perhaps a bathing suit, offering tactility and colour in two directions, pastness and futurity. In remembering, I notice that my clothes tend toward black or grey, greedy colours that don't reflect back the other wavelengths in the spectrum of light. Instead, I hold their catalyzing flow next to my skin, needing the materiality and intensity of their kaleidoscopic charge. They are good-enough clothes for the time being, while I use them in learning how research rewrites me. In both of the remembered situations in my own *currere* (bathing suit and summer professor), a powerful desire was temporarily loosed from social structures of identity or differentiation and the myths that support them. I tottered on the edge of a space that must remain an indeterminate totality, an event of my self as utterly alive. In the smell of algae at a prairie lake in August – in the intensity of a classroom realization of magnetic attraction – foolishness, incomplete ideas, the ignition of a self was, "erotically potentialized by the entire extensive world that *infolds* and *unfolds* around it" (Lambevski, 2005, p. 582, italics in original). For Lambevski, the body re-engineers itself from technical machines, substances, buildings, images, words, sound smells, textures, colours, materials, landscapes, oceans, rocks, animals and plants – all bits of the gigantic machine that regulates the flows of life.

There are certain words, of course, that readers will look for in my accounts of feeling the materiality of the self in the midst of change: inclusions of already-determined sexualities, genders, labels, moments of assuming certain identities, the finding of my 'true' self, 'coming out', or 'retreating into'. There are easier ways to tell stories to myself and to others but they are ways that I seem to resist. These constructions of cultural significations have a limited sphere of applicability and in their immediate applicability they limit other movement. They are predicated on other forms of fiction: the self as a "back-formation from cessation" (Massumi, 2002, p. 7), formations that also move forward to effectively "backform their reality" (p. 8).

The body, explains Sasho Lambevski (2004), has little to do with prefabricated social discourses, or how the "relations between the large aggregates – genders, sexes, sexualities, races, classes, nations, age groups – are organized on a molar level" (p. 305). The moving self, as it comes undone, only coincides with its "transition to elsewhereness" (p. 307). Its relational feeling in movements of indeterminate potential may help to establish limits of a self, finding them both inside and outside our bodies. Phantasy contaminates this coursing with feelings of potential unseparated from the world already in process, a creative act, as encouraged by Alvesson and Skoldberg (2009) that implies going beyond "consensual views regarding empirical material" (p. 306) and furthermore:

The generative capacity for this kind of research is the capacity to challenge the guiding assumptions of the culture, to raise fundamental questions regarding contemporary social life, to foster reconsideration of that which is taken for granted and thereby to furnish new alternatives for social action. (p. 307)

Massumi (2002) argues that what is at stake in the movement of the body is not factuality and its profitability but, rather, relation and its generativity. Though the sensual tends towards the erotic – it is an erotic that is deeper than subjectivity, more abstract than objectivity – it is more diffuse than desire, more about intensity, ferocity, extremity, magnitude, wind, and gravitational force. It nurtures fire, obsession, ecstasy, misery.

Lambevski (2004) describes the self in relation's generativity as:

A transsensual, transsignified, synesthetic, mesoperceptive sexuality in which stimuli gathered by all five senses meet well below ideology as a script for subjecting oneself to the usual erotic power games we tend to call sexuality. This sexuality belongs neither to the subject nor to the world exclusively. As such, it is not ownable, qualifiable, recognizable, or amenable to critique. (p. 308)

Unownable sexuality is a flow attached to a nomadic desire that "does not take as its object persons or things, but the entire surroundings that it traverses, the vibrations and flows of every sort to which it is joined, introducing therein breaks from subjectivity and new syntheses of bits and pieces from the world" (Deleuze in Lambevski, p. 308).

Rather than describing *currere* as a framework, perhaps it is more suitably termed a tensile force-field that returns one to the past, feels for the future, and brings distance and difference together around resonations of new affectivities. *Currere's* tensile nature is key: flexible, fictile, pliable, capable of being shaped, bent, drawn out, twisted, and always – lured beyond its felt limits. It conduces a re-emerging self, not by requiring factual accuracy but by inviting response that is as immediately abstract as it is concrete, as much fiction as truth, "an additive space of utter receptivity" (Massumi, 2002, p. 57). The method of *currere* seems a derivative of the movement of the self, its edges waiting to be defined by the felt reality of relation. Encountering this additive space of attunement may provide what Donald Winnicott (in Ellsworth, 2005) describes as a certain sense of aliveness that is the most important work of a life. This sense of aliveness gains intensity from its intimate access to the world, the extent to which we compose ourselves in attunement to the jolt of being re-aroused in a moving world. Ultimately it will carry us through traumatic experiences and help us survive.

If the present, as Deleuze (2003) suggests, is the most attenuated or narrowed degree of the coexistent past, then this same present is the precise point at which the past can be hurled toward the future. The use we make in the present of the materiality of autobiographic consciousness can be defined as that which changes nature – the always new, the perpetuity of the oldness of life. *Currere* gathers and surpasses its moments as it inquires into the conditions of body in world, in an embodied production of newness, a newness that uses older times, newly arriving places and perhaps, forgotten modes of self-making.

I am coming, rather late in life to appreciate words, to understand their potential for experimentation and generativity rather than interpretation. In every stuttering sentence there is possibility to re-compose the movement from which the words emerged. Although I lost my language in that summer classroom, my autobiographical writing is now spattered with the intimate knowledge of sensing and making sense. Barbara Kennedy (2003) writes that engagements with our materiality prior to language and subjectivity may arouse "new affectivities, new intensities between people [that] might provide a mutant sensibility which could prove more significant in changing people's experiences of themselves and the world than any macro-defined politics" (p. 13). The continuity or *truth* of the self in *currere* writing is more abstract and more concrete that can be expressed in a single story about a single experience. Massumi (2002) explains, "The personal is not intentionally prefigured. It is instead, rhythmically re-fused in a way that always brings something new and unexpected into the loop. The loop is always strangely open" (p. 26). Truth, as Britzman (2006) suggests, "resides in the farthest thing from one's mind ... within the utterance, 'I would have never thought of that'" (p. 31). Igniting, imagining, inventing sensations at our limits – at our exterior and interior edges, might respond to Lasch's (1984) concern for the hope of survival resting on a reconstruction of a self. Instead of defining our edges, we may be encountering the aliveness of sensing them.

References

Abram, D. (1996). *The spell of the sensuous.* New York, NY: Vintage Books.

Agamben, G. (2005). *The coming community* (M. Hardt, Trans.). Minneapolis, MN: University of Minnesota Press.

Alvesson, M., & Sköldbert, K. (2009). *Reflexive methodology: New vistas for qualitative research.* Thousand Oaks, CA: Sage Publications.

Britzman, D. (2006). *Novel education: Psychoanalytic studies of learning and not learning.* New York, NY: Peter Lang.

Deleuze, G. (2003). *Desert islands and other texts 1953–1974.* Cambridge, MA: MIT Press.

Ellsworth, E. (2005). *Places of learning: Media, architecture, pedagogy.* New York, NY: RoutledgeFalmer.

Kennedy, B. (2003). *Deleuze and cinema: The aesthetics of sensation.* Edinburgh: Edinburgh University Press.

Lambevski, S. A. (2004). Movement and desire: On the need to fluidify academic discourse on sexuality. *GLQ: A Journal of Lesbian and Gay Studies, 10*(2), 304–308.

Lambevski, S. A. (2005). Bodies, schizo vibes and hallucinatory desires: Sexualities in movement. *Sexualities, 8*(5), 570–586.

Lasch, C. (1984). *The minimal self: Psychic survival in troubled times.* New York, NY: W.W. Norton.

Massumi, B. (2002). *Parables for the virtual: Movement, affect, sensation.* Durham, NC: Duke University Press.

Miller, J. (2005). *Sounds of silence breaking: Women, autobiography, curriculum.* New York, NY: Peter Lang.

Morton, T. (2012). Mal-functioning. *The Yearbook of Comparative Literature, 58*, 95–114.

Paderno, A. (2012). *English language & usage stack exchange* (Q&A online site). Retrieved from http://english.stackexchange.com/

Park, J. (2005). *Writing at the edge: Narrative and writing process theory.* New York, NY: Peter Lang.

Pinar, W. F. (1975, April). *The method of currere.* Paper presentation at the American Educational Research Association Annual Meeting, Washington, DC.

Pinar, W. F. (1994). *Autobiography, politics and sexuality: Essays in curriculum theory 1972–1992.* New York, NY: Peter Lang.

Pinar, W. F., & Grumet, M. R. (1976). *Toward a poor curriculum.* Dubuque, IA: Kendall/ Hunt Publishing Company.

Pitt, A. (2003). *The play of the personal: Psychoanalytic narratives of feminist education.* New York, NY: Peter Lang.

Robertson, R. (1987). *Somewhere down this crazy river.* Producer D. Lanois, Geffen Records.

Smith, S., & Watson, J. (2001). The rumpled bed of autobiography: Extravagant lives, extravagant questions. *Biography, 24*(1), 1–14.

Sorensen, M. (2018). *Attending to the quantum leap: New materialism and field experience in teacher education* (Unpublished doctoral dissertation). Faculty of Education, University of Regina, Regina.

Thrift, N. (2008). *Non-representational theory: Space, politics, affect.* New York, NY: Routledge.

CHAPTER 11

Who Are You? Developing Teacher Identity Through an Ethics of Intersubjectivity

Lana Parker

I propose that teacher identity ought to be examined and constructed in response to an ethical premise. The ethical premise is based on a pre-ontological responsibility for the Other, an intersubjective relation, and an epistemological stance rooted in wisdom (Levinas, 1989). Using these conditions for ethics as a point of departure for teacher identity has implications for how teachers engage in their own learning, with the curriculum, and with students. After offering a description of the ethical conditions in more detail, I discuss what these conditions mean for teacher identity through three acts of facing the Other. Finally, I propose an extension of reflexive inquiry that simultaneously calls the self into question while making space for the Other.

Articulating an Ethics of Intersubjectivity

An ethics of intersubjectivity, as elaborated here, emerges from Levinas' (1989) "Ethics as First Philosophy." For the purposes of this discussion, it is useful to develop three fundamental considerations for an ethics of intersubjectivity: first, it begins with a pre-ontological responsibility to the Other; second, it is rooted in the self/Other relation; third, it suggests that meaning is not fixed, and that there is a distinction between knowledge and wisdom.

Responsibility

The first condition determines that responsibility for the Other begins before an individual becomes aware of laws or societal norms. It is a pre-ontological responsibility that emerges from a complex awareness that: in being, one is; but in being, one also has to account for one's right to be. Levinas (1989) clearly summarizes the pre-ontological responsibility as follows:

> Language is born in responsibility. One has to speak, to say *I*, to be in the first person, precisely to be me (*moi*). But, from that point, in affirming this *me* being, one has to respond to one's right to be. (p. 82)

© KONINKLIJKE BRILL NV, LEIDEN, 2018 | DOI:10.1163/9789004388901_011

It is significant that the self/Other relation is shaped by the sense of responsibility; that is, because the interaction emerges from a place of responsibility, there is an inherent asymmetry between the self and Other, with the Other always at a height and the self exposed in a stance of humility. Levinas' premise for ethics as first philosophy is notable because it begins with an acknowledgement of a commitment to the Other that plays out in an interaction of listening, which is also described as an act of facing (Hand, 2006). This responsibility, and the interaction it begets, is the path to goodness and, as discussed further below, wisdom.

The Self/Other Relation

The second condition of this ethics is positioned against individualism. Unlike neoliberal ideology, which manifests in the "guise of an individualism that privileges the rational, knowing subject as the fount of all knowledge, signification, moral authority, and action" (Peters, 2001, p. 116), the ethical premise puts the interaction between self and Other at the heart of meaning and being. For Levinas (1989), the self/Other relation is characterized by self-as-listener and Other-as-teacher. In the moment of interaction, the Other faces and surpasses us; its alterity is complete. To better understand the nature of the interaction Levinas conceptualizes, it is necessary to understand two aspects.

The first is radical passivity. If, as Levinas suggests, responsibility emerges not through law but through existence, then the state of being responsible, "pre-reflective self-consciousness" (Levinas, 1989, p. 80), and of being open to the interaction with the Other, comes not from volition but instead from a state of passivity. This state of passivity sets up the tension between the *bonne* and *mauvaise conscience*. Levinas (1989) clarifies,

> This implication of the non-intentional is a form of *mauvaise conscience*: it has no intentions, or aims, and cannot avail itself of the protective mask of a character contemplating in the mirror of the world a reassured and self-positing portrait. ... It dreads the insistence in the return to self that is a necessary part of identification. This is either *mauvaise conscience* or timidity; it is not guilty, but accused; and responsible for its very presence. (p. 81)

This vulnerable state of passivity, this *mauvaise conscience*, is responsible for the existence of the self and called upon to answer for the self. It is this call to answer, and being called into question, that moves the self into the interaction of listening to the Other. If passivity is represented by the *mauvaise conscience*, then ego, thought, identity, and certainty, are represented by the *bonne conscience*. The *bonne conscience* is self-sufficient. Unlike the *mauvaise conscience*, it does not rely on listening to the Other, but instead upon the insularity of thought.

Turning to Gibbs' (2000) analysis of Levinasian listening, of facing the Other, one discovers that 'I' do not listen with the intent to respond, but with an attitude of apology. When I speak in reply to the Other, I do not seek to colonize them with my words. Instead, my response is an affirmation of my limits, a bent knee before the teacher. The motivation for this act of listening lies within the desire for meaning.

Wisdom

The third condition is especially relevant to education and teacher identity. It is the understanding that there is a distinction between knowledge and wisdom. Levinas (1989) grapples with truth, and its relation to knowledge and being. He determines:

> the correlation between knowledge and being, or the thematics of contemplation, indicates both a difference and a difference that is overcome in the true. Here the known is understood and so appropriated by knowledge, and as it were freed of its otherness. In the realm of truth, being, as the other of thought becomes the characteristic property of thought as knowledge. (Levinas, 1989, p. 76)

Levinas is making a distinction here between truth and knowledge, laying the groundwork to differentiate knowledge from wisdom. First, he locates knowledge as a product of the interaction between self and Other; however, knowledge as it is presented here is equated with a truth that "overcomes" difference and is "freed of its otherness." The passage to truth reduces the other's alterity and knowledge becomes trapped in the self-enforcing space of thought. Truth, knowledge, and thought divest the self from the Other, and enclose existence in totality.

Contrast this with wisdom. Wisdom is born of the *mauvaise conscience*, which moves with a passivity (not an intentionality) away from the self and toward the Other. It moves away, and so cannot be enclosed in a totality; it is a radical passivity that moves toward that which is always beyond, always past the beam of light that thought and consciousness throw onto the Other. It moves toward infinity. Relating back to both responsibility and the nature of the self/Other interaction, the *mauvaise* and *bonne conscience* reflect the tensions between listening/wisdom and thinking/knowing.

2   Intersubjectivity and Teacher Identity through Three Acts of Facing

Teaching is an ongoing process of facing the Other. As such, teacher identity is subject to the Other as it is repeatedly called into question. Taken in this way, teacher identity never ossifies into a structure of correctness, nor does it coalesce into perfection. Rather, this approach to teacher identity is evoked by the image of a spiral that reaches ever outward, toward infinity, yet without particular destination. In the second component of the analysis, I investigate three particular acts of facing, taken up in the Levinasian context of self/Other interaction that is both fleeting and ongoing: teacher facing Other as a learner, particularly as enacted in identity formation at teacher education programs; teacher facing the curriculum; finally, teacher facing students.

Identity-of-Teacher Facing Self

Ostensibly, a teacher's identity begins to coalesce in a teacher education program. These might be the first moments of crisis for the *bonne conscience* as the individual is called into question, not only in the self/Other interaction but also as the self struggles with the assumption of a new identity, a new injury to the ego.

Levinas distinguishes between ego and self. As Levin (2001) observes, Levinas furnishes a self that exists as "pre-history of the ego" and that "gives to the individual some moral direction and motivation" (p. 16). Levin goes on to note that in Levinas' phenomenology, both the self and the ego are subject to wounding when faced with the Other. For teacher candidates in a teacher education program, confronting the professional identity of teacher is first a fracture to their self-perception. By assuming the role of teacher, by learning about the relational work and professional demands of teaching, the teacher candidate begins to add to the *bonne conscience* by assuming a new knowledge about teaching. By itself, this first extension of ego poses no threat to the self. We can see this as the teacher candidate who is busy memorizing the mechanics and pragmatics of lesson planning, curriculum, expectations, and instructional and assessment techniques.

But, beyond this extension of ego, there is an opportunity for morality and ethics when one considers the ego as distinct from the self, with a responsibility not simply to Other but also to what lies beyond totality. A key aspect of teacher education, the site of nascent identity formation, is the work of separating ego from self, and totality from potentiality. This second step requires that a bright beam of light be shone upon what is not yet known and what cannot be mastered: potentiality. Teacher education programs that ask teacher candidates to confront the self distinguish between what can be learnt (adding to the *bonne conscience*) and the ongoing responsibility to listen and evolve (the *mauvaise conscience*) that comes through listening to students, parents, and other teachers. By becoming aware of this distinction, teachers are pulled away from certainty to the moral obligation to listen. They become aware that every act of facing opens the sense to trauma ("I must change") but also possibility ("I will become aware of more than what I currently perceive"). This first step of recognition of the cleavage between self/ego, *bonne* and *mauvaise conscience*, and knowledge/wisdom constructs the premise for ethical conditions for teaching, and prepares the teacher for wisdom through future interactions with the Other.

Teacher Facing Curriculum

Another act of facing occurs between a teacher and curriculum. While Levinas resisted the idea of non-human others as Others in the ethical interaction, he deliberated text as Other in selected poetry and literature (1991, 1996). I suggest that an aspect of teacher identity evolves in response to the curricula that the teacher works with on a daily basis. That is, the teacher is called not only to enact the curriculum with students in a classroom, but is called to see the curriculum as a document that contains plurality as well as absence. There is a danger in seeing the curriculum document as codified knowledge. The teacher must avoid colonizing students with the curriculum, but must also see the curriculum as an Other that cannot be fully possessed.

Teachers must bring a sense of listening to the curriculum as an Other. This might be slightly more difficult since there can be a tendency to perceive text as monolithic and true, especially for a standardised curriculum document which ostensibly contains facts that students ought to master or skills that students should perfect. But a teacher's first task with curriculum planning is to perceive the curriculum, where "perception is first of all a solicitous, caring bringing-to-light, before it is appropriation, possession, domination" (Levin, 2001, p. 17). A "caring bringing-to-light" suggests that teachers review the curriculum for both what is contained and what is missing, for what is prioritized and for what is diminished. This is in direct contrast to reading the curriculum as a text to be mastered, contained, or performed in its entirety. As a listener, the teacher becomes vulnerable to the curriculum and aware of all the potentiality that exists beyond what is readily apparent on the surface.

It is also important that, as teachers enact the curriculum, they avoid using it to claim ownership, colonize, or inculcate students. The space between teacher and curriculum and curriculum and student must be maintained. In this act of facing, it is the curriculum, as moderated by the teacher, that faces students. The teacher becomes responsible for a nuanced offering of the curriculum: on the one hand, the teacher employs the curriculum to trouble the students' own *bonne conscience*; on the other hand, the teacher must remind the students that even a curriculum can be incomplete and that there is always more to be questioned, perceived, and provoked.

Teacher Facing Student

A further act of facing emerges through the teacher and student interaction. Traditionally, this interaction has been asymmetrical, with the teacher holding power and the student in a position of vulnerability. An ethics of intersubjectivity inverts this relationship, requiring humility and listening from the teacher who sees the *student as teacher*. Teacher identity is not only challenged with respect to its usual power dynamic, but is subject to constant revision in response to each student interaction.

This is perhaps a teacher's most salient and prevalent act of facing. Each student becomes an Other who broadens the teacher's thought as a patrol of consciousness. Each student fractures the *bonne conscience* anew, deepening a teacher's wisdom, and freeing the teacher to respond. Instead of engaging in reflection that turns inward, the ethical premise engages teachers with the Other in an ongoing process of listening and responding. This process presents an aporia for teacher identity: the basis of its formation, listening to the Other, is also the basis for its destruction. Listening is both formation and re-formation, building of self and resistance to ego. A teacher identity is then as susceptible to wounds as any manifestation of ego/self; the challenge is to begin to see the process of trauma and revision as desirable – as the manifestation of an ethics of responsibility and care – rather than as weakness.

What is most notable in this power inversion is the vulnerability and humility required of the teacher. This is not an easy shift and many teachers, especially those coming with their own experiences of traditional schooling, may be resistant to the change. Not only does this condition for an ethics of intersubjectivity ask the teacher to relinquish the traditional stance of "teacher," but it also asks the teacher to see the student as an Other who is inherently above the teacher. Gibbs' (2000) analysis offers several characteristics of the power balance self/Other interaction that will be helpful for educators in particular. First, that the responsibility to listen is primary: "I listen to the other speak, and am called to respond to and for the other person" (p. 29). In this sense, an educator is first a listener to students in the classroom. Any decisions with curriculum, instruction, assessment, and community ought to stem in response to what the Other/student has shared. The second notable characteristic is the asymmetry of the interaction: "The other speaks to me from a height, with an authority that instigates my need to listen and to respond" (p. 33); also, "listening is the performance that struggles with otherness" (p. 36). As an educator, then, I am called to be responsible for a form of listening that can never claim full knowledge or understanding of my students. They will always retain the authority to teach me. This leads to the final relevant characteristic of the interaction: it is necessary in order for me to know not only my self but also the world. As Gibbs (2000) points out,

> The self is first of all in relation with other people. ... If one is looking for a definition of myself, of what I really am in myself, then the answer will require the inclusion of something that is not myself. ... I need to listen to be questioned in a way I cannot question myself – and in listening to the question I am shown the questioner. (p. 32)

Students become the way for teachers to know themselves and to know the profession. There is a commitment here to students first, before curriculum and before assumptions of best pedagogic practice. This is the key for an ethics of intersubjectivity in the classroom: no decision can be made, no clear way forward can be determined, and no teacher identity can be formed, without listening to students.

Be/Coming

An ethics of intersubjectivity suggests a shift in traditional constructs of teacher identity. At its heart this ethics decenters the subject; as Ruitenberg (2011) notes, "[this ethics] does not ask 'Who am I?' but instead responds to the question 'Who are you?'" (p. 30). In this final section, I propose a variation of reflexive inquiry that acknowledges the ego/self, but that also turns purposefully outward, facing the Other.

Reflexive Inquiry Be/Coming

In a way, asking questions of oneself can become the insular trap of ego, thought, and knowledge Levinas criticized. On the other hand, teachers are often asked to engage in reflection in teacher education programs and throughout their careers. Reflexive inquiry helps transition from a stance of inquiry for knowing, to inquiry as a process of becoming or emerging (Armitage, 2012; Lyle, 2009). Reflexive inquiry sets the stage for tenuousness over ossification.

In this approach, reflexive inquiry is called to be/come more, marrying tenets of criticality, subjectivity, and relationality (Armitage, 2013) with ethics of intersubjectivity that decenters the subject. The educator may be called upon to engage with the question "who am I?" but only as a secondary function of first receiving the Other. Inherent to the question "who are you?' is the impossibility of ever knowing the answer. This tension presents a space between what is perceived and how it is processed into wisdom. An ethics of intersubjectivity moves reflexive inquiry into direct engagement with this space, bringing to bear elements of criticality and relationality, in combination with an understanding that there should be no claim made on the Other's alterity. The question becomes: how does one navigate a complex space as a person and as an educator?

Maclear's (1999, 2003) work on a parallax vision for art can be helpfully adapted here to develop a mode of inquiry that reflects on teacher identity, but also turns outward to the irreducible spaces between self and Other. Maclear (1999, 2003) aims to draw an audience's attention to the complexity of art by sustaining a space for witnessing that refutes certitude and necessitates vulnerability. Maclear (1999) describes parallax vision as comprising two levels of seeing: "At one level it is *corrective* – encouraging us to ask what counts as evidence, how testimony is socially framed; at another level it is *contemplative* – affording us passages through which we may revisit our own perceptual and epistemic assumptions" (p. 86). These corrective and contemplative gestures of witness resound with elements of an ethics of intersubjectivity: to resist foreclosure, to move beyond the evidentiary, and to maintain a sense of wonder and humility at all that cannot be captured according to our existing frames of knowing. Maclear (1999) contends, "for visual arts to testify differently, to different realities and knowings, we need to be open to looking as a process of defamiliarization and dehabituation" (p. 86). It is this sense of uncertainty, of defamiliarization, that is of most use when contemplating an ethics of intersubjectivity and teacher identity.

Extending Maclear's thematic of parallax vision to teacher identity and reflexive inquiry, I suggest two types of questions, constitutive and intercessive, that reflect a decentering of the subject. Constitutive questions probe a teacher's existing patrol of consciousness. That is, these questions provoke a teacher, when faced with an Other, to question how a subject or issue is socially constructed. What are the reasons why something counts and other things do not? Intercessive questions preserve the space for alterity between self and Other by redirecting educators to examine their own responses, emotions, and experiences when faced with the Other. As Lyle (2009) contends, "because teaching and teacher development are rooted in the personal, reflexive inquiry involves the study of how the personal influences the professional" (p. 294); it is therefore necessary to grapple with questions that not only examine personal responses, but that also examine how the Other shifts or traumatises the self into spaces of increasing wisdom. Intercessive questions play with these tensions, asking: Why do I believe this? Why am I reacting this way to this experience? Is there another perspective? What am I called to see, hear, and do by this Other? How can I respond? These twin pillars of inquiry are applicable in each of the three instances of facing delineated above.

In the first case, teacher facing teacher identity, constitutive questions ask teachers to engage with the pervasive narratives of teaching and to examine them critically. For example, how are teaching "excellence" and student "achievement" discourses shaped? In whose interests? What are the implications? Intercessive questions provoke the teachers to reflect on their own reactions to multiple perspectives: what ideas cause them the most discomfort and why? What are their personal beliefs about the teacher-student relationship? About curriculum? Assessment? What blind spots does their existing perspective create? How do their own experiences of education affect their beliefs? How do those beliefs shape their pedagogic philosophy? Here, the parallax vision serves to set the stage for an identity that is persistently troubled by new experiences. It introduces teachers to their responsibility to the Other and to responsiveness by problematizing the certainty of "best practices" and by encouraging discussion about dominant hegemonies.

When facing and teaching the curriculum, constitutive questions ask educators to examine standardized expectations in the greater context of their construction. These questions might include: Whose interests are reflected in and served by this curriculum and these existing resources? Who has been marginalized or silenced? What are the opportunities for diversification? Where are there spaces for debate, dissent, and questioning? Intercessive questions ask the educators to reflect on their biases and affinities. What areas of the curriculum and resources do I value? Why might that be? What does that mean for my teaching and for students and parents that express other interests? Where are my personal areas of challenge? How do I maintain space to teach those areas well despite my discomfort? In addition, when enacting the curriculum, educators must be sure not to render the curriculum monolithic to students. This requires an extension of constitutive and intercessive questions into student practice. In lieu of asking mostly content-based or mastery-oriented questions, an educator would include parallax questions about the curricular content for students to explore. This would encourage the students to also begin to see learning as a process of interaction, rather than something that can be perfected or claimed.

The most significant act of facing requires the most diligent and persistent form of reflexive inquiry. When in the classroom, each student and each day is a new call out of certainty and into the humble space of listening. Because of the inverted power dynamic this type of interaction is likely to be most difficult for educators to sustain. Nonetheless, if listening (and reflexive inquiry) are about being and becoming, the aporia of *what is* and *what is not yet*, then a beam of inquiry ought to continue to illuminate the spaces of teacher-student interaction. The constitutive and intercessive questions are less easy to exemplify here, as they will emerge organically from what is said and unsayable in each act of facing. What is notable is that the questions are not aimed at the student; they are instead aimed provocatively at the constructions of knowledge that comprise the ego and world. They are aimed at how the educator's self is called into question. The questions might include: how can I better understand without claiming? How can I see you as an Other and not as a manifestation of stereotype? How is what you are saying calling my beliefs into question? How might I respond in ways that reflect my learning? The guiding motif is, as Ruitenberg (2011) avers, "Who are you?" In this way the spotlight of reflexive inquiry dances between self and Other, but is always shaped by responsibility and humility.

References

Armitage, A. (2012). *Silent voices in organisations: Conscientization as a reflexive research methodology*. Paper presented at the 34-IX. Retrieved from https://search.proquest.com/docview/1346926394?accountid=15182

Gibbs, R. (2000). Why listen? In R. Gibbs (Ed.), *Why ethics? Signs of responsibilities* (pp. 29–46). Princeton, NJ: Princeton University Press.

Hand, S. (2006). *Facing the other: The ethics of Emmanuel Levinas*. New York, NY: Routledge.

Levin, D. M. (2001). The embodiment of the categorical imperative: Kafka, Foucault, Benjamin, Adorno and Levinas. *Philosophy & Social Criticism, 27*(4), 1–20.

Levinas, E. (1989). *The Levinas reader*. Oxford: Blackwell.

Levinas, E. (1991). Jean Atlan et la tension de l'art. In C. Chálier & M. Abensour (Eds.), *Cahier de l'herne: Emmanuel Levinas* (pp. 509–510). Paris: Herne.

Levinas, E. (1996). *Proper names* (M. B. Smith, Trans.). Stanford, CA: Stanford University Press.

Lyle, E. (2009). A process of becoming: In favour of a reflexive narrative approach. *The Qualitative Report, 14*(2), 293–298.

Maclear, K. (1999). *Beclouded visions: Hiroshima-Nagasaki and the art of witness*. New York, NY: SUNY Press.

Maclear, K. (2003). The limits of vision: Hiroshima mon amour and the subversion of representation. In A. Douglass & T. A. Vogler (Eds.), *Witness and memory: The discourse of trauma* (pp. 233–248). London: Routledge.

Peters, M. A. (2001). *Poststructuralism, marxism, and neoliberalism: Between theory and politics.* New York, NY: Rowman & Littlefield.

Ruitenberg, C. (2011). The empty chair: Education in an ethic of hospitality. In R. Kunzman (Ed.), *Philosophy of education 2011* (pp. 28–36). Urbana, IL: Philosophy of Education Society.

CHAPTER 12

Self-Defining as Professionally Secular in the Public Space: Reflecting on Teacher Identity and Practice

*Melanie Bennett-Stonebanks and C. Darius Stonebank*s

> When I do not know myself, I cannot know who my students are. I will
> see them through a glass darkly, in the shadows of my unexamined life –
> and when I cannot see them clearly I cannot teach them well. When I do
> not know myself, I cannot know my subject – not at the deepest levels of
> embodied, personal meaning.
>
> PARKER J. PALMER (1998)

∴

Introduction

We have a vision of teaching as an intricate act – an intricate act that cannot
be broken down to a set of skills or a recipe of strategies. Like many others
who have confidence that education has the capacity to be transformative,
socially just, and emancipatory, we believe that teachers do not enter the field
simply to put into practice the instructions or implementations from a curriculum guide or textbook. Teachers are dynamic beings, each with their own
framework of understanding and knowledge in regard to personal, linguistic,
cultural, and social composition. Their experiences, beliefs, ethical values,
motivations, and commitments are part of their frameworks of knowledge
and contribute to their stances and identities as teachers (Scarino, 2007).
We, as educators, need to recognize that we have more than one self-identity
that connects us to the world or, conversely, the world to us. Identities are
co-constructed and ever changing (Hendrix, Jackson II, & Warren, 2003) and,
given this, teachers need to be in ongoing and critical reflection on their self-
identities as they negotiate their relationships with their peers, their pupils,
and their workspace. The student, the classroom, the school, and society are
always in change and, if it is our intention to be facilitators of students' growth
as active participants in a socially just world, then we have the responsibil-

ity to be reflexively aware of our subjectivities when it comes to professional stance. Stance, as adopted by Cochran-Smith and Lytle (1999), refers to:

> ... the positions teachers and others who work together ... take toward knowledge and its relationships to practice. We use the metaphor of stance to suggest both orientational and positional ideas, to carry allusions to the physical placing of the body as well as the intellectual activities and perspectives over time. In this sense, the metaphor is intended to capture the ways we stand, the ways we see, and the lenses we see through. Teaching is a complex activity that occurs within webs of social, historical, cultural and political significance ... Stance provides a kind of grounding within the changing cultures of school reform and competing political agendas. (pp. 288–289)

Teaching from the vantage point of a professional stance "is a way to live one's life as an educator to maximize impact, making life and learning conditions better for all the children we teach. It is a way to transform the profession of teaching" (Dana, 2015, pp. 164–165).

The following chapter will examine how teachers navigate the challenges of defining and enacting a professionally secular stance by means of reflexive inquiry. This is an especially important consideration within the post 9/11 Global North context, as the increased debate and implementation of secular public spaces, including public schooling, has left educational stakeholders uncertain of what this means in a multicultural society like Canada. Through examining interviews from a four-year pan-Canadian research study on teachers' perceptions on secularism in public schools, a portrait has emerged revealing how self-defined secular teachers negotiate their identities, their stances, and the implications of these negotiations on the students they are teaching.

Background

The 1982 Canadian Charter of Rights and Freedoms guaranteed the fundamental "... freedom of conscience and religion" (section 52, 2a) and, since then, teachers have struggled to reconcile changes in public schools that gradually shifted from a religious base to a secular orientation (Bafesky & Walden, 2006). Compounding the topic for teachers is the use of secularism as political fodder in anti-immigrant platforms (Stonebanks, 2017), leaving the social justice oriented educator wary of their positions in such attacks. Since 1982, provinces and territories across Canada have slowly made changes from heavily religious-entrenched school systems, like Quebec's Catholic School Board and Protestant School Board, to those that are now touted in that province as being "entirely non-religious structures" (MELS, 2008). This pedagogical transformation required schools to adopt and advance a curriculum wide view and study of religion that is not based on proselytizing or promoting a single perspective in favour of students' and teachers' abilities to use their analytical skills to critically and respectfully examine both religious and secular viewpoints. Keeping with the Quebec example, from the Proulx Report (1999) to the Bouchard-Taylor Report (2008), there has been a decade of preparation for schools to move from their religious foundations to secular orientations open to the variety of its students' beliefs and philosophies. Despite this time, however, implementation of Quebec's secular program has been fraught with resistance and confusion amongst many education stakeholders (Knott, 2010; Stonebanks & Stonebanks, 2008). Our research has consistently demonstrated that, in relation to perplexity on meaning making of the teacher's stance in secular education spaces, many of the norms and privileges associated with North America's Christian and Eurocentric public education heritage are central (Carr & Lund, 2007; Stonebanks & Stonebanks, 2010; Stonebanks, 2008, 2009, 2010). In an increasingly religiously, spiritually, and world-view diverse Canada, what then are teachers' perspectives on the division between church and state inside of Canadian public schools? For our research team, the pressing question emerged: *From the secularist teachers' perspective, what does secularism in public education mean and to what extent are Canada's public schools secular?*

Purpose of the Study

The purpose of the study was to examine the perceptions of teachers within Canadian public schools who define themselves as *secularist* (atheist, agnostic, spiritual, religious, or otherwise) concerning the mandated secular nature of their province's education system. We looked to develop a sense, through the daily experiences of teachers who have adopted this professional stance, of public schools across Canada with regard to secular mandates. Using a snowball sampling recruitment strategy (where a group of people recommend potential participants for a study, who, in turn, recommend other participants), we recruited one hundred teachers (legally recognized and a member of their teacher's union) throughout the provinces and territories across Canada in order to better understand how our schools function nationwide in relation to secularism.

Methods

Teachers were asked to participate (on their own time, outside of their school hours) in three open-ended interviews over the course of the school year, utilizing remote communication technology (telephone, video conferencing, etc.) where they told their story in relation to the perceived realities of school. As all members of the research team were affiliated with the teaching profession (all possess a minimum Bachelor of Education degree), the dialogic nature of the interviews was evolving and not subject to static interview questions.

In these interviews, the teacher participants told their stories in relation to the perceived realities of their school and the researcher also contributed in order to catalyze the power of difference in knowledge production. Engaging in this process with one hundred participants, reflecting proportional representation based on total population for each province and territory, gave the research team profound insights into the intersection of different experiences around a similar phenomenon – insights that help reshape the understandings of all participants and all readers of the research produced (Barton & Darkside, 2005; Kincheloe, 2005; Roth, 2005). This initial, but in-depth, data gathering methodology was particularly useful to our research because it was "... designed to reveal how participants conceive of their worlds and how they explain these conceptions" (Goetz & LeCompte, 1984, p. 126). It also allowed the researchers to "... assess the participants' definition of social situations and recognize the images of selves contained in these definitions" (Barrows, 1988, p. 20), which fit securely into our critical framework. By applying this methodology to our work, we developed a picture of the participants' workplaces as well as their places within those schools as secularist professionals. Our interview format was grounded on an interview-based qualitative inquiry model that followed the guidelines of such authors as Goetz and Lecompte (1984) and Seidman (1991), along with the narrative-inducing interview formats and considerations of Reissman (1993) and Nelson (2001), in which there was an explicit recognition that the participant's self was intertwined with their surroundings, whether these contexts were interpersonal or institutional.

The year following the individual interviews, participants were asked to participate in an online, blog-based Professional Learning Community (PLC) with the research team. Participants had pseudonyms (with broad geographic location definers that would only refer to the province of employment) that would assure anonymity. Participation in this PLC entailed posting autoethnographic journal entries fairly regularly (approximately every month throughout the first year) that related to the topics being researched, as well as dialoguing with both the research team and other participants of the research project.

In participating in this PLC, we developed an understanding of how our public schools engage in the concept of secularism. By chronicling their thoughts, the participants developed autoethnographic journals about their schools' culture regarding religion and world-views. As they built upon what they articulated during the first year's interviews, the participants further revealed their positioning within their public schools, creating "... charged moments of clarity, connection, and change" (Holman Jones, 2005, p. 764). Finally, the dialogue between teacher participants created a textual, interactive description of our participant teachers' perspectives of the culture of Canadian schools over an entire school year.

Participants

For the study, our aim was to document and analyze primary and secondary school teachers within the public sector who are self-described as having secularist perspectives (regardless of their religious affiliations or world-views) towards the role of public education in Canada. Participants all fell under the category of adults (over 18), professionals (possessing provincially recognized certification) working within their field who belong to a professional union or association, and who were interested in investigating their work environment as it related to the mandated policy requirements using a professional stance. We identified these candidates by contacting multiple Canadian education organizations (e.g. religious teacher associations working in public schools, School boards, Teacher unions, Provincial Ministries of Education, etc.), as well as organizations that are self-described as "secularist" (e.g. Provincial Secular Movement associations, provincial branches of the Humanist Association of Canada, etc.), and departments of education within Canadian universities to reach in-service teachers who were continuing their professional development. By the time interviews were to begin, we had a total participant tally of one hundred proportionally represented primary and secondary teachers from across Canada.

Data Collection

During the first set of the three interviews, a series of questions was asked to contextualize each participant's teaching history and milieu as well as begin a discussion on their understanding of secularism. A fundamental question was posed to shed light on how each participant considered their place in relation to secularism and their professional identity: *You define yourself as a secularist teacher; can you explain in what ways?* This was followed up with a query to encourage each participant to reflect more deeply not only on their perception of what it means to be professionally secular, but also on how they demonstrate this in their day to day teaching. This introspection was prompted by the following question: *What does this mean to you and how is it lived in the professional context?* The intent for this line of inquiry was to build a base on which further interview themes such as the state of secularism in education on a provincial and national level (interview 2) and the future of secularism and consideration of directions to be taken towards a successful secularist curriculum (interview 3) could be addressed. It also allowed for reflexive responses to ensue as often the latter interview questions spiraled back around to touch on aspects of previous interrogations in relation to social and educative contexts. This recursive method was revisited when we began our year-long online Professional Learning Community. In order for the participants to reflect and reconsider their identity as self-declared secularist teachers, the first question that was posted on the forum and which brought about conversations nationwide was: *Why have you identified as professionally secular, and is it a personal choice, a professional obligation, a combination of both or based on an entirely different reason?* As the dialogue between professionals took root, it was interesting to see the variety of responses which shaped each participant's understanding of what it meant to be professionally secular and how this identity was formed, at times reshaped, and essentially lived out in their professional landscapes.

Results

Through reviewing the interviews and the PLC, one thing that became clear was the wide variety of experiences that led these teachers to identify as professionally secular. Some cited their upbringing stating that how they see themselves now and their responsibility in the classroom is due to the multicultural nature of their childhood.

> I grew up in a school where it was very multicultural and I lived in a neighbourhood that was very multicultural. And as such, I was always in a very diverse world/neighbourhood. So, to me I always embraced all cultures and religions ... which brings me to why I believe I am secular professionally ... for me, secularism isn't necessarily about just eliminating all discussions of religious things/religions/faiths ... for me, it's about embracing all religious things/religions/faiths. No one is more important than another .... It's just part of who I am. (Wongy, QC)

Others simply shared that they did not have a religious upbringing in any way so they did not see any reason to bring religion into their curriculum. One participant described having had negative experiences with religious groups as they were growing up and therefore had turned against the idea of infusing any aspect of their teaching with a religious perspective.

> Personally, religion is not very important. I don't really believe in religion and have never considered myself a religious person. In my experience, most people who claim to be religious are often judgmental and critical of others. This belief comes mostly from my experience in the small town in which I live. I have had many negative experiences with people who claim to be religious but look down their noses at people who aren't. I have also had experiences as a teacher where parents and students have criticized novels I teach based on religion. I have experienced some rather nasty and critical reactions and judgments from these people. The whole thing has left a sour taste in my mouth regarding religion. (Mae, AB)

There were some who revealed that their positioning on living out a professionally secular life was due to the reality that they were atheists and brought a scientific understanding to the world in which they live.

> I identify professionally and privately as a secular person. I'm an open atheist with no spiritual belief or identity. In my private life I am an unwavering atheist with respect for knowledge and learning within the realms of observable science and data driven theory ... In my professional practice, as a Canadian, accepting the social norms and legal requirements of our Charter of Rights and Freedoms, I know that I cannot discriminate, nor judge others for their religious/spiritual beliefs. I am an open atheist. I never balk from mentioning this fact in my English classes but I also openly note that a variety of faiths, beliefs, and understandings exist within my classroom. I need to be mindful and respectful of this. (WildRose, AB)

On the opposite end of this spectrum were those who said it made sense to instruct their students with a secular lens due to having gone to university and studied world religions. This educational training allowed them to have a deeper understanding and appreciation for various world-views and beliefs. One teacher echoed this notion stating that she was professionally secular because she was a person of faith.

> I believe in teaching in a secular setting precisely because I'm a person of faith. I believe that we should all be free to follow our own faith, anywhere from a traditional form to atheism (provided, of course, that it's not harmful to ourselves or others) ... I feel that spirituality should be allowed in school, but not a focus. There are other venues that focus on that (places of faith and home) ... I think a secular system is the only one that makes sense. (BigNickel, ON)

There were also a number who asserted that being professionally secular was both their personal choice and their professional obligation. Some teachers maintained that they had to be professionally secular because they were working in a secular school and this was the pedagogical expectation for all the staff members. As we continued our dialogue with participants, their explanations as to how they linked their professional identity with what they professed was a secular curriculum deepened and intensified.

> I define myself as a secular teacher merely because I teach in a secular context. I am open and honest about my own religious beliefs as they arise in discussions and content related to the course; however, I will staunchly defend each individual's right to have their own beliefs. I protect the self-worth of individuals in my classes and I encourage critical thinking. To think critically, students must be exposed to as many diverse perspectives as possible, really. In addition, when presenting religious related content in say, a History course, I do not promote one perspective over another or ridicule any secular or non-secular perspectives. Each is presented rationally and fairly to the best of my ability. (SK 3)

As diverse geographically as our country, so are the experiences of students across Canada. We can confidently state at this point that there is no one archetype of a secular teacher or a nationwide understanding of secular pedagogical practices. The spectrum of what is occurring in our classrooms is quite vast, moving from secular teachers who believe that there should be no religion brought in at all –

> I just feel that public education and religion should be kept separate. (RedRockCanyon, AB)

to those who see a need for students to have a space for spirituality even if they, themselves, are atheists.

> I tried to believe, but with four years immersed in science thinking,
> I just couldn't find it in me to suspend the ability to think critically. I am
> not merely secular, but atheist. And yet, in my classroom, I recognize
> the needs of my students to have a spirituality. So, in my classroom it is
> inclusive and accepting all forms of spirituality. (Tiarna, BC)

Many participants believed conversations that fostered inclusivity were a
necessary component of their classroom directives in order to promote a deepening of understanding of various beliefs and perspectives. Their curriculum
was purposely designed to build awareness and empathy towards others.

> When I think of secularism I don't really think of it as eliminating religion
> from the classroom, I see it as broadening the conversation to be more
> inclusive ... I think there is value in conversation so long as it is not
> divisive, offensive. Am I professionally secular? Maybe not in the way
> many might consider it, but I feel that none of what I teach comes from
> any religious perspective but rather is open to including conversations
> about the realities of religion so that my students end up with a broader
> perspective on subjects overall. (Mirandus, BC)

Even in this space where teachers encouraged sharing of perspectives and the
prospect of learning other viewpoints, there were still variances in how this secular instruction should be approached. Some believed that this area of the curriculum should not be discussed unless students brought it up. Others were adamant
that it was their professional responsibility to offer students the tools to explore
diverse perspectives. More often than not, teachers forwarded the practice of presenting all religions and beliefs equally with a neutral stance. They believed that
bias could be removed if lessons were not based on a holy book or deity as being a
single "truth" or reality, rather that it is a reflection of a perspective.

> It means that I don't ever promote any kind of religion or anti-religion.
> I try to be neutral about it. In discussion I try to encourage students to
> be respectful of each other's points of view, whether it's Christian, non-
> Christian, Buddhist, whatever. (BC 8)

The area surrounding bias was intriguing as, again, there was a range of voices.
Some promoted the opinion that teachers needed to recognize their own
personal bias and model to their students how to recognize it and work against
it, sharing openly their thinking process.

> So, teaching in a secular way, you can't really be devoid of all bias ... everybody has a bias. I think part of being a secular teacher is being upfront about those biases and state that and state why I might have those biases and then model that kind of discussion with students because the thing about good teaching is that there's a lot of meta-cognitive stuff. (AB 2)

Others were firm in that there is never a point in their teaching where they share their personal lens as this would influence the thinking of their students and potentially sway them from developing their own judgments.

> I would not share, I think on a basic level, I think I would not share my religious or non-religious views with the students. I don't believe it necessary or whether or not it's appropriate. (AB 12)

Participants took their roles and responsibilities very seriously. They reflected, they shared, and they reflected some more, all the while purposefully analyzing their role and responsibilities in their secularly mandated teaching contexts.

> I think what it means to be a secular teacher, it means that I make a conscious and avid effort to present myself as a person who I guess promotes the ideals of inclusivity. How that translates into my practice? I try to be fair and evenhanded. Having said that there is always going to be subjective choices I am always going to choose ... Those choices are obviously going to be informed by my own biases but I think a part of identifying myself as a secular teacher, I think a very important step here is to realize that there is a subjective component to what I am choosing to teach about and how I am choosing to teach about it ... Also, I think being a secular teacher, part of what that means in practice is taking an interest in your students and being attentive and sensitive to their own background, their own values and understand that yes I represent the state as a public school teacher ... If I am going to be a secular teacher, I think the first step is to be aware of my own situatedness and being aware that in the process of teaching I am making subjective choices and to reflect on what those choices are and through those choices what messages are transmitted here. Does this align with what I feel are the ideals of inclusivity and fairness? If the answer is no then I need to re-evaluate and go back to the drawing board. (QC 20)

Conclusion

As Canadian public schools alter from their historical Christian roots to models that either have secular options, or structures that are entirely non-religious, teachers attempt to live secular mandates in a public space that Taylor (2007) believes should be locations for openness and tolerance. As teachers ourselves, who have worked for years in the field, we wanted to discover what this meant in theory and what this looked like in practice. Through our research, we found that teachers often work in silos and, at times, feel isolated and alone as their professional stance might be in opposition to the demands of their administrators, colleagues or parents. Connecting teachers across the country who identify as professionally secular allowed us to individually and collectively "negotiate and co-create similarly meaningful points of reference for learning and development within which we reflect and extend our understandings" (Schnellert, Richardson, & Cherkowski, 2014, p. 234).

Pillow (2003) advances the use of reflexivity based on "uncomfortable reflexive practices" (p. 175). Her standpoint is that, "reflexivity and the reflexive text not only trace and challenge the constructs of the author but also challenge the reader – pushing the reader to analyze, question, and re-question her/his own knowledges and assumptions brought to the reading" (Pillow, 2003, p. 189). For us, this stance speaks loudly as we are engaging with what Marcus (1998) refers to as "reflexive, messy texts" (p. 392). Through this engagement, we hope to question our work and encourage questioning in others. Ultimately, this work will take time. We have simply started the conversations. In trying to define and characterize oneself and one's professional identity, we offer no singular answer to the daily challenges of teaching and learning a secular curriculum. However, the discussions have begun and a community is coming together with a generative mindset.

In examining how a variety of teachers nationwide reconciled their personal and professional viewpoints, we facilitated an organic process that encouraged teachers to have an active voice in societal, institutional, and organizational change. By means of reflexive inquiry there is rigour in our attempts to engage in innovative and critical practice. It has, through candid dialogue, provided much needed clarity to a professional group's comprehension and definition on what a secular professional stance means while, at the same time, revealing the existing realities of Canada's non-religiously affiliated public education system to all the stakeholders. In an increasingly diverse Canadian population, this is an essential dialogue for our common good.

References

Bafesky, A. F., & Waldman, A. (2006). *State support for religions in Canada: Canada versus the United Nations*. Leiden: Martinus Nijhoff Publishers.

Banes, L. C., Martinez, D. C., Athanases, S. Z., & Wong, J. W. (2016). Self-reflective inquiry into language use and beliefs: Toward more expansive language ideologies. *International Multilingual Research Journal, 10*(3), 168–187.

Barrows, H. S. (1988). *The tutorial process*. Springfield, IL: Southern Illinois University School of Medicine.

Barton, A., & Darkside, N. V. (2005). Greater objectivity through local knowledge. In W. Roth (Ed.), *Auto/biography and auto/ethnography: Praxis of a research method*. Rotterdam, The Netherlands: Sense Publishers.

Bouchard, G., & Taylor, C. (2008). *Building the future: A time for reconciliation* (Report of the consultation commission on accommodation practices related to cultural differences). Québec: Gouvernement du Québec.

Canadian Charter of Rights and Freedoms, Part I of the *Constitution Act, 1982*, being Schedule B to the *Canada Act 1982* (UK), 1982, c 11.

Carr, P., & Lund, D. E. (Eds.). (2007). *The great White north? Whiteness, privilege and identity in education*. Rotterdam, The Netherlands: Sense Publishers.

Cochran-Smith, M., & Lytle, S. L. (1999). Relationships of knowledge and practice: Teacher learning in communities. *Review of Research in Education, 24*, 249–305.

Dana, N. F. (2015). Understanding inquiry as stance: Illustration and analysis of one teacher researcher's work. *Learning Landscapes, 8*(2), 161–171.

Goetz, J. P., & LeCompte, M. D. (1984). *Ethnography and qualitative design in educational research*. New York, NY: Academic Press.

Gouvernement du Québec, Ministère de L'Éducation, du Loisir et du Sport, Religion in Secular Schools: A New Perspective for Québec. Quebec, 1999.

Hendrix, K. G., Jackson II, R. L., & Warren, J. R. (2003). Shifting academic landscapes: Exploring co-identity negotiation, and critical progressive pedagogy. *Communication Education, 52*(3–4), 177–190.

Holman Jones, S. (2005). Autoethnography: Making the personal political. In (Eds.), *Sage handbook of qualitative research* (pp. 763–791). Thousand Oaks, CA: Sage Publications.

Kincheloe, J. (2005). Critical ontology and auto/biography: Being a teacher, developing a reflective teacher persona. In W. Roth (Ed.), *Auto/biography and auto/ethnography: Praxis of a research method*. Rotterdam, The Netherlands: Sense Publishers.

Knott, N. (2010). *Teacher professional stance in the Québec ethics and religious culture program*. Montreal: McGill University Library.

Krishnamurthy, S. (2007). Reflexive inquiry and reflexive practice: Critical reflection and pedagogy in English language teaching. *NAWA: Journal of Language and Communications, 1*(2), 14–22.

Marcus, G. (1998). What comes (just) after "post"? The case of ethnography. In N. Denzin & Y. Lincoln (Eds.), *The landscape of qualitative research: Theories and issues*. Thousand Oaks, CA: Sage Publications.

Ministère de l'Éducation, du Loisir et du Sport. (2008). *Ethics and religious culture: Programme de formation de l'école québécoise: Éducation préscolaire, enseignement Primaire*. Québec: Gouvernement du Québec.

Mockler, N., & Sachs, J. (Eds.). (2011). *Rethinking educational practice through reflexive inquiry*. London: Springer.

Palmer, P. (1998). *The courage to teach*. San Francisco, CA: Harper & Row.

Pillow, W. (2003). Confession, catharsis, or cure? Rethinking the uses of reflexivity as methodological power in qualitative research. *Qualitative Studies in Education, 16*(2), 175–196.

Pinar, W. (2015). *Educational experience as lived knowledge, history, alterity: The selected works of William F. Pinar*. New York, NY: Routledge.

Riessman, C. K. (1993). *Narrative analysis*. Newbury Park, CA: Sage Publications.

Roth, W. (2005). Auto/biography and auto/ethnography: Finding the generalized other in the self. In W. Roth (Ed.), *Auto/biography and auto/ethnography: Praxis of a research method*. Rotterdam, The Netherlands: Sense Publishers.

Scarino, A. (2007). Words, slogans, meanings and the role of teachers in languages education. *Babel, 42*(1), 4–11.

Schnellert, L., Richardson, P., & Cherkowski, S. (2014). Teacher educator professional development as reflexive inquiry. *Learning Landscapes, 8*(1), 233–250.

Seidman, I. E. (1991). *Interviewing as qualitative research: A guide for researchers in education and the social sciences*. New York, NY: Teachers College Press.

Stonebanks, C. D. (2010). On critical thinking, indigenous knowledge and raisins floating in soda water. In J. Adams, D. Tippins, M. Mueller, & M. van Eijck (Eds.), *Cultural studies and environmentalism: The confluence of ecojustice, indigenous knowledge systems and a sense of place*. New York, NY: Springer.

Stonebanks, C. D. (2017). Multiculturalism and the Canadian pre-service teacher: Made in the USA? In E. Lyle (Ed.), *At the intersection of selves and subject: Exploring the curricular landscape of identity*. Rotterdam, The Netherlands: Sense Publishers.

Stonebanks, C. D., & Stonebanks, M. (2008). Religion and diversity in our classrooms. In S. R. Steinberg (Ed.), *Diversity: A reader*. New York, NY: Peter Lang.

Stonebanks, C. D., & Stonebanks, M. (2010). Religious identity in schools and the looking glass self. In D. Chapman (Ed.), *Teaching social theory*. New York, NY: Peter Lang.

Taylor, C. (2007). *A secular age*. Cambridge, MA: Harvard University Press.

Visweswaran, K. (1994). *Fictions of feminist ethnography*. Minneapolis, MN: University of Minnesota Press.

CHAPTER 13

Sharing Stories: Duoethnographically Evoking Mathematics Teacher Identities through Narratives

Derek Markides and Sandy Miller

Teaching like learning is not about convergence onto a pre-established truth, but about divergence – about broadening what can be known and done.

DAVIS AND SUMARA, 2007, p. 64

∴

Pitre, Kushner, Raine, and Hegadoren (2013) propose that all narrative writing comes from our own personal experiences, histories, cultural influences, language, and knowledge. Given that all these experiences are social constructions, written narratives are inherently socially informed. Pitre et al. (2013) go on to suppose that narratives hold within them, a positioning that provides insight into power structures, ideologies, biases, and beliefs of the participants, and that knowledge generation can be accomplished through dialogue and reflection whereby, "storytellers locate themselves within the conditions that influence their choices and actions as social agents" (p. 118). They recognize that the reader can be the one who takes up action as a result of an engagement with the narrative.

Creating opportunities for discussion, we believe, allows for educators to share what they are thinking about, struggling with, or feeling troubled by in a "space of possibilities that is opened up through the exploration of the current space of the possible" (Davis & Sumara, 2007, p. 58). Through narratives, educators may negotiate and re-negotiate concepts in a recursive manner, allowing for an attendance to tacit formulations of their identities and making explicit what they hope to connect to, attend to, or struggle with. We believe this is a more holistic attempt at sense-making, as Walker (2007) suggests that "the exchange of stories challenges our complacency as interpreters 'outside' the story and makes us aware that our own place in the world plays a part in the interpretation and shapes the meanings we derive from them" (p. 302).

© KONINKLIJKE BRILL NV, LEIDEN, 2018 | DOI:10.1163/9789004388901_013

Kovach (2009) posits that "in co-creating knowledge, story is not only a means for hearing another's narrative, it also invites reflexivity" (p. 100). Becoming more open to listening – listening as the active attendance to the narratives of those whom we are in the presence – will disrupt our desire to hear-to-respond and challenge us to reconsider our own understandings through a co-creational means. Through open dialogue, we are able to push back on our previously understood *truths*, whereby, we as educators, may (re) negotiate our understanding of who we are as individuals and as teachers. With this focus on more critical reflexive pedagogies, "we are being asked to consider identity not so much as something already present, but rather as production, in the throes of being constituted as we live in places of difference" (Aoki, 1993, p. 260).

Engaging Duoethnographically

As humans we are both storymaking beings and beings who are constituted through the act of storytelling – beings who in telling the tale create and re-create the self, knowledge of the self, and knowledge of the world. (Krammer & Mangiardi, 2012, p. 43)

The following chapter is the beginning of a duoethnographic conversation. Through this reflexive process, we look to consider how our identities have been transformed, our beliefs about learners have changed, and our understandings about knowledge formation have expanded. In the following duoethnography, which was undertaken in the same spirit as Sawyer and Norris (2013), we challenge prescriptive positivist paradigms that have become normalized within Western mathematics classrooms while considering the role that our identities play in our pedagogies.

Through this dialogical process, we hope that our stories, as considered through a non-linear lens of our past, may elicit a more vivid (re)collection of thoughts. As Krammer and Mangiardi (2012) posit, "a solitary act of reflection can engender only limited understandings; but the dynamic interplay of two critically questioning minds can transform, create, and expand each participant's understandings" (p. 43). It is this dialogical process – a diffuse revisioning of the past through the lens of the present in tension with another – that allows us to reconstruct our memories and thoughts. As Walker (2007) suggests, "we get to put our stories next to those of other, to experience the shock of recognition and 'the appeal to the heart', to listen and hear differently" (p. 300). This way of knowing – a reflexive understanding of ourselves – requires us to question what it is that we see and know as *truth*. For us, engaging duoethnographically allows "different individuals ... to make meaning of their life histories and then reconceptualiz[e] those meanings" (Nabavi & Lund, 2012, p. 177). Our hope is that, by participating in this duoethnography, the possibility to reflect widens and the landscape upon which our experiences have influenced both our practice and identity may invite others to consider and explore reflexively their own identities.

Our Shared Narrative

It's a snowy Saturday morning in Calgary; I arrive at the coffee shop early. I feel the warm air scented of coffee as I pull open the door. I look for a table in the crowded room and find one near a window at the back. I sink into the upholstery covered armchair, running my hand over its arm, admiring the intricacy of the patterned fabric as I consider the journey that Derek and I have shared as colleagues in high school math education and as students in post-graduate classes. Minutes later Derek arrives, and we each order a coffee; we begin talking about how we met years ago at a conference in Edmonton for Advanced Placement (AP) Calculus.

We happened to sit beside each other. The desks were aligned in rows, all facing the front of the class. The AP facilitator began discussing math concepts that were important outcomes of the program. Derek and I were both competitively engaged in completing the questions that were written and displayed on a large white screen at the front of the class. We worked alone on our calculations, regularly checking in with each other by asking "What did you get?" "Did you do this?" "Are you done yet?" This was a narrative which echoed conversations had by our students in our high school math classes. Five years later, we completed our Masters in Mathematics Education at the University of Calgary, and we are currently doctoral students, once again completing the program together. The time spent as educators, students, and friends has given us pause to consider and reconsider topics of math education through many conversations and from a variety of perspectives. Throughout our ten-year friendship we have discussed issues of teacher education and mathematics curriculum; however, the opportunity to engage in a discussion about our identities has never arisen until now.

Derek: So, I think that we should start with the past, share where we came from. Remind me about where you are from and what your education was like?

Sandy: So where to begin? Okay, well, this feels a bit awkward. Who am I? I am a fifty-five-year-old woman and have been teaching high school math for over ten years. I was born in Montreal, Quebec. I am White, was raised in a middle-class family, and I have one older brother. I am married; I have two grown sons and a dog. I liked school; no, let me clarify – I loved school. As a small child, I remember playing school with my friends. When I was old enough to attend, it was a place where I felt comfortable, where I was encouraged, by grades that were systematically assigned to work I had completed.

Derek: How would you describe your formal education?

Sandy: The way that I experienced my education was in a very mechanistic way, very much like the way I was taught to swim: each day an expert would demonstrate, with precision, the required movements. There were basic skills that needed to be mastered in order to stay afloat. Practice was expected in order to get stronger and faster. Everyone swam going up and down, in an assigned lane, completing the list of drills that were posted on a board at the front of the pool. There was no talking, no changing pace, and no deviation from the list of drills. Bobbit (2013) describes this technical approach to curriculum as a "series of experiences which children and youth must have by way of attaining ... objectives" (p. 13) and may only be represented in one specific form. I have known you for ten years, but I am not certain that I really know who you are. What is your story?

Derek: I enjoyed school as well, however, I think that it was the rote, mechanical nature of some aspects of school that I found challenging. Math and sciences were easy, but likely not for the reasons that many enjoyed the subjects. Math always made sense despite the dehumanized and "isolated and inhuman piles of axioms and algorithms" (Hersh, 1990, p. 105) that my teachers often perpetuated. For me, math was not a subject that was out there for us to discover; it was a sense making activity. Math was a space of beauty and elegance that started from a feeling, the space of a potential coherence that was messy and disorganized behind the scenes and appeared organized and formalized on paper (Hersh, 1991). When it came to writing, well, that was a different story. Throughout my schooling I was convinced that effective writing needed to be formulaic. The five paragraph essay, keyhole entry, appropriate comma placement, no run-on sentences, and the proper use of parts of speech were a must. To this day I struggle to write. It is something that I am learning to enjoy. Perhaps it is because writing can be taken up in so many different ways. I find that as I read more my writing changes and evolves. The diversity of authors and writing styles has given me license to find my own style and voice. This seems to be a lead-in to a discussion about fundamental pedagogical beliefs around learning. I am interested in exploring the embodied behaviours that teachers enact, as insights into what they believe about learners. What are your fundamental beliefs about mathematics and the teaching of mathematics? What do you think are the entailments of these beliefs as they relate to your students? What I struggle with every day, is how I explain various math concepts. I wonder if it is possible to explain ideas with great enough clarity so that all students understand them? As Davis and Renert (2014) state, "the simple (yet utterly complex) point is that mathematical concepts are comprehensible, but that comprehensibility demands continuous elaborative work" (p. 75). I wonder, do I create coherence of concepts for the students?

Sandy: I agree with you about the struggle to represent concepts in ways that all students can grasp, and I am not sure I have an answer. What I am certain of is that there can be no singular way to interpret mathematics and mathematics education. Over the last fifty years, educators and curriculum specialists have attempted to bridge the divide that exists within the discipline of mathematics and curriculum development and, still today, here we are talking about the same issues. Finding common ground is difficult when looking at how people teach and learn mathematics. There are people who like math and those who do not; those who find it easy, and those who struggle with concepts; those who need direct instruction for clarity and those that prefer open-ended questions.

Derek: It appears that we are both wondering what really matters in a high school mathematics classroom. We both see that mathematics requires creativity and thoughtfulness along with formality and coherence (Hersh, 1991). Is the important thing to create an environment where learning can happen? Do we put too much weight on what the teacher is doing? How does this help students to understand their own understanding? To think critically? Maybe focusing the lens on creating relationships is more important?

Sandy: I think that it is both. If learners aren't submerged in a culture within a classroom that draws attention to reasoning and analysis their ability to continue to discuss ideas is reduced to calculations. Creating experiences that model the incompleteness of mathematics helps students understand it from that perspective – thinking of mathematics as a "continually expanding field of human creation and invention, not a finished product" (Romberg, 1992, p. 751). The longer that I teach, the more I come to see the incompleteness of my own knowledge. I am always seeing things in a new light.

Derek: This seems to imply that you don't teach the way that you described your own education and maybe it has been an evolving process. Can you explain how this thinking of incompleteness might be changing how you now think of math education?

Sandy: Until a few years ago, I was teaching in much the same way that I was taught. I would write a series of problems on the whiteboard, work through them one at a time and, at the end, ask students if there were any questions. My teaching practice was focused on mathematical processes. About three years ago, I began to really think about how I was teaching, about relationships between curricular outcomes and what mathematics means to me. I worked to understand myself and my understanding of mathematics in a different way, which I had not done before. It is not something that is supported in practicums or professional development; both seemed to have a focus on lesson planning, specific activities, and student behaviours.

Derek: So, you think that this time spent reflexively examining your own beliefs about mathematics changed your practice?

Sandy: Yes. I think it did. I realized, through introspection, that delivering information from the front of the class, in a way that I had been taught, did not always equate to learning. Using journaling as a way to reflect on things that happened in the class, I became aware that there was no way of knowing if my actions would or would not trigger something for a particular student. I could not identify at what moment which pedagogical theory or which response would affect learning. This served to "represent a rejection of the notions of linear causality that were transposed from the analytic sciences onto discussions of teaching. Cause-effect interpretations make little sense when learners are understood to engage in recursive and elaborative processes" (Davis & Sumara, 2007, p. 59). As a result, both teaching and learning mathematics have come to mean more to me than questions from a textbook, assessments, and report cards. I have come to understand that "teaching is not about what the teacher does, it is about what happens to the learner" (Davis, Sumara, & Luce-Kapler, 2008, p. 158). It is important to be attentive to students' experiences, while working to build student-teacher relationships. I believe that this supports a departure from thinking of the teaching mathematics as linear – a way to attain knowledge through skills and practice – to an emerging system where complexity exists in relationships both between others and with mathematics, and where attentiveness to these moments is contingent upon care. My views on assessment have changed, I spend less time marking assignments and more time talking with students individually. I try to build a culture of *being with* mathematics in all/any conversations in the classroom. The time spent listening to each other in this way seems to matter, it seems to grow the collective knowledge much more than the isolated student working through problems on their own. This cultural shift within the classroom points to mathematics as more than a discipline; to me, it is a way of being.

Derek: I agree. We need to recognize education as cultural. We must become more comfortable with messiness. Decreasing our emphasis on the commensurable. As Marie Battiste (2013) advocates, "modern educational thought finds actual human consciousness too messy to be studied, which may account for why youth get the facts but not the discussion of what their own purpose is within the life in which they are submersed" (p. 31). Education must become more about relationships and coherence, connection and sense-making, empathy and care. You said it perfectly: mathematics and education (I would add) are ways of being. A pedagogical journey of walking beside.

Sandy: What about you? If you look back, what is one thing that you know differently about yourself and your teaching?

Derek: It is hard to define a moment where things changed for me. I see myself as a very different educator and person than I was when I started. Looking back, I find it problematic that, as part of my teacher education, I was never challenged to struggle with just what it was that I understood mathematics or teaching to be. By disrupting what I knew to be true, or by "rendering the familiar strange" (Davis, Sumara, & Luce-Kapler, 2008, p. 28), I had to (re)consider my own beliefs. The entailments of such transformations and their realizations would likely have helped me to see my early teaching identity in a more dynamic way. I suppose the change that I see in myself is a more cautious recognition of how our actions and language, as teachers, can solidify a student's identity as a learner of mathematics. Using less absolute language feels as though it may allow for the subsummation of present schema for future schema.

Sandy: I think of this as growth in my ability to hear/know selectively and intentionally. What I mean by that is, I hear/know what I am able to, at this moment, in this moment, and this speaks to the fluidity of identity. Is this what you might mean by seeing your identity more dynamically?

Derek: As a concrete example, I was always taught that multiplication *is* "groups of" something, like 2x3=6 can be represented as 2 groups of 3. While this is an adequate schema because it builds from the idea of repeated addition, it becomes inadequate when we discuss ideas such as groups of something or -3 groups of something and quickly becomes an insubsummable schema. For me, it is a change towards an emphasis on the non-absolute use of language such as: *in this case*, or *can be*, instead of *is*. This language choice can be applied throughout mathematics but is pedagogically contradictory to the ways in which I was taught, and it has the potential to take away the comfort associated with absolutist and dehumanized understandings of math. This way of thinking has been an evolutionary journey.

Sandy: Do you think that this shift in paradigm causes dissonance for math educators? What happens when you don't conform to established norms defined by an institution or your peers? The idea of belonging seems to be bubbling up in many readings. Dei (2008) describes "the ability to call on wider social support" (p. 355), while Hieu, Calhoun, Worthington, Pyrch, and Este (2015) consider "an unravelling of ... their sense of belonging" (p. 76).

Derek: I do think that these fundamental changes in pedagogy put me at odds with teachers in mathematics departments. Sometimes it doesn't feel like we are speaking the same language. It makes for some frustrating dialogue. I can understand your perspective on not belonging because, as hooks (1994) mentions, as we learn more it can be challenging to think in the same manner or to be around those who do.

As an administrator, I am constantly being asked to answer questions of accountability and how and why I know teachers are having a positive impact on students and their learning. As teachers, we are also asked to address these issues. I am of the same mindset that achievement scores (while they are certainly a piece of important data) are less important than student growth, wellbeing, and agency. However, achievement scores and wellbeing are not mutually exclusive. We could think to connect this to Nel Noddings (2002) work around care and replication of educational moments. This seems to be part of the reason why teacher interpretation, enactment, and embodiment of prescriptive Program of Studies Specific Learning Outcomes (Alberta Education, 2008) can look so very different even by teachers with similar educational context. My fear is that we ignore the complexity of reality as educators. I like the idea of giving more recognition to situation, context, and complexity.

Sandy: I understand what you are saying. There is value in examining our identities through the lenses of past experiences and socially-influenced relational exchanges. What I thought to be linear might not be, and what I have understood as advantageous may have traumatic effects on learning. There is great difficulty in this unpacking of where we are from, and where we are positioned now. The realization of our hidden histories is unsettling. There may be incommensurability in shifts in ideologies when they do not align with where someone is situationally, developmentally, or emotionally.

Derek: It is always a challenge to identify what we claim as our beliefs, but even more complex to question them. These beliefs are a large part of who we are. They provide the lens through which we have observed the world and then made sense of our realities. Lately, I have found myself struggling with the concept of a non-absolute reality. Not that I have felt that what I have experienced is what others experience; rather, I think that my perception was that similar experiences occurred in similar contexts. As a result of my exploration of complexity in my masters, I now realize just how minuscule differences in initial conditions can create drastic changes in future events.

Sandy: Your reference to the complexity of ideals and tightly held beliefs really resonated with me. If I were to summarize my current positioning I would say that my ultimate aim is to help students recognize and analyze patterns and structures in the curriculum of lived experiences. I do sometimes feel that I live with a split personality of sorts, both internally and externally. I am clumsily making my way through understanding learning and mathematics. My history pulls at my perspective yet, simultaneously, the idea of story and care, and individuals having voice, are things that I lean on and bring into my classroom every day. These tensions are pushing me to think deeper, ask more questions, and listen more.

Derek: I have come to understand that "this close attention to life making is slow, patient work" (Lessard, Caine, & Clandinin, 2015, p. 212) and that my experience with tough concepts reflects the care and time needed to unpack and come face-to-face with my strongly held beliefs. Interrogating the *truths* of education and imagining complex issues through the lenses of a math teacher, parent, and learning leader, provided the opportunity to expand my perspective to include "a movement toward connectivity" (Donald, 2009, p. 19).

Sandy: And, remember, according to Greene (2013), "the reader, using his imagination, must move within his own subjectivity and break with the common sense world he normally takes for granted" (p. 129), and "the constraints of the imagination tell us things about human life that we don't get in any other way" (Willinsky, 1998, p. 235).

Where Are We Now?

We understand our identities to be contextual, situational, and time-dependent – an ever-changing flux – "shifting, and volatile construct, a contradictory and unfinalized *social relationship* [emphasis added]" (Britzman, 1995, p. 68). Our identities are in a constant state of dynamic existence, and they are challenging to reconcile at any one moment. Through reflexivity these changes are recognizable, if only as differences from a former identity. The dialogical experience of duoethnography has evoked a (re)collection of our affective histories allowing us to gain better insight into the evolution of how we understand ourselves. Our identities are enmeshed within the complexities of our lived interactions and experiences. We recognize "that our experience is always incomplete" (Greene, 2013, p. 137) and, as a result, identity is in a dynamic state of existence. This fluid sense of (our)self(ves) comes as the result "of incorporating [the] reassembled past, seeming present, and anticipated future into an internalized dynamically changing story of self" (Kraehe, 2015; McAdams, 2001, 2013, as cited in Lyle, 2017, p. 3).

We have seen parallels between the evolution of curriculum development and our journey, moving from linear thinking to a more complex understanding of mathematics education, one that is rooted in discourse and care. We understand, that when taken up effectively, education "offers the space for change, invention, spontaneous shifts, that can serve as a catalyst" (hooks, 1994, p. 11) – a catalyst for hope, opportunity, and empowerment. The (re)collection and disruption of our memories has been a reflexive process: giving rise to altered perspectives of ourselves, increasing focus on opening possibilities, and fostering awakenings to new epistemologies. Through this dialogue, we have considered *pathways* (see Cajete, 1994) as the journey within a cultural framework as part of a collective learning experiences "both planned and unplanned" (Noddings, 2002, p. 283).

With much focused effort, we can now imagine possibilities that were not conceivable in our pasts. As Greene (1995) posits, "imagination may be a new way of decentering ourselves, of breaking out of the confinement of privatism and self-regard into a space where we can come face to face with others" (p. 31). It is by opening space for dialogue and actively perturbating our mathematical paradigms that we were able to disrupt what we had lived as students, in order to construct our identities as educators. This reflexive journey has given voice to our shared experience and has enabled us to link where we began teaching to where we see ourselves today. It has helped us to see how student learning experiences were changing, with us changing along-side.

References

Alberta Education. (2008). *The Alberta 10–12 mathematics program of studies with achievement indicators 2008*. Edmonton: Alberta Education.

Aoki, T. (1993). Legitimizing lived curriculum: Towards a landscape of multiplicity. *Journal of Curriculum and Supervision, 8*(3), 255–268.

Battiste, M. (2013). *Decolonizing education: Nourishing the learning spirit.* Saskatoon: Purich.

Bobbit, F. (2013). Scientific method in curriculum-making. In D. J. Flinders & S. J. Thornton (Eds.), *The curriculum studies reader* (4th ed., pp. 11–18). New York, NY: Routledge.

Britzman, D. (1995). What is this thing called love? *Taboo: The Journal of Cultural Studies Education, 1,* 65–93.

Cajete, G. (1994). *Look to the mountains: An ecology of indigenous education.* Durango: Kiviki Press.

Davis, B., & Renert, M. (2014). *The math teachers know: Profound understanding of emergent mathematics.* New York, NY: Routledge.

Davis, B., & Sumara, D. (2007). Complexity science and education: Reconceptualizing the teacher's role in learning. *Interchange, 38*(1), 53–67. doi: 10.1007/s10780-007-9012-5

Davis, B., Sumara, D., & Luce-Kapler, R. (2008). *Engaging minds: Changing teaching in complex times.* New York, NY: Routledge.

Dei, G. J. S. (2008). Schooling as community: Race, schooling, and the education of African youth. *Journal of Black Studies, 38*(3), 346–366.

Donald, D. (2009). Forts, curriculum and indigenous métissage: Imagining decolonization of Aboriginal-Canadian relations in educational contexts. *First Nations Perspectives, 2*(1), 1–24.

Greene, M. (1995). *Releasing the imagination: Essays on education, the arts, and social change.* San Francisco, CA: Jossey-Bass.

Greene, M. (2013). Curriculum and consciousness. In D. J. Flinders & S. J. Thornton (Eds.), *The curriculum studies reader* (4th ed., pp. 127–138). New York, NY: Routledge.

Hersh, R. (1990). Let's teach the philosophy of mathematics! *The College of Mathematics Journal, 21*(2), 105–111.

Hersh, R. (1991). Mathematics has a front and a back. *New Directions in the Philosophy of Mathematics, 88*(2), 127–133.

Hieu, V. N., Calhoun, A., Worthington, C., Pyrch, T., & Este, D. (2015). The unravelling of identities and belonging: Criminal gang involvement of youth from immigrant families. *Springer, 18,* 63–84. doi: 10.1007/s12134-015-0466-5.

hooks, b. (1994). *Teaching to transgress: Education as the practice of freedom.* London: Routledge.

Kovach, M. (2009). *Indigenous methodologies: Characteristics, conversations, and contexts.* Toronto: University of Toronto Press.

Krammer, D., & Mangiardi, R. (2012). The hidden curriculum of schooling: A duoethnographic exploration of what schools teach us about schooling. In J. Norris, R. D. Sawyer, & D. Lund (Eds.), *Duoethnography: Dialogical methods for social, health, and educational research* (pp. 41–69). Walnut Creek, CA: Left Coast Press.

Lessard, S., Caine, V., & Clandin, D. J. (2015). A narrative inquiry into familial and school curriculum making: Attending to multiple worlds of aboriginal youth and families. *Journal of Youth Studies, 18*(2), 197–214.

Lyle, E. (2017). Autoethnographic approaches to an identity conscious curriculum. In E. Lyle (Ed.), *At the intersection of selves and subject: Exploring the curricular landscape of identity* (pp. 1–8). Rotterdam, The Netherlands: Sense Publishers.

Nabavi, M., & Lund, D. (2012). Tensions and contradictions of living in a multicultural nation in an era of bounded identities. In J. Norris, R. D. Sawyer, & D. Lund (Eds.), *Duoethnography: Dialogical methods for social, health, and educational research* (pp. 177–198). Walnut Creek, CA: Left Coast Press.

Noddings, N. (2002). *Starting at home: Caring and social policy.* Los Angeles, CA: University of California Press.

Pitre, N. Y., Kushner, K. E., Raine, K. D., & Hegadoren, K. M. (2013). Critical feminist narrative inquiry: Advancing knowledge through double hermeneutic narrative analysis. *Advances in Nursing Science, 36*(2), 118–132.

Romberg, T. A. (1992). Problematic features of the school mathematics curriculum. In P. Jackson (Ed.), *Handbook on research on curriculum* (pp. 749–788). New York, NY: Macmillan.

Sawyer, R. D., & Norris, J. (2013). *Duoethnography.* New York, NY: Oxford University Press.

Walker, M. (2007). Action research and narratives: 'Finely aware and richly responsible'. *Educational Action Research, 15*(2), 295–303. doi: 10.1080/09650790701314999

Willinsky, J. (1998). *Learning to divide the world: Education at empire's end.* Minneapolis, MN: University of Minnesota Press.

CHAPTER 14

Becoming Community: Ranya's Story of Intergenerational Teaching and Learning in Art Education

Anita Sinner

Getting to Know One Another

As artwork scholarship, this story of becoming-community is written from an arts-based research perspective, one of many dispositions to take up reflexive inquiry. In this case, Ranya, a mature student in her mid-thirties who immigrated to Canada years earlier, returned to university to earn a degree in art education, and that is where we join her in this conversation. Ranya was a student-teacher assigned to the community group commonly known as the Concordia Seniors. The Concordia Seniors met weekly on campus to partake in informal learning opportunities organised by continuing education, which included our dedicated studio class. Along with a second student-teacher and six of the seniors in that class, she was part of a larger study in art education investigating the experiences of third-age learners.

During the course of the year, Ranya's story emerged as a mediation of an intergenerational experience of teaching and learning that offered insight to the interplay of public-private, self-other, student-teacher, and younger-older. Verbatim quotes drawn from interviews conducted with Ranya are woven together into story form to highlight how she mapped her identity as she undertook responsibility for planning, designing, and delivering curriculum for the first time. Through ongoing reflexive inquiry, Ranya cultivated an emergent self, where becoming a teacher in community required continual dialogue about beliefs, perceptions, emotions, and rationale, in relation to conditions and events in the classroom, to inform understandings of professional and personal practice. As an expression of life writing, her story charts the dynamics of exchange residing within such relationships of learning and demonstrates how reflexive inquiry is central in articulating epistemological qualities of the art of teaching and learning as an ongoing negotiation of self-always-in-relation.

© KONINKLIJKE BRILL NV, LEIDEN, 2018 | DOI:10.1163/9789004388901_014

Why Reflexive Inquiry?

Reflexive inquiry may be imagined as an eclectic rhizome, inclusive of hegemonic discourses that contextualizes our individual stories and our worldviews, and our resulting modes of inquiry in curriculum and instruction. Reflexivity provides a means of sustaining the teaching self through continuous negotiation of positionality, encouraging "intuitive and/or transient ways of knowing" (Rolling, 2018, p. 584). Such practice recognises the vitality and validity of voice by encouraging candor, vulnerability, and self-criticality, enabling us to enter deliberation on aspects of learning experiences that are essential to a healthy teaching culture.

Historically traced in the genealogy of scholarship by Dewey (1933) and Schön (1983) among others, reflection and reflexivity are long-standing cornerstones of teacher education. In this case, reflection is defined as the act of becoming self-aware, a necessary state of inner objectivity that leads to reflexivity; reflexivity in turn is a process of engaging in relational contexts, of inter-subjectivity with a critical perspective, examining how we are always implicated in shaping events and experiences (see Brown, Sawyer & Norris, 2016; Freda & Esposito, 2015; Cunliffe, 2004; Matthews & Jessel, 1998). The focus of this chapter concerns how intense reflexive practice combined with arts-based inquiry produces stories of becoming based on social reality. Much as Richardson (2001) advocated, such storying defines the nature, enactment, and idealism formative in teacher identities, and it is incumbent on researchers concerned with the nature of teaching to listen to, and respond to, those who are living the experience to ensure our field remains robust. In this story we trace how Ranya is becoming-community, drawing our attention to the tensions, challenges, and in-betweenness that emerged while navigating changing definitions of self in relation to the teaching profession, and how that self is implicated in community art education as public pedagogy, which necessitates a unique blend of responsibility, dedication, caring, and responsiveness in the classroom.

In this way reflexive practice serves as a form of verification, to borrow from qualitative approaches for a moment, in that the process of continually reflecting upon teaching provides a means to navigate, balance, and check inner biases that manifest in identity construction. Reminiscent of Lather's method of *getting lost* (2007) as an ontological starting point, Ranya's reflexive journey "produce[d] different knowledge, and produce[d] knowledge differently" by "inducing breakdowns in representing experience," returning to that which was "missed the first time" as part of the responsibility we hold as teachers (pp. 13, 157). With a view that reflexive inquiry underlies identity construction, the value of reflective practice in the course of learning to become a teacher is at the heart of the following story.

Ranya: Reflectivity-in-Relation

I love doing this. I just want to do more, more, and more. I think teaching is a talent that you need to develop. I see teaching as an academic responsibility, and ethical responsibility as well. You have to be aware of everything you say and you do in the classroom. The Concordia Seniors come from different backgrounds. Most of them are immigrants. Most of the class never made it to university, and they come to school with the sense that they're having a university class, even if it is informal. Most of them live alone, away from their families, so they go to community activities, mostly those that relate to their age group. Although they are in the same stage of life, their lives are very different. They kind of feel segregated from the rest of society. When they come to Concordia, they work with younger people, and they're exposed to the new culture. So to take them into a different space and expose them to different experiences, I think they needed the shift.

Because it is a community setting, the practice itself is the subject. I have the entire class based on fine arts teaching without the curriculum restrictions of schools. Learners are not being graded, which gives them the chance to be more relaxed, free, and more receptive. They come to class and want to really work with you. They're into it. I think it's more creative. Community teaching allows me to research methods of teaching, and think about how to create a paradigm for that particular class, and what to teach, how, and why it is important to be taught. It's the kind of job that helps me to keep building up my knowledge and expanding my experiences, not only as a teacher, but also as an artist. We can do whatever we want, and I can go crazy inventing things with them. So it's a different world. All I needed to do was learn about my learners and know their needs and their abilities, and if they had any special needs. The only reason I'm in the classroom is because of them and for them. It's not the opposite. They're not here for me.

One of the things that helps me to feel comfortable in class is being prepared. I work hard on my lesson plans and I never introduce students to something I'm not completely aware of and capable of providing answers for in class. I like the idea of being a resourceful teacher. I see my students every week so I try and encourage each person in class specifically. I know they have different needs and I started to learn more about that. In class I make observations and take a lot of notes. I learn about the students and the circumstance that I'm dealing with, and then decide how I'm going to work with that situation. I like to challenge my students. I want them to ask themselves questions and look for answers and find solutions. That's why in my lessons, I'm very aware of the examples I'm using. I choose something that is so doable for them, and that is easy to get the impression of what to do, so it is not that difficult.

But one woman who comes, she's just tired. She's so stressed out and she can't relax. She comes and she is a little bit intimidated. They're able to produce art and she's not. She'd wonder, "Why can't I do that like everybody else?" So she needs to know it's not about the product. She also needs someone to understand and to respect her space. Teaching seniors is different. And all of a sudden, two or three will pop up, "We don't like that. We don't want to do it." And you're working so hard to satisfy everybody and to accommodate everyone's needs. Working with them requires taking risks, making different approaches, and, of course, some stress but, in the end, as a student, artist, and teacher, I tend to take risks because I want to learn more in depth.

At the beginning of the semester, I realized most of them did not really know each other. They've been in the same group in previous classes, but they rarely talked to each other. So in the first few classes, when we finished the project and the activity, I encouraged each of them to step out and talk about their work. It was really hard to convince them to participate. It was so difficult, and comments like, "No, no, I have nothing to say about this artwork, it's just a drawing, it just came to me," were common.

I prompted, "Ok, just tell me about your painting. Just talk about anything that comes to your mind, not too long, only one to two, three minutes maximum. Just say whatever you have. Tell me anything."

It took time, but that is when they started to talk about themselves, step by step. Reto told us about his grandfather's home in Switzerland and the dog he used to have. So just bit by bit, you help, you inspire, you give ideas that they can share with each other. One lady mentioned that it's the first time that they learned about each other's stories. So, I think this was a major change. By the end of the semester, the closure was the best time of the class. They really loved it and enjoyed the idea of expressing their thoughts and sharing it with each other. And it became my favorite part, too. I loved to hear their feedback because I learnt from their comments, and I came to know what the difficulties were, and what we can avoid in the next assignment. I want them to move forward, I want them to know that they're productive, that they're capable of learning new things. I talk with them all the time, to get to know them, learning about their needs and also respecting their diversity. These are things we need to acknowledge as educators.

In addition to coursework, I have spent a lot of time researching seniors and learning. I learned that seniors have deeper cognitive abilities as they grow older, and they develop deeper experiences; however sometimes they are unable to concentrate, or less able to accumulate knowledge and use it for different projects. In one article, the author suggested that educators ask the students for self-reflections on activities, how they feel about the classroom, and so art educators can gain knowledge for creating class objectives. The author spoke about the need for educators to be flexible, and understand that a lesson plan is not always final. So much can occur in the classroom that can oblige us to make changes, maybe radical changes, in order to accommodate the moment. That was also something that I had to understand and work on, because once I have already worked to prepare a lesson plan, I am completely focused and dedicated and want to do it until the end. I want to do it perfectly. But it's more about the process itself, and I started to learn that. I was very focused on the final product in the beginning, and that was one of the very important things that I learned: it is not about the final product. It is about community.

So I included this theory in my lesson plans to reinforce their self-study through art. I want them to look inside of themselves. What do they want to do? Where do they want to go? What do they really like to do? And I talked to them openly, "The best thing about art practice is to make mistakes. Make mistakes. Make ugly drawings and ugly paintings. That is how you'll learn. You don't have to worry about being graded! So enjoy your mistakes, have fun with them." So that's what I'm talking about, being comfortable in the setting. They know they are not being judged, and so they're enjoying the process. I think the teacher creates that environment. If the students are not enjoying it, they won't come. They are not obliged to in community. To be honest it's a lot of fun!

The seniors are fantastic, but I have had difficulties with some students who have been very resistant to everything. They want to control the class, and seem to want us to do the things they want. But I also need to balance that want with learning about my teaching process. This is my chance to experiment. I need to break through and move forward, make new ideas, and to be more challenging, so I can learn, and they can learn as well. It is an exchange and an experiment for both of us. In one class, we started with a very relaxing activity, and students were not required to represent any product, they were just playing in the medium.

All of a sudden, one of the seniors said, "This is very easy. We are not supposed to do this."

"Okay; what do you think we should be doing?"

And she replied, "Learning."

I was amazed because that was my point of view, too. That's when the challenge begins and they start to face difficulties. Learning how to use watercolours, for instance, does not mean that you can draw or paint with watercolours. The challenge starts when you are really doing paintings using watercolours. Then you start to learn more about it. So exploring the art medium is not the art making process. It's practicing. At the same time, I have discovered that every student has a different difficulty, and a different perception of our learning together. And they come every week in different moods, so it's hard to manage sometimes. I learned to say, "Okay, you can sit on your own, do whatever you want, just let me know whenever you need me back." Most of the time, when I open the door for them to decide on their own whether to do the activity or not, they actually end up doing it. I had to learn when to push for more, and when to stop and let go. And I'm still learning that actually.

In the first term, only traditional artwork was art for them. So I had to help them change this kind of concept and say, yes, this is art, but it's not all art. They finally began to make a shift and again, yes, there was a lot of resistance. So I started working with them individually, ensuring that they don't have to achieve anything out of this and it's mostly about playing with materials. Taking the obligation from their shoulders was a big thing for them. In the second semester, when we took the theme, 'Spontaneous Artwork,' I found so many artists who never received any art education in their lives. Most of the artists were older, so it was kind of like a motivation for my students, real life examples to learn from, and the transfer of techniques was somehow easier. This led me to realize I needed to differentiate between being a teacher and a facilitator. To learn when and how to do this is one of my biggest objectives.

In community art, making art is not just the responsibility of the student anymore; it's my responsibility to understand when and how to interact with the students, to show flexibility, to change objectives, to lower the fence sometimes so they can jump in and achieve something. I need to balance that with studio art making expectations. So teaching community is very challenging and interesting. As the teacher, you're the one who sets the curriculum, and you're the one who does the schedule. However, you have to understand what's going on around you, and not all students are expecting the same thing from you. Some of them really want to do art and really want to understand and get something from it, and some, they just simply don't care. You have to appreciate both and work both approaches at the same time. So it's like wearing two hats, switching all the time. It's kind of tricky.

And you can never tell what the workshop will turn out to be so I think working with a fixed curriculum with them would be a very huge challenge. Instead, I think the best thing is to take them very slowly. In one of my lesson plans I wanted them to integrate two different techniques on the same canvas, an oil marbling technique and a decal technique. In the presentation, I had both techniques outlined, but I said to myself, "No. I'm not showing them both techniques at the same time. I'm giving them only the marbling technique, and I'll wait and I'll see how it goes. And then, if it works well with them and we still have enough time to explore something different, I'll get the other one in the process." I introduced them to the marbling technique, and then the image transfer technique, and how layers can be added on top of each other. This really helped Maria, who loves art, but at the

beginning of the year, like the others, she felt she wasn't an artist. After these pro-
jects, she said, "Finally I don't have to worry of producing art." That shows growth
I think, and it meant a lot to me.

Building personal relationships with seniors is crucial if you really want to
achieve something. If I kept the hierarchy of the teacher-student, they would not
show up. They kept coming because they felt there was something worthwhile
going on. They kept coming to the class even in the snowstorms and bad weather. I
respect that, and I show that I'm aware of this. And because they're older and they
come from very traditional backgrounds, that was also a privilege for me. They
appreciated the respect I gave them. And they gave that back to me. This is how I
see it. I learned, too. We have actually moved into a whole new seeing together. It's
kind of like a reciprocal relationship. You are giving and you are receiving at the
same time. You see the results in their eyes, how they approach you, how they ask
you about things, and you need to give them that sense of self-confidence, and say
"You can do it! Just give it a try, give it a try!"

Responding to Ranya's Story

Although the intent of artwork scholarship is that the art stands alone as
research, or in practice, the story speaks as a rendering of data, interpretations,
and findings; in this case responding to Ranya's story focuses our attention on
the dialogic of becoming-community at the heart of reflexive inquiry. Ranya's
story represents a carefully considered account of her disciplined yet emergent
practice. By fostering a high degree of ongoing reflexivity as the backbone of
an evolving teacher identity, her story reflects a fluid composition of teaching
strategies, art techniques, personal beliefs, and personality. In this story, reflexive competencies outlined by Freda and Esposito (2015) provide a framework
to interpret Ranya's story in terms of critical events that created discontinuity;
internalized self-observation and emotional responses; translation of reflexive awareness into agency; and the inter-subjective exchange between teacher
and students, all aspects that resonate epistemologically as dispositions of a
teacher's identity.

Encountering Educational Emergence

Ranya viewed herself as experimental and her teaching as an experiment, and
this denotes a predisposition to an analytic orientation that underscores her
identity development. Bringing together her age and the generational gap with
seniors, Rayna invested much time and consideration to better comprehend
the values and beliefs the seniors held toward art and learning, and how she
might broaden the scope of that conversation, making her role that of both
an interpreter and interrupter of curriculum. For instance, social encounters

were initially critical events that created discontinuity, yet those encounters provided a means to develop intellectual exchange that facilitated greater inclusion. By the end of the academic year, encounters were central in how learners assessed their own capacities and kept themselves engaged and motivated with self-awareness.

In much the same way as Ryan and Bourke (2013) argue for principled practice, Rayna embodied a similar vision for effective teaching that was also built upon her self-directed inquiry, such as reflecting on the classroom activities and reading articles related to seniors and learning. The flexibility of community art education curriculum and instruction was an emergent factor of this praxis because it allowed Ranya creative freedom without the restrictions of set benchmarks like grading. In the process, she organically developed individualised, sustainable teaching strategies that were dependent on context, that is, that group of learners at that point in time, and through experimentation, this practice became integrated into her professional identity.

Reflectively Refining Practice

Proximity was essential in Ranya's capacity to identify pedagogic methods that translated into increasing agency for her and her students over the course of the year. Valuing the individual characteristics of each senior played a significant role in determining art activities and, as a mature student, Ranya grasped the importance of finding common ground and mediating that space in the classroom. In turn, Ranya's attentive support and encouragement helped shift the group from initial sedimentary ideas of art to a more expansive, receptive attitude, open to spontaneous and experimental art practice.

Ranya frequently mentioned observing classroom activities to learn how seniors experienced her teaching and, in the course of ongoing reflection, she internalised self-observations and reflected on emotional responses as a way to improve her instruction. With a strong social justice orientation, she maintained a critical perspective on her decision-making and judgements, while creating a holistic learning environment that mediated lifelong learning for seniors. This tension was often present in conversation with Ranya, who meticulously described how she deconstructed the instructor-student dynamic in ways that facilitated intergenerational learning. LaBelle (2017) suggests that such an ethical stance "leads to social and political transformation" in community through civic engagement, grounded in "real-life observation and participation in teaching and learning processes" (p. 689). Indeed, the satisfaction Ranya derived from the challenges she set for herself suggest the transformative potential of personal accountability is an essential component in teacher identity development.

Discerning Degrees of Distinctiveness

Evident in her story is how she systematically and comparatively examined inter-subjective moments between teacher and students concerning issues relating to the learning context, pedagogic considerations, and art techniques and materials. Arguably these moments informed her self-efficacy as a creative and resilient teacher (LaBelle, 2017). Ranya's responsiveness and willingness to meet the needs of her learners demonstrated how teaching and learning operated as reciprocal acts for both Ranya and the seniors, as they experienced the roles of teacher-student defined by age and life experience. As communal understanding was constructed through reciprocity, the seniors became aware of the dynamic and new learning opportunities they were being offered, and they became more adaptive to new ways of experiencing art. As such, reciprocity facilitated the transition from one step to the next in the evolution of learner-teacher relationships.

Through ongoing introspection Ranya identified patterns of behaviour in the spaces between self-place-other, mapping interconnections between networks of relations in the classroom – individual students, aspects of teaching and learning in flux, and personal development as a professional teacher. It was her detailed, preparatory work for each art activity that directly contributed to this progressive movement. Discerning degrees of distinctiveness in her identity development helped Ranya articulate a more socially informed and tailored practice and solidified her sense of ability and effectiveness as a teacher, with an awareness that learning to teach, much like the seniors learning to make art, is foremost a commitment to lifelong learning.

Becoming-Community: Composing a Teacher's Identity

Most evident throughout Ranya's story is her humility as an artist and teacher, and how she translated that humility to respect and caring for the individual seniors. With a high degree of sensitivity, she frequently described the nuances inherent in hierarchies of power that can define classrooms, and how she explicitly averted that dynamic in her time with the seniors, as a mark of respect, but also as a statement of belief she holds as a teacher. It is in such reflexive decisions that Ranya is in effect, becoming-community.

Building on Cunliffe (2004), three core dimensions of identity negotiated through reflexive inquiry include: the existential (who am I and what kind of teacher do I want to be?); relational (how do I build relationships of trust and good communications with my students?); and praxis (what actions will I undertake based on past activities?). If we enter Ranya's story with appreciation of this complexity, it can serve as an exemplar to student-teachers

who may seek affirmation when the dissonance between the real and imagined teacher identity gives cause for concern (Warin, Maddock, Pell, &
Hargreaves, 2006). Written in the first-person with the intimacy of conversation, storied accounts like Ranya's promote verification of practice and
establish a collective commons that invite understandings of teacher identity as an intuitive, contemplative practice, where failures and successes are
defined foremost by an investment of the authentic self in explicit self-study.
This prioritises curriculum and instruction as an enactment of deeper introspection and self-awareness, where no single story concretely establishes
identity, but where stories are adapting, conflicting, and multiplying as the
effect of teaching is manifest over time and place. In so doing, stories, as artwork scholarship, acknowledge that readers may each draw on different salient moments that resonate more fully with their own relational and reflexive
experiences.

Teacher stories aid in creating empathetic characters, and this is particularly important for student-teachers planning to dedicate their working lives
to community contexts where the potential vulnerability of learners and the
transitory nature of learning differ from formal environments. In this way,
Ranya's story provides a mechanism to raise questions, rethink social assumptions, re-evaluate teaching methods, and improve upon art activities. As an
art educator, she charts a pathway to deeper and more expanded reflexivity,
attentive to the fact that each activity she introduced that year focused on individual vision where each learner was given options to explore self-expression,
along with ongoing one-to-one support. Art making was both a purpose and
an objective that gathered all learners to a common ground. Creating this kind
of accessibility shifts thinking from presumptions and/or prescriptions that
often define initial student-teacher identity, to a way of being a teacher that
embraces self-motivation within a collaborative context, built upon increasing
levels of trust in learning relationships that then enable effective teaching to
take place.

As a result, Ranya's story holds many dimensions and qualities that highlight the nature of intergenerational exchange as unanticipated moments of
emergence. It is from accounts like her story that we may begin to identify
pedagogic pivots, and move towards a reconceptualising of how we teach
teachers in higher education. Stories as artful inquiry and a mode of intimate
expression are particularly helpful when learning about a teaching life, and
to include Ranya's story in our conversations about teacher identity expands
the parameters of the profession, and offers a means for student-teachers and
educators alike to appreciate the potential of the act and action of teaching

and learning. Stories from the community classroom serve as one of many ways student-teachers may begin to formalise a teaching life and, in the process, find greater meaning-making at the heart of their identity as they compose their personal and professional identities in-between theory and practice.

Acknowledgements

Since participating in this study, Ranya completed her Bachelor's degree, a Master of Arts degree, and she is now pursuing a PhD in Art Education.

This study was generously supported by the Social Sciences and Humanities Research Council of Canada.

References

Brown, H., Sawyer, D., & Norris, N. (2016). *Forms of practitioner reflexivity: Critical, conversational and arts-based approaches.* New York, NY: Palgrave.

Cunliffe, A. (2004). On becoming a critically reflexive practitioner. *Journal of Management Education, 28*(4), 407–426.

Dewey, J. (1933/2010). *How we think: A restatement of the relation of reflective thinking to the educative process.* Boston, MA: D.C. Health.

Freda, M., & Esposito, G. (2017). Promoting reflection and reflexivity through narrative devices: Narrative mediation path qualitative multimodal method. *Qualitative Research Journal 17*(1), 2–19.

LaBelle, J. (2017). Ethical and political implications of reflective practice among preservice teachers. *Reflective Practice, 18*(5), 688–698.

Lather, P. (2007). *Getting lost: Feminist efforts toward a double(d) science.* Albany, NY: State University of New York Press.

Matthews, B., & Jessel, J. (1998). Reflective and reflexive practice in initial teacher education: A critical case study. *Teaching in Higher Education, 3*(2), 231–243.

Richardson, L. (2001). Getting personal: Writing stories. *Qualitative Studies in Education, 14*(1), 33–58.

Rolling, J. (2018). Arts-based research in education. In P. Leavy (Ed.), *Handbook of arts-based research* (pp. 493–510). New York, NY: Guilford.

Ryan, M., & Bourke, T. (2013). The teacher as reflexive professional: Making visual the excluded discourse in teacher standards. *Discourse: Studies in the Cultural Politics of Education, 34*(3), 411–423.

Schön, D. (1983). *The reflective practitioner: How professionals think in action.* New York, NY: Basic Books.

Warin, J., Maddock, M., Pell, A., & Hargreaves, L. (2006). Resolving identity dissonance through reflective and reflexive practice in teaching. *Reflective Practice, 7*(2), 233–245.

CHAPTER 15

Symbolic World, Reflexivity, and Intentionality in the Construction of Academic Professional Identities (APIS)

Evelyn Morales Vázquez

> How could I disaggregate the polarized emotions I felt while I was living, and dying in, my academic dream?

∴

The purpose of this chapter is to consider the role that personal life history plays in the development of academic identity. In an attempt to reconceptualize the current homogenous understandings about academic identity, I rely on *personal reflections* (Bochner & Ellis, 2016; Denzin, 2013; Trahar, 2009), reflexive inquiry (Cunliffe, 2003), and identity theory (Burke & Stets, 2009) to recognize how my symbolic world, reflexivity, and intentionality have influenced the development of my academic professional identity (API). I employed personal reflections to layout and conceptualize API based on: my experiences as female first generation student; experiences derived of situational chages during my doctorate; and the challenges I have encountered as a graduate student as a result of the feeling norms in academia.

Epiphanies and the Attribution of Meanings

I understand reflexive inquiry (RI) as both as an internal process and as a disruptive practice that allows individuals to reflect upon themselves in a constructive and dynamic way (Cunliffe, 2003). It is because of RI that I became aware of how my frames of reference, positionality (e.g., female, the oldest daughter, Mexican international student, and first-generation student), and lived experiences inform and contextualize my imagined future selves, my intentionality, and my behaviours as a future professor. Because of reflexivity, individuals attribute meanings to their lived experiences, modulate their attitudes, behaviours, and emotional reactions in relation to the different roles they play, as well as the social interactions and experiences they have (Bloomber & Volpe, 2016; Creswell, 2006; Lyle, 2009; Patton, 2002; Slay & Smith, 2011). Reflexivity also allows individuals to think about themselves across time (Eakin, 2008). Individuals can reflect on their memories and perceptions of particular events while they imagine various imagined future selves based on their symbolic world, intentionality, and frames of reference (Slay & Smith, 2011).

> In 2015, I was living the beginning of my academic dreamlife: I got a fellowship to study a Ph.D. abroad. But the sweetness and excitement of that beautiful dream brought its own crisis and poisons. Two weeks after classes started, I got a call from my sister: Abuelita (Grandma) is dead. This is the last sentence I remember from that call. I cannot remember any other day in my life when I felt such a strong current of pain emanating from myself. I ended the call. I stopped listening. I stopped thinking. I was there: just feeling. When I recovered my sense of being and realized I was in my office, I decided to go outside and sit under a tree. As I sat under a tree on campus, I became a completely emotional being. My emotions took over me and they threw away, or maybe destroyed, my frames of reference, my expectations, and even some of my motivations, about who I was and who I wanted to become, in an abrupt, disruptive, and painful way. However, in that morning, in that isolated and painful moment, I took some of the most precious gems of myself, I relied on my symbolic world – I took memories, I reflected on lived experiences of my childhood – to heal my adult wound.

In the above passage about my personal life, I attributed meanings to myself in a specific and significant event through my capacities of reflexivity and introspection (Patton, 2002). The meanings attributed to that event were linked to my personal history, cultural background, and positionality in the social structure. Surrounded by intense sadness and uncertainties about my life, I realized that I needed to reconstruct a new imagined academic self. It was through this epiphany (Denzin, 2013), understood as a huge realization of a perceived reality, that I was intentionally reconstructing myself. Without noticing it, I became a radical-reflexive entity.

> Radical-reflexivity turns the reflexive act upon ourselves to deconstruct our own constructions of realities, identities, and knowledge, and highlight the intersubjective and indexical nature of meaning (i.e. accounts are ongoing discursive social accomplishments taking place in shared, taken-for-granted interactions between people). Radically reflexive

researchers explore how we as researchers and practitioners constitute meaning through our own taken-for-granted suppositions, actions, and linguistic practices – our own reflexive accomplishment from the perspective of becoming-realism. This means recognizing that we are working within a number of linguistic communities (e.g. academic, business) and need to unsettle our forms of reasoning and any claims of objectivity or truth. (Cunliffe, 2003, p. 989)

Identity theory (Burke & Stets, 2009), from a structural symbolic interactionism perspective, proposes that the meanings that individuals use when they reflect about themselves narratively are a result of the interaction of the multiple experiences, interpretations, and emotional attachments that individuals hold in their subjective worlds. Aligned with the notion of the ways in which RI deconstructs our pre-conceptions, and creates room to re-construct ourselves, identity theory helped me to explain the different meanings I can rely on when I think or define myself as a graduate student and as a future professor. Going back to my previous passage, the loss of my grandmother became an epiphany because it interrupted my academic identity; that loss became my first personal-professional crisis. It was a personal-professional crisis because it was the first time when I noticed my incapacity to fragment my academic-professional life from my personal life.

> Loyal to my beloved Grandmother, I went back to Mexico for the funeral. After I came back from that trip, I was another Evelyn. I was raised by my Grandmother, I did not just lose a family member, I lost the woman who sowed in me seeds of academic motivation and love for learning. I lost the woman who nurtured me and took care of me until I was nine years old. She was the woman who, without formal education herself, took me every day to school during my first five years of schooling. I read my first words to her. I learned how to write by her side. I constructed an imagined future professional self because of her.

When I returned to graduate school, my performance as a student was hurt. After losing the one person who inspired me throughout my life to pursue an academic career, I was unable to meet the academic expectations of my environment. I could not focus on anything. Some classmates and professors even thought that I was not really interested in the Ph.D. They were just looking at my academic performance with no knowledge of my personal struggles. The identity that was assigned to me did not match my own perceptions. It was at this moment when I became interested in the study of academic identities.

The Study of Academic Identities

When higher education scholars explore and describe the academic profession, they have typically relied on fragmented categories. Rather than recognize the richness of the interwoven meanings used when individuals think about the many components that make up who they are, this approach compartmentalizes the self through the usage of categories such as academic disciplines (Clark, 1987), faculty appointments (Gappa, Austin, & Trice, 2007), institutional characteristics (Finkelstein, Conley, & Schuster, 2016), or institutional rank (Neumann, 2009). One of the main issues in the study of academic identity is that a large number of studies attempt to explain academic identities as merely determined by the roles and activities that faculty members perform. This reductionist perspective fragments the identities of academics by ignoring the central elements that give meaning to the subjective world of individuals, particularly their symbolic world, reflexivity, and intentionality as aligned to their professional pathways. This perspective reproduces the use of sociological and organizational lenses to explore academic identities, thus limiting exploration to the meso level (between groups) and macro level (social structure) at the expense of the micro level (the lived experiences of faculty members).

Some of the lived experiences of faculty members are reflected in their performances as professors. However, I argue that performance is not identity. The narrow focus on the performance of the academic profession (professional roles, duties, and behaviours) as the main source of identity fails to consider the influence of the symbolic world, such as the meanings, symbols, and values attached to the roles and activities of the academic profession. Based on my notions of RI as a transformational process that is aligned to my intentionality (of what I would like to be as a future professor), it was necessary to reconceptualize higher education notions of academic identity through the recognition of academic workers' humanity, defined in this chapter as the personal history and symbolic world of faculty members.

In order to do this, I turned to micro-identity theories to gain an understanding of the ways in which individuals attribute meanings to themselves and to their social structures. Micro-identity theories, from a symbolic interactionism perspective, proposed that the symbolic world, language, and social interactions of individuals inform the different roles they perform in their social structures. One's symbolic world is the set of meanings, motivations, cognitive processes, and emotions used to reflect on oneself and one's social realities. Thus, the symbols and meanings that individuals have about themselves are learned, internalized, and shared through social interactions.

Identity Theory and the Construction of Academic Professional Identities

According to identity theory (Burke & Stets, 2009), individuals characterize their identities through the meanings, symbols, and perceptions that they have about the different roles they play in their social structures. These symbolic meanings and understandings are constructed as individuals interact with others. Through these interactions, individuals gain understanding of the meanings, behaviours, and roles that they play in the various positions they hold within their social structure.

An individual's self-concept is constructed of shared symbols and meanings derived from their social interactions and symbolic interchange of meanings. Identities are categorized based on the different roles individuals play in their social positions. In addition, this categorization is also related to identity hierarchy. Burke and Stets (2009) argue that there are three bases of identities: "role identities are based on the different social positions individuals hold; social identities are based on individuals' memberships in certain groups; person identities are based on a view of the person as a unique entity, distinct from other individuals" (p. 112). All of these bases of identities are repositories of meanings and have identity standards that guide the behaviours of an individual in specific situations. These three bases of identities serve as points of reference to the specific roles that a person plays. In relation to the hierarchy of identities, personal identities, such as gender and ethnic background, tend to have higher levels of salience. This means that personal identities tend to influence the kind of meanings and intentions that individuals have in specific roles they play within their social structures. Thus, contrary to the traditional conceptualizations of academic identity, considered as a role identity, APIs are strongly linked to personal identities of faculty members. These bases of identity have informed the construction of my API – all of which were impacted by the loss of my grandmother and my ensuing reflexivity.

My Journey of Becoming a Professor

The loss of my grandmother not only changed how I perceived myself as a graduate student, but it also altered the intentionality and motivations of my future self. The personal and existential crises I have experienced since I started my doctorate have constructed, modulated, and altered my academic professional identity. It has been through these multiple adjustments and periods of instability that I have been constructing my future self as a future professor. This journey of becoming a professor has been characterized by multiple dilemmas about who I am, who I might be, and who I am becoming.

The crisis of losing my grandmother was a disruption that led me to recognize the constraints academia places on self-expression: I felt stifled and disconnected from my supposedly collegial community, which did not embrace me but instead left me isolated. I learned that my isolation was, in and of itself, not remotely an isolated incident (Bloch, 2002).

Some scholars conceptualize this disruption in our ways of thinking and feeling as situational changes (Burke & Stets, 2009) or turning points (Wheaton & Gotlib, 1997). These alterations influence the meanings that individuals attribute to themselves when they reflect on their life's journey. To recognize my symbolic world as an active entity in my professional life that influences my meanings, motivations, attitudes, and roles, I must recognize and accept the multiple selves I rely on when I think and behave as a future professor. Just the same way unexpected events changed my sense of being, my future students can be affected similarly.

The Conceptualization of Academic Professional Identities (APIs)

After ongoing personal reflection and extensive reading of conceptual and empirical studies on academic identities, I became motivated to describe the academic profession in a radical way. Who are the faculty members? In which ways do personal experiences inform the APIs and professional behaviours of faculty members? I began to reconceptualise the academic identity by developing the concept of academic professional identities (APIs). On the one hand, I am a Ph.D. student with academic responsibilities but, on the other hand, I am learning the institutional expectations, rules, and norms of the academic profession. I consider APIs to be amalgams of multiple meanings, reflected in cognitive processes, such as reflexivity and intentionality, which are used when individuals construct their narratives about themselves as professionals. Faculty members use these amalgams of meanings interchangeably when they reflect on themselves as professionals. These amalgams permit faculty members to meet their motivations, goals, and needs linked to their profession.

Consistent with identity theory (Burke & Stets, 2009), APIs are grounded in the three bases of identities (Figure 15.1). APIs are reflected in the meanings, perceptions, and symbols that faculty members use to describe themselves as professionals, as well as the ones they use to maintain or change their social structures. The personal identity base of APIs, conveyed through the autobiography of the participants, includes meanings related to their ethnic and cultural background, personal history, and personal experiences. The role identity base of API is composed of academics' professional background and present professional position, which allows them to learn the meanings, norms, values, and expectations of their academic profession. Finally, the social identity base

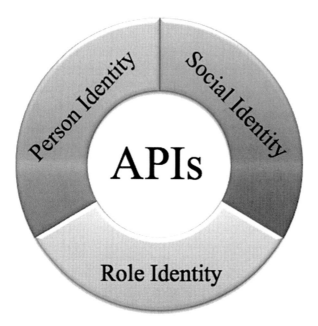

FIGURE 15.1   The components of the academic professional identities

of APIs is composed of institutional membership, and includes institutional culture, institutional expectations about the academic profession, and the institution's reward system.

Conclusions

It was after I encountered a situational challenge, the death of my grandmother, that I became radically reflexive. The notions I have about my future as a professor rely primarily on the consequent reflections, learnings, and future selves I have constructed during my last three years as a Ph.D. student. Reflexive inquiry allowed me to understand the symbolic and subjective aspects I used in the construction, establishment, and change of my academic professional identity. I realised that my API, as an amalgam of meanings, could help me to establish a more empathetic and human relationship with my research participants and also will influence my relationship with future students and colleagues. I hope that my personal reflections, my motivations as a graduate student and as a future professor, help to demystify the lack of acknowledgement of the ways that our personal histories influence our understandings, notions, and expectations as students, scholars, and as future professional selves.

This new concept of APIs suggests that the professional identities of faculty members are a product of their reflexivity and their capacity for introspection (Lyle, 2009). Individuals' cognitive capacities (Burke & Stets, 2009), such as reflexivity, allow them to think about who they are retrospectively and negotiate this sense dynamically. When I articulate, organize, and express meanings about my API, I put an emphasis on my history, my lived experiences, and my professional expectations and desires.

Contrary to the scholarly literature that highlights the role of academic discipline and institutional context in the formation of academic identities, my personal reflections underscore the fact that both personal story and professional expectations inform the construction of my API. My personal life history has influenced the motivations, values, behaviours, and strategies that I use when I describe myself as a Ph.D. student and as a researcher, as well as when I think about my future self as professor. This investigation recognizes that academic disciplines and institutional context do play significant roles in the values and norms that I can learn as a future faculty member. Yet, my personal characteristics influence the cognitive processes, meanings, and symbols that I rely on to construct my narratives as a graduate student and as a future professor. It was through my symbolic world and reflexivity that I projected and gave intentional meanings to myself as a graduate student and as a future professor. From this perspective, identity could influence certain behaviours and roles that individuals have about their profession, but the roles and activities that professionals have do not explain by themselves the symbolic world (meanings, intentions, and purposes) attached to these performances. Thus, reflexive inquiry allowed me to understand the interplay within the complexities and multiple meanings that give meaning to the symbolic world of academic professional identities (APIs).

References

Bloch, C. (2002). Managing the emotions of competition and recognition in academia. In J. Barbalet (Ed.), *Emotions and sociology* (pp. 113–131). Malden, MA: Blackwell Publising.

Bloomber, L. D., & Volpe, M. (2016). *Completing your qualitative dissertation: A road map from the beginning to end.* Thousand Oaks, CA: Sage Publications.

Bochner, A., & Ellis, C. (2016). *Evocative autoethnography: Writing life and telling stories.* New York, NY: Taylor & Francis.

Burke, P. J., & Stets, J. E. (2009). *Identity theory.* New York, NY: Oxford University Press.

Clark, B. R. (1987). *The academic life: Small worlds, different worlds.* Princeton, NJ: The Carnegie Foundation for the Advancement of Teaching.

Creswell, J. W. (2006). *Qualitative inquiry and research design: Choosing among five approaches.* Thousand Oaks, CA: Sage Publications.

Cunliffe, A. L. (2003). Reflexive inquiry in organizational research: Questions and possibilities. *Human Relations, 56*(8), 983–1003.

Denzin, N. K. (2013). Interpretive autoethnography. In S. H. Jones, T. E. Adams, & C. Ellis (Eds.), *Handbook of autoethnography* (pp. 123–142). New York, NY: Routledge.

Eakin, P. J. (2008). *Living autobiographically: How we create identity in narrative.* New York, NY: Cornell University Press.

Finkelstein, M. J., Conley, V. L., & Schuster, J. H. (2016). *The faculty factor: Reassessing the American academy in a turbulent era.* Baltimore, MD: The Johns Hopkins University Press.

Gappa, J. M., Austin, A. E., & Trice, A. G. (2007). *Rethinking faculty work: Higher education's strategic imperative.* Hoboken, NJ: John Wiley & Sons.

Holstein, J. A., & Gubrium, J. F. (2000). *The self we live by: Narrative identity in a postmodern world.* New York, NY: Oxford University Press.

Lyle, E. (2009). A process of becoming: In favour of a reflexive narrative approach. *The Qualitative Report, 14*(2), 293–298.

Neumann, A. (2009). *Professing to learn: Creating tenured lives and careers in the American research university.* Baltimore, MD: The Johns Hopkins University Press.

Patton, M. Q. (2002). *Qualitative research and evaluation methods* (3rd ed.). Thousand Oaks, CA: Sage Publishers.

Seidman, I. (2013). A structure for in-depth, phenomenological interviewing. In I. Seidman (Ed.), *Interviewing as qualitative research: A guide for researchers in education and the social sciences* (pp. 81–114). New York, NY: Teachers College Press.

Slay, H. S., & Smith, D. A. (2011). Professional identity construction: Using narrative to understand the negotiation of professional and stigmatized cultural identities. *Human Relations, 64*(1), 85–107.

Trahar, S. (2009). Beyond the story itself: Narrative inquiry and autoethnography in intercultural research in higher education. *Forum: Qualitative Social Research, 10*(1), 1–13. Retrieved from http://www.qualitative-research.net/index.php/fqs/article/view/1218/2654

Webster, L., & Mertova, P. (2007). *Using narrative inquiry as a research method: An introduction to using critical event narrative analysis in research on learning and teaching.* New York, NY: Routledge.

Wheaton, B., & Gotlib, I. H. (1997). Trajectories and turning points over the life course: Concepts and themes. In I. H. Gotlib (Ed.), *Stress and adversity over the life course trajectories and turning points* (pp. 1–26). Cambridge: Cambridge University Press.

CHAPTER 16

Critical Conversations on Reflexive Inquiry in Field Experiences

S. Laurie Hill, Amy Burns, Patricia Danyluk and Kathryn Crawford

Introduction

The task of preparing student teachers for the profession of teaching is a complex and dynamic process. The many dimensions that support the development of thoughtful, qualified, and skilled professionals are not easily identified and, at times, unevenly applied in teacher education programs. Student teachers must grapple with developing and identifying their goals and priorities and must determine their approaches to instruction, assessment, and classroom management while also developing a professional identity. As teacher educators, we value deep learning and transformation of understanding and self for our pre-service teachers and acknowledge that teacher education should pay close attention to the meaning making processes of pre-service teachers (Gallchoir, O'Flaherty, & Hinchion, 2018).

Pre-service teachers bring unique experiences, understandings, and early enactments of teaching (Sexton, 2008) to their studies in a Bachelor of Education (B. Ed.) program. "Drawing upon different arrays of social positioning, experiences and resources to enact their professional selves in particular ways" (Sexton, 2008, p. 75) pre-service teachers play an active role in the formation of their professional identity (Sutherland, Howard, & Markauskaite, 2010). The development of professional identity involves an ongoing process of interpretation and reinterpretation of experiences (Coldron & Smith, 1999) that necessarily involves pre-service teachers' sense of self and agency. Incorporating reflexive inquiry into our education programs is a way to provide opportunities for our pre-service teachers to engage in a conscious process of identifying areas of growth in their practice, exploring potential actions and solutions, and developing an understanding of self as an emerging teacher.

This chapter explores the development of pre-service teachers' professional identities through practices designed to encourage reflexivity, utilized in three (3) B. Ed. programs. The development of a reflexive stance is also referred to here as reflexive inquiry. We stress the active engagement by pre-service teachers in their learning and in the development of their teaching practice. As colleagues across institutions who collaborate to strengthen field experiences for our student teachers within our individual programs, we consider practices that support the development of a reflexive self to be an essential aspect of pre-service teacher development. We discuss various practices implemented in our teacher education programs that support the practice of reflexivity and contemplate the impact of these practices for our student teachers. Our stories, however, go beyond the ways in which we seek to engage our students in developing a reflexive self; we also explore individual perspectives on our work with students and identify elements of our professional selves (Baxter Magolda, 2009, 2010) in our roles as practicum directors.

Background

Frèire (2003) suggests that teaching requires constant preparation and critical self-reflection. We interpret 'critical' here to mean "looking below the surface, particularly in relation to how knowledge is constructed from a particular position with particular interests in mind" (Tarc, 2013, p. 5). Critical reflection is the process, then, of questioning, analyzing, and revisiting experiences in order to arrive at a deeper awareness and understanding. Reflexivity is a shift from a deep awareness to one of connectedness. "The term 'reflexive' is used to denote actions that direct attention back to the self and foster a circular relationship between subject and object" (Probst, 2015, p. 38). While the act of reflection is usually individual in nature, reflexivity is relational.

During time in field practicums, when pre-service teachers are placed in classroom settings with a partner teacher, pre-service teachers are given the opportunity to observe, consider, and act on a variety of professional dilemmas and practices. They are asked to think carefully about the educational contexts they are part of and to apply professional judgment in responding to the learning needs of students and their professional responsibilities. A reflexive stance can support pre-service teachers in developing a more complete understanding of their teaching practices and of who they are becoming as practitioners. When pre-service teachers engage in reflexive inquiry, they are applying critical reflection to their experiences and following up with action rooted in understanding. This active stance and self-conscious consideration can prompt further growth in thought or behaviour (Danielewicz, 2001).

A pre-service teacher's past experiences of being a student inform her ongoing development as a teacher and become altered and shaped as she encounters new information, university faculty, peers, learners, and teachers in the practicum setting. Leavy, McSorley, and Bote (2007) suggest that the attitudes held on entry to pre-service training programs greatly influence what pre-service teachers learn and has a significant impact on their classroom practices. Leavy et al. (2007) propose that one of the goals of teacher education should be to transform naïve, undeveloped beliefs into informed ideas through examination of such beliefs. The epistemological beliefs held by pre-service teachers about teaching become building blocks in the construction of their teaching practice. In turn, their ability to teach well is dependent on the development of a reflexive capacity. van Manen (1991) maintains that every situation in the classroom requires a response from the teacher and it is this response that illuminates "how one is oriented to children and how one lives up (or fails to live up) to one's responsibilities" (p. 15).

A reflexive approach to practice necessarily involves issues of identity. Real-life challenges in teaching require student teachers to re-examine their beliefs and values, which help to shape a sense of professional self. Baxter-Magolda's (1992) research on 'ways of knowing', suggests to us that pre-service teachers will construct their perspectives and beliefs based on judgments and reflections on best evidence in a particular context and that these beliefs and perspectives will inform their sense of efficacy as a professional educator. While changes in long held beliefs are not easily made (Brookfield, 1987), opportunities to engage in reflexive inquiry can encourage changes to the professional self (Campoy, 2010).

Inquiry Design

This inquiry reflects our values and perspectives as teacher educators. We draw on elements of duoethnography (Norris, 2008) and "critical dialogue" (Lund & Veinotte, 2010, p. 5) to share and understand the ways in which reflexive practices are developed and applied within our teacher education programs. Additionally, we illuminate how our identities as teacher educators have been influenced by this work.

While duoethnography usually implies two voices or authors, in this chapter, the tenets of duoethnography are expanded to include the perceptions of four rather than two directors of field experience. Developed by Richard Sawyer and Joe Norris (Sawyer & Norris, 2013; Norris, Sawyer, & Lund, 2012; Norris, 2008), duoethnographic inquiry allowed us to engage in conversation not only about the development of student teacher reflexive thinking, but of our re-interpretation and understanding of our teacher educator identities. The text format of our conversation "follows the model of representation in duoethnography"; that is a text written as a dialogue between four individuals, without integrating the four perspectives into one text, and "without relying or drawing extensively on exterior voices or texts for substantiation" (Seidel & Hill, 2015, p. 51).

Our shared inquiry into pre-service teacher reflexive inquiry was guided by the insights on learning partners developed by Baxter Magolda (2009, 2010). Baxter Magolda explains how shared investigations into particular phenomena may provide opportunities for individuals to develop more sophisticated ways of knowing. These ways of knowing are framed as epistemological patterns that encourage the development of self-authorship or voice. Baxter Magolda (2009, 2010) describes the manner in which learning partners may challenge each other to develop self-authorship through three principles. First, learning partners respect the thoughts and beliefs of their partner and so affirm the value of their perspectives. Second, learning partners help their partner to view their experiences as an opening for growth and new understanding. Finally, learning partners collaborate with each other to help understand and analyze problems and dilemmas. This model provided a framework for thinking about our work together, for arriving at new perspectives, and for considering particular dilemmas that arise in implementing practices that support reflexivity with our pre-service teachers.

Inquiry into Practices Supporting Reflexivity

As individuals in the role of field director in each of our institutions, we often experience isolation in our positions. Originally we came together as a group to understand how to meet the challenges of finding field placements for our pre-service teachers. We were seeking affirmation of the challenges in doing this work and looking for potential solutions. The opportunity to develop professional relationships with others in a similar role was an added reward of our conversations. This professional collaboration has allowed us to continue to investigate areas of teacher education that are significant to us all.

For this inquiry, we met initially to discuss and refine our thinking as a group on how pre-service teachers are encouraged in reflexivity. Dialogue is the foundation of duoethnography (Sawyer & Norris, 2013) and our conversations provided a means for exploring the manner in which reflexive inquiry was woven into our respective B. Ed. programs. In order to guide our conversations, we developed four questions:

1. How do we provide opportunities for our student teachers to engage in reflexive inquiry in our programs?
2. What successes and challenges do we face in developing and implementing reflexive inquiry in our B. Ed. programs?

3.   What are the challenges for student teachers in developing a reflexive capacity and a strengthened sense of professional identity?

4.   How has our own practice/sense of professional identity been impacted by this work?

After our initial meeting and conversation, we went away and responded individually to our questions in writing. These written reflections were shared within our group and we met again to consider the complexity of our individual and shared experiences with regard to implementing practices that encourage reflexivity among our pre-service teachers. We then shaped our notes and conversations into a written dialogue that we exchanged with each other for further exploration and clarification. The final edited dialogue is presented here, with each section focusing on the themes that emerged in response to the questions we posed.

Themes and Discussion

Although our programs vary in purpose and size, each stresses the interconnectedness between university courses in pedagogy and practicum experiences in classroom settings.

Pre-Service Teacher Reflexive Inquiry

Laurie: Welcome everyone. Perhaps you could begin with a brief introduction of your program and the opportunities it offers for reflexive inquiry by your pre-service teachers.

Kathryn: My program is a small one in the city and this size allows us to know each student very well. Our pre-service teachers are required to critically reflect through field journals during each of their practicum placements. They are encouraged to make connections between their experiences, theory, and identity formation through shared praxis with their partner teacher, field experience instructor, and peers.

Amy: This is the same for me, but the scale is slightly different. My program has approximately 1200 student teachers per semester and all are asked to critically reflect on their practice through face-to-face meetings with both their partner teacher and field experience instructor and through D2L, our online learning platform. In the discussions that occur with partner teachers and field experience instructors, pre-service teachers are asked to consider a teaching experience that has often just occurred, and to identify elements of what has gone well, what requires improvement, and the way in which they can actively address areas for growth. This reflexive inquiry is incredibly important as it mimics the kind of thinking required of teachers as they negotiate the moment-to-moment requirements of the profession.

Laurie: Patricia, you and Amy are in the same university faculty, but your programs are quite different. Do you follow a similar format?

Patricia: The community-based program is unique in that it is smaller in size, but we place pre-service teachers all over the province, allowing them to stay in their home communities. Many of my students do not have recent school experiences; this makes the development of a reflexive stance even more critical as they come to terms with the ways schooling has changed since they, themselves, were students. In their first field experience, pre-service teachers post a response to a question and respond to one of their classmate's postings each day. In subsequent field experiences, when pre-service teachers begin to lesson plan, the requirement for postings and responses shifts from daily to weekly. Pre-service teachers are then required to write about what went well for each lesson taught, what didn't, and to identify what they could do differently.

Kathryn: That sounds very similar to what we do also. The conversations pre-service teachers have are guided by their observations and questions about what worked in their lessons and are posed in their field journals and in the classroom during a weekly seminar class on campus. Walker (2007) suggests, "by listening to others, ... more accountable and responsible knowledge [is produced]" (p. 296).

Patricia: That is so true. Reflections on their lessons often lead to the most powerful learning and, yet at the same time, they are the part of the lesson plan that students often skip. There is a tendency for students to think they will remember what worked and what did not, but only by writing down their reflections are they able to see patterns in their practice and to reflexively consider other strategies for addressing student learning needs.

Laurie: I think that we have many similar opportunities for reflexive inquiry. My program is smaller, with approximately 200 pre-service teachers. Ideally, reflective conversations should be happening on a daily basis with the partner teacher and on a regular basis with the field experience instructor. Our pre-service teachers are also required to respond to new understandings of practice and professionalism in a weekly written reflection. These practices encourage reflexivity on the part of the pre-service teachers, but are sometimes resisted by a small number of them who feel vulnerable or judged.

Successes and Challenges Developing and Implementing Reflexive Inquiry

Patricia: Let's share some of our successes and challenges in trying to promote reflexive inquiry with our pre-service teachers.

Kathryn: I can identify one significant challenge I experience in our program. First, partner teachers and field experience instructors do not hold consistent expectations for pre-service teachers in developing reflexive thinking. Because of the diversity of classroom environments, partner teachers' skills with reflection and pedagogical conversations, and field experience instructors' commitment to engage in reflection with the pre-service teacher, pre-service teachers are held to different standards during their practicum.

Amy: Yes, expectations definitely vary among practitioners in the field. One challenge I see in our program is that when pre-service teachers are grappling with the demands of field experience, it can be difficult for them to see the importance and value in doing the more detailed, more theoretical reflective writing required for online discussion posts.

Laurie: I also find that the biggest challenge in our program is persuading pre-service teachers that critical reflection is a worthwhile task – one that should be prioritized as it leads to a deeper understanding of the issues they are grappling with. When the demands and expectations of field experience become overwhelming, reflective writing is usually the first thing to be dropped and the opportunity of developing or deepening a reflexive stance is lost.

Kathryn: That situation sounds similar to the second challenge I have observed that relates to buy-in from pre-service teachers. Pre-service teachers are often slow to grasp the value of critical reflection, and struggle to reflexively engage with meaningful moments in practice, especially if they lack modelling and support. In my experience, the development of reflexivity in most pre-service teachers develops through conversation with others who play the catalyst to encouraging a reflexive stance.

Patricia: I find most pre-service teachers need to be taught how to reflect and question their assumptions so that they can act in new and informed ways in their practice. In the teaching strategy reflective assignment, I have broken down into steps how to reflect. By including these steps, I have found that most students are able to engage in reflection in a meaningful manner. Critical reflection becomes less successful when pre-service teachers are unclear what they are to reflect on or how to reflect and they often express anxiety about the quality of the postings. Reflection is an important first step to engaging reflexively with the dilemmas and challenges of developing teacher practice.

Kathryn: I agree, Patricia, but I think field experience instructors and partner teachers also share the lack of clarity about reflexivity as a process that goes beyond reflection. I think I need to expand my role to include ongoing conversation between everyone (field experience instructors, partner teachers, and pre-service teachers) in order to foster increased understanding about a reflexive stance so that an alignment in expectations is achievable.

Amy: I find that our pre-service teachers sometimes struggle with discussing what needs to be improved with their partner teachers. Instead of seeing this as an opportunity, it is experienced as criticism, and pre-service teachers can become defensive. This scenario makes it difficult for pre-service teachers to be genuinely reflexive. As well, pre-service teachers often struggle with how to dig deeply into elements of practice that they need to examine. This challenge has been somewhat ameliorated by teaching about a reflexive stance in our on-campus courses. Pre-service teachers, in their first year, have been taught to consider first the way in which the topic under reflection is informed by their previous experience, then to examine the literature that they have been reading and make connections to theory, and finally to question their responses and actions to the topic.

Laurie: We all agree that reflexive inquiry should be prioritized in our education programs and that these practices should be taught to, encouraged in, and lived by our pre-service teachers. The development of a reflexive capacity in pre-service teachers really depends on their ability and willingness to question the assumptions, beliefs, and values that they already hold. Baxter Magolda (1992) explains that students require an appropriate "balance of confirmation and contradiction" (p. 27) to support them in examining meaning found in experiences. Field experiences give pre-service teachers the opportunity for doing both of these things: they are encouraged to integrate previous knowledge to new experiences; and they are required to evaluate new understanding. Making these opportunities count is a big part of our role.

Challenges for Pre-Service Teachers in Developing Reflexive Capacity and Professional Identity

Amy: I feel sure that each of you experience this as well, but I really do believe that some of the greatest challenges for our pre-service teachers in developing a sense of professional identity lay in the mismatch of experience in on-campus courses and field experiences.

Kathryn: I find that, too. In fact, a significant difficulty in expressing professional identity for our pre-service teachers is the language of ownership. Pre-service teachers often attribute tensions in their emerging practice to the difference in pedagogy between their partner teacher and themselves, whereas our recent graduates who are beginning teachers must consider their tensions through the lens of their own decisions. Pre-service teacher identity formation is often described in relation to the practices of the partner teacher. Those who tend to be able to reflect on their sense of emerging practice through the actual practice of teaching, task design, and relationship with students are those who are provided more autonomy over the course of their practicum. Those who struggle to identify their own sense of self as a result of practice often describe their experience in relation to the practices that are already in place. As a result, they tend to be critical of the instructional design and teaching practices instead of on their own learning and understanding.

Amy: That makes sense. For us, it sometimes happens that pre-service teachers begin to develop a strong sense of the kind of teacher they want to be during on-campus courses but, when they go out into their practicum, they don't see that image exactly reflected and can't necessarily recognize it. Although this is a challenge for them, I believe it is critical that they bring these two realities together. It is in this mismatch that changes, and growth in understanding and practices are realized.

Patricia: That happens all the time in the community-based program as well. There are some pre-service teachers who are unable to engage in reflexivity for reasons that are not entirely clear. Once pre-service teachers are in the classroom, they need to be mindful about everything they do, including how students in their classroom are responding to their teaching and what implications this has for their teaching. Pre-service teachers who are unable to develop a reflexive stance often view others as being non-supportive. At this point in the field experience, they begin to believe that they have been matched with a teacher who doesn't understand them or who is unwilling to support them. These pre-service teachers begin to blame others for their lack of success in the placement. They see their partner teacher, their students, or their field experience instructor as the problem. Such individuals are often not well suited to the teaching profession. Alternatively, those who begin to understand the need for a reflexive stance may be temporarily disappointed in their lack of success, but are often able to rally by accepting responsibility for their role and adapting their teaching to better meet the needs of their students.

Kathryn: A frequent conversation I have with our pre-service teachers is around their struggle to engage in authentic critical reflection, knowing their partner teacher or field experience instructor who are also evaluating their competency development will read it. There is vulnerability in articulating their thoughts and reflections on experiences that are valued by another person.

Laurie: One strategy that we implemented this year was to take away the requirement that partner teachers should read the reflective writing by pre-service teachers. It meant that pre-service teachers' reflections became a conversation between two individuals; themselves and the field experience instructor. This change has encouraged a trusting relationship between the pre-service teacher and the field experience instructor and has facilitated a deeper consideration of the complexity of teaching by the pre-service teacher. Most pre-service teachers were able to move beyond just looking back at their work to consider the ways they could actively address and apply new knowledge in the classroom.

Professional Identity and Impact of this Work

Patricia: In the classroom the same problems are often encountered on a daily basis. In many ways, being an instructor is like Groundhog Day, in that the same student will likely react the same way until we do something differently. In my work, I engage in constant reflection about what I am teaching and what I am writing. I am, however, cognizant of the crippling effect of too much reflection. Most instructors are reflective by nature, but too much reflection can prevent us from taking action. The value of a reflexive stance is the opportunity to be aware of our positionality as an instructor and to act on our knowledge and beliefs in a manner that will best support our students.

Laurie: One of the challenges I think we all face is time – time to use reflexive inquiry as a process to understand the way that we feel about ourselves in relation to our practice.

Kathryn: My practice has benefited from shared praxis with pre-service teachers, partner teachers, field experience instructors, faculty, and other stakeholders in pre-service teacher education. I try to make time for these conversations with others. I am more effective at asking questions that foster reflexivity and introspection than I was before engaging in this work. I have drawn upon my work with pre-service teachers to inform my teaching, guide my own reflections in course content, and create opportunities for more diverse assignments that allow pre-service teachers to articulate their evolving understanding of learners and learning, teachers and teaching, and their own professional identity.

Amy: My practice and sense of professional identity has been impacted significantly by my work with pre-service teachers and I have come to two realizations. First, I tend to be less reflexive than I believe I should be as my personality is one of task completion. In an effort to solve issues for students, I find it difficult to allow them to solve those issues for themselves. If I engaged more in reflexive thinking, I believe this would come more naturally to me. Second, I have come to realize how important the process of reflexivity was in my work as a K-12 teacher. It is for this reason that I feel strongly that pre-service teachers must be explicitly encouraged to engage in inquiry that moves them towards reflexivity. In teaching my students to hold a reflexive stance, I have had no choice but to be reflexive in turn.

Laurie: A focus on implementing and supporting reflexivity with my pre-service teachers has reminded me about the importance of articulating the reasons for my own teaching decisions and actions. Reflexivity is a useful tool for growth, and it has made me more aware of the pedagogical context of my practice and how my beliefs and values shape my interactions with the students.

Conclusions

Our collaborative writing and dialogue allowed us to examine our roles as practicum directors and the ways that we support pre-service teachers in developing a reflexive stance. As a group, we agreed that it is vitally important to encourage pre-service teachers to move beyond reflection to embrace reflexivity in examining their experiences of teaching and learning in a B. Ed. program. We view reflexive inquiry as a process that is cultivated within our educational programs and one that allows pre-service teachers to frame their practice based on professional values and sense of professional identity. It is a way for pre-service teachers to transform their teaching practice and professional selves. One of the important aspects of reflexivity is the self-knowledge that comes from knowing why we do something. We encourage pre-service teachers to step back from their assumptions about teaching and their habits of practice to think deeply about particular perspectives they hold and actions they have taken in the classroom; this process helps them recognize that they are not alone but connected to others through shared experiences, perspectives, and practices. Our wish is that, as they move through the B. Ed program, they are continuously re-imagining and re-enacting their professional selves and teaching practice.

Our shared dialogue has reminded us that, along with our students, we are also learners and our relationships with each other support us in learning. Baxter Magolda (2009) refers to this process of connecting self to practice as *authoring your life,* a process best done with others. In reflexively examining our practices as teacher educators in distinct educational contexts, we have a clearer understanding of our responsibility for designing and implementing meaningful and rounded field experiences for our students. This work is vital for the development of pre-service teacher identity and practice. While it is often invisible work done in the isolation of our individual roles, our collaboration has provided us with a shared understanding of our work across institutions, a re-examination of our practice, and has provided possibilities for the future work we do together.

References

Baxter Magolda, M. B. (1992). *Knowing and reasoning in college: Gender-related patterns in students' intellectual development.* San Francisco, CA: Jossey-Bass.

Baxter Magolda, M. B. (2009). *Authoring your own life: Developing an internal voice to navigate life's challenges.* Sterling, VA: Stylus Publishing, LLC.

Baxter Magolda, M. B. (2010). A tandem journey through the labyrinth. *Journal of Learning Development in Higher Education, 2,* 1–6.

Brookfield, S. D. (1987). *Developing critical thinkers: Challenging adults to explore alternative ways of thinking and acting.* Milton Keynes: Open University Press.

Campoy, R. (2010). Reflective thinking and educational solutions: Clarifying what teacher educators are attempting to accomplish. *SRATE Journal, 19*(2), 15–22.

Coldron, J., & Smith, R. (1999). Active location in teachers' construction of their professional identities. *Journal of Curriculum Studies, 31*(6), 711–726.

Copeland, W. D., Birmingham, C., La Cruz, E. D., & Lewin, B. (1993). The reflective practitioner in teaching: Toward a research agenda. *Teaching and Teacher Education, 9*(4), 347–359.

Danielewicz, J. (2001). *Teaching selves: Identity, pedagogy, and teacher education.* Albany, NY: SUNY Press.

Frèire, P. (2003). Reading the world/reading the word. In A. Lieberman (Ed.), *The Jossey-Bass reader on teaching* (pp. 52–61). San Francisco, CA: Jossey-Bass.

Gallchoir, C., O'Flaherty, J., & Hinchion, C. (2018). Identity development: What I notice about myself as a teacher. *European Journal of Teacher Education, 41*(2), 138–156.

Leavy, A. M., McSorley, F. A., & Bote, L. A. (2007). An examination of what metaphor construction reveals about the evolution of preservice teachers' beliefs about teaching and learning. *Teaching and Teacher Education, 23*(7), 1217–1233.

Lund, D. E., & Veinotte, C. (2010). Researching a social justice course in a charter school: A duoethnographic conversation. *Education, 6*(2), 5–14.

Norris, J. (2008). Duoethnography. In L. M. Given (Ed.), *The Sage encyclopedia of qualitative research methods* (pp. 233–236). Los Angeles, CA: Sage Publications.

Norris, J., Sawyer, R. D., & Lund, D. (Eds.). (2012). *Duoethnography: Dialogic methods for social, health, and educational research.* Walnut Creek, CA: Left Coast Press.

Probst, B. (2015). The eye regards itself: Benefits and challenges of reflexivity in qualitative social work research. *Social Work Research, 39*(1), 37–48. Retrieved from https://doi.org/10.1093/swr/svu028

Sawyer, R. D., & Norris, J. (2013). *Duoethnography.* New York, NY: Oxford University Press.

Seidel, J., & Hill, S. L. (2015). Thinking together: A duoethnographic inquiry into the implementation of a field experience curriculum. *Education, 21*(2), 49–64.

Sexton, D. M. (2008). Student teachers negotiating identify, role and agency. *Teacher Education Quarterly, 35*(3), 73–88.

Sutherland, L., Howard, S., & Markauskaite, L. (2010). Professional identity creation: Examining the development of beginning preservice teachers' understanding of their work as teachers. *Teaching and Teaching Education, 26*, 455–465.

Tarc, P. (2013). *International education in global times: Engaging the pedagogic.* New York, NY: Peter Lang.

van Manen, M. (1991). *The tact of teaching: The meaning of pedagogical thoughtfulness.* London: The Althouse Press.

Walker, M. (2007). Action research and narrative: 'Finely aware and richly responsible'. *Educational Action Research, 15*(2), 295–303.

CHAPTER 17

Preservice Teachers Explore Their Development as Teachers of Reading

Beverley Brenna and Andrea Dunk

It is late summer. Prairie sun shines down but, at night, crisp air reminds us that fall is approaching. Apples ripen. Rose petals fall. Course instructors at our university are putting the finishing touches on syllabi, anticipating a new year of incoming students. In the College of Education we are thinking about the teacher candidates we have taught in the past, professionals who are now practicing teachers in our school divisions. What do they remember from previous instruction? How might we further fill in gaps for our incoming teacher candidates so that they become their best teacher selves? We look at our elementary literacy courses and think about Ministry of Education expectations related to curriculum and teacher education. What shifts will our students make in defining and actualizing literacy pedagogy in their time with us? How might we explore and encourage these changes? How might reflexive inquiry support us all?

The year ahead beckons. We connect as a potential research team, both interested in literacy instruction in early childhood, both hoping to think about an undergraduate course as a context for expanding our learning about post-secondary teaching, and both wishing to maximize instruction for the teacher candidates enrolled in our College's elementary B.Ed. program. Bev is a faculty member whose assignment this year includes two consecutive required courses in literacy instruction. Andrea is a PhD student working with Bev as a research assistant as well as a seminar leader later in the year. Conversations between the two of us sparkle – we brainstorm, we pass questions back and forth, and we think about what we want to explore in the context of teacher education and how we might do it.

Purpose of the Study

After a period of time playing with ideas, we settle down to the serious choices ahead. We decide to collect data from voluntary participants in Bev's first term English Language Arts (ELA) course – an introductory ELA course that will be followed later in the year with a second curriculum course deepening the ELA subject matter. We wonder what is most impactful about this initial course in terms of transformative pedagogy, acknowledging Mezirow's (1997) notion that expanding a frame of reference – the structures of assumptions through which we understand experience – will be important as part of our learning journey together with undergraduate students. In particular, we want to understand how Bev's students define and re-define aspects of literacy teaching and learning and how they begin to delineate their roles as educators with a specific focus on reading in early childhood classrooms. This study will no doubt also connect to how we see ourselves as teacher educators. Bev wonders:

> What if we study transformation and the teacher candidates in this course do not demonstrate or reflect on change – will I have failed as an instructor? What will I do with that?

Although a new methodology for us, we selected reflexive inquiry as a source of information within this course-based study. While we initially suspected that our research might also enhance student learning for our preservice teachers through its focus on reflexive thinking, little did we know how critical the self-assessment components would become to the 38 teacher candidates who volunteered for this study.

Our College has, over time, embraced different models related to curriculum instruction in English Language Arts. The framework around these models has included a standard two (2) three-credit courses required by the Ministry of Education related to teacher certification. Twenty-five years ago, we recall a time when elementary students were delivered, fresh-faced and excited, to our classroom doors so that our teacher candidates could practice lesson delivery as part of these courses. Through restructuring, we recall a shift to lecture-only frameworks, with ELA units and lessons planned as part of course content but not applied until later field experiences in schools. For the past few years, our undergraduate students have had field experiences that run within Terms I and II, offering two days each week through which to observe, explore, and experience life in schools as well as deliver course-based lessons. In addition to questions about transformative possibilities within the framework of our courses, we wonder about the value of these field experiences for our teacher candidates.

Perspectives

Reflexive Inquiry
Our first task was to define for ourselves as researchers the scope of reflexive inquiry that we would be adopting for this study. The definition we adopted

supports the idea that, as researchers, we are critically conscious of our positionality throughout the research process including the analysis phase of the research (Pillow, 2003). Our research is influenced by the relationship between ourselves as researchers and the relationship with our participants, and we recognize that "meanings are seen to be negotiated between researcher and researched within a particular social context so that another researcher in a different relationship will unfold a different story" (Finlay, 2002, p. 531). Of the two types of reflexive inquiry mentioned in the literature: epistemological and methodological (Finlay, 2002; Popoveniuc, 2013), we selected methodological in order to capture understandings about the *process* of becoming reading/literacy teachers.

Early in the development of our literature review, Bev posed the question, *how is reflexive inquiry different from reflective thinking?* Our journey through the literature has led us to think about how reflexivity connects the personal and the professional, in our case considering and re-considering definitions and teaching practices related to literacy education (Cole & Knowles, 2000). Through reflexive practice we attempt to shift or strengthen self-knowledge (Lyle, 2009) in the capacities of our teacher candidates and ourselves, supporting future practice as literacy teachers and teacher-leaders. Andrea likened this approach to Palmer: *It's about refining our practice stemming from identity and integrity*, connecting to Palmer's (1997) statement that "teaching holds a mirror to the soul" (p. 15). Bolstered with these readings from reflexive inquiry viewpoints, we moved closer to actually designing our study.

In addition to thinking about how our research questions fit well within a framework of reflexive inquiry, we also thought about methods. We knew that pre- and post-course surveys could assist us in understanding changing beliefs, and we adapted an existing survey (Gove, 1983; Vacca, Vacca, & Gove, 1991) to use at the beginning and end of Bev's course in Term 1. We also wanted to help students think narratively about transformation throughout the course – and this is where the idea of including mid-course "exit cards" emerged as another tool for data collection. The exit card is a formative assessment strategy described by Hume (2010) consisting of written answers on an index card submitted anonymously at the end of class. It allows students to summarize their understanding while instructors gain a snapshot of learning at that moment in time.

We examined data from the semi-structured teacher survey, given pre- and post-course delivery (Appendices A & B), as well as the mid-course exit cards, looking for conceptual categories related to shifting understandings of literacy teaching and learning in education with a particular focus on the teaching of reading. In addition to definitions of reading and understandings about how it should be taught in early elementary classrooms, the TCs were also asked to reflect on the experiences that underpinned their beliefs, and identify which experiences related most strongly to their changing understandings. We wondered: *given that it's these TCs' first year of Education courses, how do we demonstrate respect for what they are bringing without making them feel self-conscious about their knowledge or lack of knowledge around literacy practices? How do we foreground their previous experiences in schools and open a space for change?*

Although the study was developed as part of our course content, all of the surveys and exit cards were completed on a voluntary basis with flexible submissions of the pre-course survey and the exit cards into a basket the instructor brought to class for this purpose. For the final response on the post-course survey, where perhaps the most pressure might exist on participants to conform to what they thought the instructor wanted to hear, the departmental secretary exchanged places with Bev at the end of class and collected student responses in an envelope that was subsequently sealed and retained in the secretary's locked filing cabinet. This envelope was provided to Bev and Andrea only after final marks were distributed to the students.

Of the 38 possible participants in this survey, 100% chose to submit responses during class time, on all instruments. The TCs attached pseudonyms to the surveys and the exit passes were submitted without any identifying names at all. We wanted to maximize student safety through the anonymity of these responses and were aware that relational structures between instructor and students could be a place where honesty was eclipsed by duty or expectation. In this way we attempted to minimize bias to the data and support students' freedom to participate although we acknowledge the shaping hand of the researcher in this, as in other, qualitative research (Lawrence-Lightfoot & Davis, 1997).

Goals beyond Simple Qualitative Endeavour

Our current study was designed to attempt to fill gaps in contemporary understandings in the field. But our research questions called for special treatment. While a general qualitative study would offer findings related to participant definitions and assessment of experiences, we wanted to offer our teacher candidates the opportunity to consider and re-consider definitions and aspects of classroom practice that we guess are shifting over time. Because of this desire to invite our preservice teachers into a place where they could consciously sift through and acknowledge possible areas of challenge and transformation, the delivery of our study was best imagined in an embedded sense within course content, with multiple points of more formal invitation and data collection on the key questions below:

– What definitions of reading and understandings about the teaching of reading do preservice teachers bring with them into an introductory English Language Arts class related to elementary education?

- What shifts in definitions and understandings occur throughout this course, delineated towards future classroom practice?
- What experiences are identified by the teacher candidates as catalysts to their changing beliefs about the teaching of reading?

The pre and post survey data was elicited through semi-structured questions from which we analyzed narrative answers for meaning – looking for the "what," "the why" and "the how" of literacy instruction and TCs' related beliefs. By selecting qualitative methodology, we were free to deeply explore these responses rather than strictly sort responses into categories, although we do use numbers to catalogue responses related to TCs' prioritization of various influences on their developing course-based understandings. We were also seeking to analyze these responses in time for a second ELA course required in Term II – hoping that perhaps our initial findings could inform the syllabus development for this connected course offering.

Flash Points Connected to Literacy Instruction

The term *flash point* is more conventionally understood as a place, event, or time at which trouble flares (flash point, n.d.). While some circles may not recognize the potential for *flash points* in literacy education, we are conscious of many diverse and even opposing viewpoints related to literacy instruction, particularly early literacy instruction. Similarly, we are mindful of differing recommendations in terms of best practice in preparing teacher candidates as early childhood literacy teachers. From our previous work, we anticipated that some students might enter this course with outdated or narrow views about literacy teaching and learning, and we wanted to make space for those views to be honoured as well as the shifts we hoped might occur over time. As one of TCs stated: "... The whole process of learning to read is so much more than I realized ..." (Michelle).

While it is widely recognized that literacy instruction is crucially important to children's development (Malatesha Joshi et al., 2009), and that particular preservice methods in literacy instruction improve performance assessments of teacher candidates (Pomerantz & Pierce, 2010), it is acknowledged that high quality teaching of reading occurs across the curriculum and is a "complex, multidimensional phenomenon" (Croninger & Valli, 2009, p. 101). Teachers in the field consciously promote a wide range of skills and strategies through diverse practices (Brenna & Chen, 2013). The importance of examining pedagogical growth in teacher education related to the teaching of reading, as well as gaps in research, has been well documented (Hoffman et al., 2005; Maloch et al., 2003; Pomerantz & Pierce, 2010; Timperly & Alton-Lee, 2008; Risko et al., 2008). Clift and Brady (2005), members of the American Educational Research Association (AERA) panel on research and teacher education, reviewed research occurring between 1995 and 2001 that targeted the impact of methods courses, with some of their work specifically examining studies of reading and English Language Arts teacher education coursework.

In a subsequent literature review, Risko et al. (2008) utilized reading teacher education research as a specific lens to examine broad themes of teacher educator practices specific to the teaching of reading. Conclusions propose that preservice teachers' pedagogical knowledge increases within structured teaching formats and opportunities to practice this pedagogical knowledge with children. Drawing on this literature, Andrea wondered about *the experiences that teacher candidates have that develop their identity as literacy teachers*, while Bev asked about *a safe space to unpack outdated or narrow views of literacy teaching and learning.*

A contemporary research study connecting theory and practice reminds us of the importance of preservice teachers' existing knowledge and the necessity of helping them revise previous assumptions about literacy learning (Massey, 2002), findings that support a *developmental stage* model of adult learning. Massey (2002) conjectured that teacher candidates' previous experiences had produced concepts that took time to unpack and shift, including a tendency to ask their students strictly recall questions after reading rather than exploring other types of comprehension teaching and assessment.

Clift and Brady (2005) also talk about the differential change that happens in preservice English Language Arts coursework when methods courses and field experiences introduce ideas that preservice teachers do not initially accept. *But how does it happen? What experiences support the necessary transformation of ideas and understandings? And how valuable is actually thinking about transformation as it happens?*

A Pedagogy of Love

As we thought about change and transformation, we also thought about an overarching pedagogy that would make it okay for our students to have differing viewpoints. We also recognized that, as researchers in the field of literacy education, we might have differing philosophies as well. Our goal was not to produce teacher candidates as cookie-cutter replicas of anyone. Our goal was to explore growth and change and understand more deeply how this kind of transformation happens. Bev recalled that: "When I was doing my PhD at the University of Alberta I heard Donaldo Macedo talk about a pedagogy of love, based on Paulo Freire's work. It completely won me over and I totally think it applies to this study and our field in general! It is what we do."

The theoretical framework of this study thus originated in the work of Freire (1983, 1991, 1998) who advocated continual explorations of teaching and learning as a pedagogy of love (Loreman, 2011). Such a framework continually reminds us that education is an act of love, and that our work here, with reflexive inquiry, must demonstrate love for our undergraduate students, just as their work must demonstrate love for the children with whom they will work.

Results, Discussion, and Implications

Preliminary Definitions and Understandings of Reading
Data from the early surveys was collated with eagerness as we were keen to explore what these TCs brought experientially to course content.

> The magnitude of the task ahead – preparing them to understand the teaching of reading, in particular – seemed suddenly daunting. Almost all of the students used phonics-only strategies to interpret a sample miscue. A few TCs even indicated that substituting a real word that was close to the textual word in letter-sounds (but different in meaning) was superior to substituting a meaningful word with different letters. They generally rated the introduction of vocabulary, and worksheets to develop skills and strategies, as more important, in terms of elementary classroom time, than setting purposes for reading, reading, and responding to reading. About a third of the group of students felt it was important to introduce *all* new vocabulary words to children prior to reading, and some of the students felt that children should be *immediately* corrected if a word was read incorrectly during oral reading. Help! (Bev)

Deep breaths were required during the examination of these initial surveys. Did most classes come into our undergraduate program with these narrow viewpoints? Probably. Did students manage the big shift to embrace the new learning expected? We didn't know. We hadn't ever compiled post-survey data before, except through more formal structures like final examinations. What were students actually learning through our program? Would this study help us? Perhaps more importantly, could it help them?

Shifts in Definitions and Understandings
By mid-term, the TCs' informal reflections submitted on exit cards had changed substantially. They offered a variety of coaching strategies to use with children in addition to *sound it out* strategies, and identified that supporting problem solving through various scaffolding techniques was often a superior choice during reading instruction. One TC stated on an exit card: "At first I thought it

was best for the teacher to immediately correct a reading or writing miscue. I have now learned that this may be discouraging, rather than helpful."

By midterm, the course instructor was seeing some interesting shifts in beliefs about reading instruction. Bev indicated: "I'm starting to feel tremendously grateful for this process and these signs of learning!" Change was happening. And it was happening in positive ways – the idea that we were shifting in our beliefs and practices seemed to be embraced rather than used for negative self-talk. The TCs talked about patience on their part as well as the importance of supporting comprehension strategies in their students, emphasizing meaning-making rather than getting every word right. One TC wrote about invented spelling as a window into a child's phonics' knowledge. Another TC wrote anonymously on an exit card: "I thought I may do round robin unrehearsed oral reading in my classroom since all my teachers did it when I was a student ... now it is not something I plan to use." Junie wrote on the post-course survey: "I have so many new ideas! And I have reasoning to back up my strategies!"

At the end of the course, more than 70% of these TCs identified, on the post-course survey, that independent/peer reading or setting purposes for reading would best develop reading skills and strategies. Many TCs felt that continuous reading allowed students to practice skills with different types of text, increase their vocabulary knowledge and awareness of sound and print, build confidence, and develop a love of reading. Setting purposes for reading would provide real world context, and instruction would be intentional and connected to the exploration of various strategies. One TC stated: "Modelling and giving purpose to reading is going to make the students excited to read and make them want to learn" (Fluffy Unicorn).

On this post-course survey, none of the TCs identified worksheets for skill and strategy development as an activity on which students should spend considerable amounts of time.

There also appeared to be a considerable shift in thinking with respect to vocabulary instruction. At the end of the term, almost 90% of the TCs felt that explicit instruction of all vocabulary prior to independent reading would be overwhelming, discouraging, and would take the fun out of reading. Instead, one TC suggested an introduction of words that might affect text meaning and understanding, while several felt students could use their schema, semantics, problem-solving, and critical thinking skills to make meaning of unknown words.

When analyzing a child's miscue on the post-course survey, TCs who assessed the substitution of a pseudoword as superior to a synonym (about two-thirds of the total number of TCs) cited the use of decoding strategies, being consistent in the miscue, and accurately identifying beginning and ending sounds as supporting their decision. Some of the TCs also suggested that in this way young children are adding new words to their speaking and listening vocabulary. Two TCs used the phonetic miscue to identify a review of vowel sounds as a specific goal for the student. In contrast, nearly one third of the TCs viewed reading for meaning as the superior strategy, a substantial increase from the pre-course survey. One TC wrote:

> They got the word right the first time, yet changed it the second time but it made sense semantically and syntactically ... They read with meaning. (Goose)

While we sometimes laughed at the choice of pseudonyms here, the research team celebrated the richness of the learning that was illuminated. We also experienced a sense of relief that the course had delivered what we hoped it would – an opportunity for conscious transformation on the part of these students.

In terms of changing definitions, key themes that emerged included the importance of reading across the curriculum and the fact that time and support contributed to the process of preservice teacher transformation occurring this term. These themes reflect findings from previous studies that promote reading pedagogy in multiple contexts (Croninger & Valli, 2009) as well as advocate for time (Massey, 2002) to allow TCs' philosophies about reading instruction to emerge and change, in addition to advocacy for support (Risko et al., 2008) in order for that process of transformation to occur.

In a number of statements on the post-course survey, TCs demonstrate key understandings about learning to teach reading and the importance of reading instruction:

> It sets up all learning in the future. (Kale)

> The reading process is long and always growing. (No Name)

> I've come to realize how important reading at a young age is. (Zee)

In a number of other statements, TCs went on to list early reading behaviors that precluded fluency with text, such as reading picture cues. Some of the TCs identified expanded definitions of the reading act itself:

> It's about strategies not about getting every word right ... modelling is important ... more than just 'sound it out' ... teaching strategies because one strategy will not support every reader. (Harper)

> ... allow students room to problem solve but make them aware you can be their safety net when struggling. Teacher modelling can be a good tool. (Alexis)

> ... I never realized how much there is to it! (Laquisha)

Many of the TCs also discussed transformation in terms of their understandings about diversity:

> I now believe that reading can be tailored to each student. (Kenzie)

> I used to think that reading could only be further developed through more reading but now I know that there are so many other methods. (Serena)

As another TC put it in a revised definition of reading: "It's a process that develops over time through a variety of experiences ... it's a process with no one way to teach it."

One minority voice stated that her definition of reading: "hasn't changed, but I do have a better understanding of how to teach it." She also indicated: "I'm actually relieved many of my philosophies were supported in this course – whew!" (Lynn).

The biggest surprise for us came in the TC's assessment of which experiences most greatly contributed to their changing views. Lecture and discussion in class time was overwhelmingly rated first, closely followed by the actual self-assessment surveys. While discussion with peers inside and outside of class, the textbook, and assignments contextualized within field experiences came next, before field experiences more generally, the impact of assessment-as-learning on our TCs was illuminating.

Our findings connect to Mezirow's (1997) conceptualization of transformative learning theory, illuminating examples of how our undergraduate students are moving past frameworks of reading based on experiences they themselves had as children and/or other experiences they have had in elementary classrooms. Broad definitions of reading, combined with interrogations regarding personal reading strategies employed as adults, as well as diverse ideas on how to teach these strategies, seem to have affected what Mezirow (1997) calls the "structure of assumptions" (p. 5) equating to a new frame of reference. Key in this process of change is what Mezirow describes as "critical reflection on the assumptions upon which our interpretations, beliefs, and habits of mind or points of view are based" (p. 7) and in our case this involved exploring negative as well as positive aspects of particular approaches and resources associated with literacy teaching and learning.

What's Next in Our Journey?

As we think about changing beliefs in relation to knowledge and practice, it appears from this study that TCs enrolled in one 3 credit course in English Language Arts instruction do indeed identify growth and transformation, and study results support the ways in which their thinking has changed. More important is the role of reflexive thinking, through self-assessment, and the way that self-assessment practices supported their changing views. There is still room for growth and discovery, and we note that while a third of the TCs acknowledged on the post-course survey the strength of a meaning-based miscue – a far greater number than on the pre-course survey – others may still see reading as equivalent to decoding letters without fully understanding the importance of comprehension. Many of those on the post-course survey who identified a strong reader based on decoding ability alone, however, also referenced how young children expand on listening and speaking vocabularies through seeing new words in context – a reasonable interpretation of that particular miscue example.

We look at the second required class these TCs will take in literacy instruction, and begin immediately to apply our learning. Just as we expect our TCs to address the needs of each individual student when they get to the classroom, as instructors we address the needs of our preservice teachers, acknowledging different ways of knowing and learning as well as building on their existing knowledge. What preconceived notions related to the new course content might we help them identify, and what kinds of ongoing reflexive inquiry might we embed in our next course towards further positive transformation?

> It's not about success or failure as an instructor – it's about an ongoing process of learning and discovery. And ongoing self-assessment, for them and for us. (Bev)

And now it is mid-winter. We are delivering the second of the two required ELA courses to these teacher candidates. We consider carefully the results of this study. We watch the snow fall outside our office windows, and look at the outcomes and activities on our course syllabi. We shift content in and out, wishing to circle back to particular concepts and nudge consideration of new understandings. We continue to think about the gaps we perceive in knowledge and strategy development and we employ Ministry outcomes as our guides, with specific attention to assessment-as-leaning. We think about the change demonstrated in Term I, and open ourselves as much as possible to creating a framework for similar changes in Term II.

References

Brenna, B., & Chen, S. E. (2013). Teacher recommendations for reading-education components of B.Ed. programs. *Journal of Reading Education, 38*(2), 10–17.

Cole, A. L., & Knowles, J. G. (2000). *Researching teaching: Exploring teacher development through reflexive inquiry.* Needham Heights, MA: Pearson.

Clift, R. T., & Brady, P. (2005). Research on methods courses and field experiences. In M. Cochran-Smith & K. M. Zeichner (Eds.), *Studying teacher education: The report of the AERA panel on research and teacher education* (pp. 309–424). Mahwah, NJ: Lawrence Erlbaum Associates.

Croninger, R. G., & Valli, L. (2009). "Where is the action?" Challenges to studying the teaching of reading in elementary classrooms. *Educational Researcher, 38*(2), 100–108.

Finlay, L. (2002). "Outing" the resesarcher: The provenance, process, and practice of reflexivity. *Qualitative Health Research, 12*(4), 531–545.

Flash point. (n.d.). *In google online dictionary.* Retrieved from https://www.google.ca/ search?q=flashpoint+definition&rlz=1C1EODB_enCA517CA518&oq=flashpoint+def &aqs=chrome.0.0j69i60j69i57j69i60j0l2.2072j1j9&sourceid=chrome&ie=UTF-8

Freire, P. (1983). *Pedagogy of the oppressed* (M. B. Ramos, Trans.). New York, NY: Continuum. (Original work published 1970)

Freire, P. (1991). The importance of the act of reading. In B. Power & R. Hubbard (Eds.), *Literacy in process* (pp. 21–26). Portsmouth, NH: Heinemann.

Freire, P. (1998). *Teachers as cultural workers: Letters to those who dare teach* (D. Macedo, D. Koike, & A. Oliveira, Trans.). Boulder, CO: Westview Press.

Gove, M. K. (1983). Clarifying teachers' beliefs about reading. *The Reading Teacher, 37*(3), 261–268.

Hoffman, J., Roller, C., Maloch, B., Sailors, M., Duffy, G., & Beretvas, S. N. (2005). Teachers' preparation to teach reading and their experiences and practices in the first three years of teaching. *Elementary School Journal, 105*(3), 267–287.

Hume, K. (2010). *50 tools and techniques for classroom assessment.* Toronto: Pearson.

Lawrence-Lightfoot, S., & Davis, J. H. (1997). *The art and science of portraiture.* San Francisco, CA: Jossey-Bass.

Loreman, T. (2011). *Love as pedagogy.* Rotterdam, The Netherlands: Sense Publishers.

Lyle, E. (2009). A process of becoming: In favour of a reflexive narrative approach. *The Qualitative Report, 14*(2), 293–298.

Malatesha Joshi, R., Binks, E., Hougen, M., Dahlgren, M. E., Ocker-Dean, E., & Smith, D. L. (2009). Why elementary teachers might be inadequately prepared to teach reading. *Journal of Learning Disabilities, 42*(5), 392–402.

Maloch, B., Flint, A., Eldridge, D., Harmon, J., Loven, R., Fine, J., Bryant-Shanklin, M., & Martinez, M. (2003). Understandings, beliefs, and reported decision-making of first-year teachers from different reading teacher preparation programs. *Elementary School Journal, 103*(5), 431–457.

Massey, D. D. (2002). Personal journeys: Teaching teachers to teach literacy. *Literacy Research and Instruction, 41*(2), 103–125.

Mezirow, J. (1997). Transformative learning in action. *New Directions for Adult and Continuing Education, 74*, 5–12.

Palmer, P. J. (1997). The heart of a teacher: Identity and integrity in teaching. *Change, 29*(6), 14–21. Retrieved from http://www.jstor.org.cyber.usask.ca/stable/pdf/40165413.pdf

Pillow, W. (2003). Confession, catharsis, or cure? Rethinking the uses of reflexivity as methodological power in qualitative research. *International Journal of Qualitative Studies in Education, 16*(2), 175–196.

Pomerantz, F., & Pierce, M. (2010). Collaborating with classroom teachers to improve performance assessments in literacy methods courses. *The Reading Professor, 32*(2), 14–24.

Popoveniuc, B. (2013). Self reflexivity: The ultimate end of knowledge. *Procedia: Social and Behavioural Sciences, 163*, 204–213.

Risko, V. J., Roller, C. M., Cummins, C., Bean, R. M., Block, C. C., Anders, P. L., & Flood, J. (2008). A critical analysis of research on reading teacher education. *Reading Research Quarterly, 43*(3), 252–288.

Timperly, H., & Alton-Lee, A. (2008). Reframing teacher professional learning: An alternative policy approach to strengthening valued outcomes for diverse learners. *Review of Research in Education, 32*(1), 328–369.

Vacca, J. L., Vacca, T. T., & Gove, M. K. (1991). *Reading and learning to read* (2nd ed.). New York, NY: HarperCollins.

Appendix A: The Teaching of Reading/Writing Self-Assessment
                  (Beginning of Term)

*Adapted from an existing self survey (Gove, 1983; Vacca, Vacca, & Gove, 1991)
Pseudonym: _____
Please circle your response to question A, and then go on to answer the other questions numbered 1–10 (point form is fine). Please do not change your answer to A (below) after you have written it.

A.   **I feel comfortable teaching reading/writing at my preferred grade level(s):**

1	2	3	4	5	6	7
Strongly disagree	Disagree	Somewhat disagree	Neither agree nor disagree	Somewhat agree	Agree	Strongly agree

Instructional Goals for Grade _____ (specify grade here)
1.   What are some important reading and writing strategies that you plan to teach your students through teacher-modelling?
     a.
     b.
     c.
     d.
     e.

Response to Oral Reading
2.   What will you do when a student is reading orally in a 1:1 reading context with you and reads a word wrong (also called a "miscue")?
     Is it good practice to immediately correct a child, in the situation above, as soon as an oral reading error is made? Why or why not?
3.   Is it good practice to immediately correct a child, in a writing situation, as soon as a spelling error is made? Why or why not?
4.   When parents ask you how you are teaching spelling, what will you tell them?
5.   Will you have your students practice unrehearsed oral round-robin reading in your classroom (in either ELA or content area textbook reading)? Why/why not?

Instructional Activities

2. Classrooms support many different kinds of activities in teaching students to read or to be more proficient readers. Which activity do you think should occupy the greatest amount of classroom time in grades 1–3 settings? (Circle it.) Why?
   a. Introduction of vocabulary.
   b. Setting purposes for reading.
   c. Reading (silently or with a partner).
   d. Response to reading activities.
   e. Worksheets to develop reading skills and strategies.

Vocabulary Words

7. Is it important to introduce all of the new vocabulary words before students read a selection independently? Why/why not?

Assessment Information

8. Tell some ways you might you assess your students in their reading development:

Rationale for "Best Reader"

9. Look below at the oral reading "mistakes" ("miscues") of three readers. The word they have not read correctly is underlined, and what they read instead of that word is written above it. Which of the three readers would you judge as the best or most effective reader based on the miscues you see here? Why?

Reader A

I live near this canal.
Men haul things up and
        channel
down the canal in big
boats.

Reader B

      2. candle
      1. ca
I live near this canal.
Men haul things up and
      candle
down the canal in big
boats.

Reader C

      2. cannel
      1. ca
I live near this canal.
Men haul things up and
      cannel
down the canal in big
boats.

B.   I feel comfortable teaching reading/writing at my preferred grade level(s):

1	2	3	4	5	6	7
Strongly disagree	Disagree	Somewhat disagree	Neither agree nor disagree	Somewhat agree	Agree	Strongly agree

My definition of literacy is the following:

Appendix B   Semi-Structured Questions to Accompany Repeated Delivery of Appendix A (End of Term)

ECUR 309 *****Please complete under a pseudonym

1.   Please indicate how your definition of the reading process has changed during this course, if indeed it did change.
2.   Please indicate how your ideas about teaching reading have changed during this course, if indeed they have changed.
3.   If your definition of the reading process, or your ideas about teaching reading, have changed during this course, please indicate which of the following supported your changing thinking. List the letters of any items in order from greatest to least, that impacted these changes, if any: A. lecture and discussion during class time; B. self-assessment conducted as part of pre and post survey questions; C. discussions with peers in class time; D. discussion with peers outside of class time; E. textbook information; F. assignments for this class contextualized in field experiences; G. other aspects of field experiences outside course assignments; H. "other experiences" (please define H if applicable)

1.   _____ (greatest impact on change)
2.   _____
3.   _____
4.   _____
5.   _____
6.   _____
7.   _____
8.   _____ (least impact on change)

CHAPTER 18

Insider/Outsider: Border Crossing, Liminality, and Disrupting Concepts of Teacher Identities through a Prototypical Lens

Christine Cho

I am a teacher, and a teacher educator, with certain privileges. I am White, middle class, Canadian-born, raised in a Christian-centric home by a mother and a father. English is my first language and I identify as cisgender, straight, and use the pronouns she/her/hers. In short, I am the prototypical teacher. Teachers in Canadian schools are over-representative of the prototypical teacher or what is commonly referred to as the "dominant group" (Causey, Thomas, & Armento, 2000; Ladson-Billings, 2005).

Why, then, do I explore issues around immigrant teacher candidates? A great body of my research involves interviews and focus groups with teacher candidates (students in the process obtaining a Bachelor of Education degree to become certified teachers) who self-identify as immigrants. Why, as a White researcher, would I wish to use the lens of Critical Race Theory (CRT) as it may be argued that my attempts to use CRT in my work could be a form of colonization (see Begerson, 2003). Despite growing diversity in the student, and more recently, in the teacher candidate population, teacher education programs continue to privilege certain types of knowledge and ways of knowing (Myles, Cheng, & Wang, 2006; Putnam & Borko, 2000). The dominant group epistemologies include Euro-Western norms in terms of standardized English (and typically monolingual) language skills, and inherent knowledge of Euro-Western cultural practices and traditions. Immigrants, especially those who are racialized or from stigmatized identity groups, disrupt the image of the prototypical teacher. I pursue my work with caution, troubling Whiteness and working consciously to listen differently to the counter-stories, spoken and unspoken, of teacher candidates who self-identify as people from stigmatized identity groups.

Radical Reflexivity

To understand how I am implicated in my research agenda and how my position as researcher, former classroom teacher, and member of the Ontario College of Teachers affects my role, I turn to researcher reflexivity (Cunliffe, 2003; Johnson-Bailey, 1999; Reger, 2001). As a prototypical teacher, to do my research with participants who self-identify as immigrants, I am crossing borders of ethnicity, nationality, positionality, and place. In this way I am an outsider. I also draw from Clandinin and Connelly's work in narrative inquiry (2000) to further understand my role as researcher: I must be willing to acknowledge the truths of my participants that may very well differ or contradict my own ways of knowing, while holding on to a research agenda. Toward that end, I draw from Cunliffe's (2003) concept of radical-reflexivity. She writes, "we need to go further than questioning the truth claims of others, to question how we as researchers (and practitioners) also make truth claims and construct meaning" (p. 985). Reflexivity is a crisis of truth and a crisis of representation (Clifford, 1986). We are constantly constructing meaning and, as Cunliffe (2003) argues, we cannot separate ontology and epistemology, nor ignore socio-cultural contexts. I see myself as both an outsider and an insider in relation to my research and my work with teacher candidates and my positionality is part of my "whys."

There exists a paradox in reflexive work. As Cunliffe (2003) writes, "self-reflexivity can be disembodying – the thinker separating self from the moment of existence. In the process of reflecting on ourselves we take an outsider-expert stance by objectifying self/feeling in the construction of causal explanations" (pp. 995–996). In terms of my positionality, I am cognizant of the fact that my research participants are sharing narratives that trouble prototypical experiences of teacher education – my experiences of teacher education, from which I have benefited. In my aim for radical-reflexivity, I have worked to dismantle the traditional relationship between researcher and participant. As Cunliffe explains, "Together, researcher and participant focus on how a shared sense of the situation unfolds in the responsive, interactive moments in the research conversation" (p. 997). The approaches I have employed include "practical theories" such as intuition and gut feelings combined with theoretical lenses to offer new ways of understanding what is happening in schools and how power is operating.

Keeping my own positionality in mind, I have to consider my participants' comfort and/or discomfort with me as a prototypical representation of the very system I am asking them about. I work to consider how my social location impacts the ways in which my participants share their stories or edit what they say and how much they share. What is left out because of who I am and what I represent? Do they tell me things they think I want to hear or know? To what extent do they censor themselves in my presence? How much do I censor my responses so as not to offend or jeopardize the data? As Cunliffe (2003) argues, "by uncovering the limitations and possibilities of our assumptions, we are less prone to becoming complacent or ritualistic in our research practices" (p. 1000). While schools are perceived to work on the basis of fairness and equality, they are sites of social domination that work to ensure dominant-subordinate positions (Dei & Kempf, 2006).

Reflective or Reflexive?

It can be easy for a researcher to lose sight of the participants' perspectives and to superimpose our own assumptions during the data analysis. Sometimes, when I reread my analysis, I realize I am *telling their stories* which is not what I set out to do. I want to *listen* to and *hear* the counter-stories (Solórzano & Yosso, 2003)[1] told by immigrant teacher candidates to expand understandings of experiences in the university and school settings and to complicate the prevailing concept of who qualifies to be a teacher. I have to be conscious of whether I am being "reflective" or "reflexive." Examining my behaviours and responses after the fact may in fact be a form of reflection (Cunliffe, 2003). There are times in my research where I find myself exposing the ways in which my participants' supposed neutrality reveals ways in which they seem to dismiss or ignore the importance and significance of their racialized and/or stigmatized bodies with respect to their work in schools. If I hide my suppositions behind my coding and use of themes without exposing how I came to the conclusion, I am not being reflexive. I may have to critique my participants, which, as a White researcher, is an uncomfortable prospect but if I do not share how this feels like a conflict of interest, I am not being reflexive. Instead, I am asking my participants to expose spaces in which they are Othered only to take the academic high ground to consider how they themselves may have acquiesced to Othering which smacks of White privilege. As Thompson (2003) argues, as White educators, "our tendency to think that we know antiracism when we see it suggests that we too have definite ideas about desirable outcomes" (p. 20). In order to engage in self-reflexivity, I have to recognize how my assumptions and values are informing my process of inquiry. To do so, I often need to recalibrate and, toward this end, I draw from Schick (2010) who asks, "whose interests are represented in this account of things?" I also ask myself three key questions: What is going on here? What is permitted? What is at stake? In my analysis, I might include my field notes, poetic musings on the side, and my own first-person account of events in order to expose the ways in which I am working to make my assumptions transparent. Throughout this chapter I will explore the ways in which reflexivity offers possibilities and insights with respect to my role and position as an instructor and researcher in a Faculty of Education.

My Positionality

My passion for this research derives from my current personal life experiences. I am married to a visible minority, who immigrated to Canada and was raised in an English Language learning household. That is, English was not a language either of his parents spoke and, as the youngest of seven children, he was distanced from the Cantonese spoken by his parents in pursuit of the English spoken at school and in the community. My mother-in-law and father-in-law immigrated twice: first to Guyana from China; and, then to Canada. My husband and his six siblings began their education in Guyana and completed it in Ontario. Along the way the siblings lost most, if not all of their first language, Cantonese, in order to assimilate into British Guyanese culture and then into Canadian culture while my parents-in-law maintained their first language and acquired just enough English to get by. I am also the mother of a mixed-race child. As such, I hold deep personal investment in the difficulties and richness of visible minority and immigrant experiences in Canadian education, and this provides the lenses through which I interact with my participants and code my data.

Research with Immigrant Teacher Candidates

Examining in-depth the role of the researcher and how my own location impacts how I view my work (England, 1994; Nagar & Geiger, 2007), I must also consider that as an instructor in the institution in which I conducted this research, given the nature of my questioning, my participants might not have wanted to disclose all their experiences. There is a complexity embedded in reflexive work. It is multifaceted, interactional, and rooted in an emergent nature of our social locations (Cunliffe, 2003). Participants in my research may have censored themselves from naming practices of racism, for example, in front of a White prototypical teacher. As well, context might have influenced the responses to be more what my participants thought I wanted to hear. I have to consider the ethical dilemma presented by myself as a member of the dominant group.

My participants and I are not necessarily learning the same things: they, as future teachers in Canada, are concerned with learning how to navigate, how to assimilate, and what they need to learn to be successful. I strive to learn how they do that. I have encountered moments when they want me, as an insider in the teaching profession, to assist them in their navigation. As a teacher and possible gatekeeper, I feel I would be remiss if I did not share and make transparent the taken-for-granted that I may be able to see (Delpit, 1995). I also look to my participants to expose aspects that I have not considered as barriers. Revealing how I position myself in relation to this work and its complexities, combined with my approach to use practical and theoretical theories, has conjured a couple of stories worth retelling.

Much of my research involves working with teacher candidates who self-identify as immigrant (ITCS). Many times, in the course of interviews and focus groups, the participants shared the subtler ways in which the perception of their race and culture impacts their experiences in schools. Some participants readily discuss the ways in which they are Othered in schools and at the university (see Cho, 2013, 2016). What I have come to learn is that much of what ITCS are expected to do centres around discerning between overt racism and microaggressions (Sue et al., 2007) and making decisions about when to address an issue and when to leave matters alone. On the whole, my participants' counter-stories reveal the ways in which they have worked to disregard racist comments, innuendos, or situations. Nigel's story is a good example of *ignoring* and exposes one of the *crises of truth* I experienced as a researcher.

Counter-Story #1: Nigel

At the time of his interview, Nigel (a pseudonym) was in his late 40's, undertaking his Bachelor of Education, part time in the evenings while he continued his day job as an educational assistant. Nigel is a Black male who immigrated from Guyana to England and then to Canada. It should be noted that the programme from which participants were recruited had a small representation of visual minority students, less than 5 percent. At the start of the interview, given that Nigel was the only Black male in the part time programme, I anticipated hearing how his positionality was informing his experience. On the contrary, Nigel was rather reluctant to discuss the role of race in his experiences. Drawing from Foucault (1977) one might argue that a Whiteness ideology has constructed a discourse that "conceals its own invention" (p. 49) whereby ITCS of colour might internalize the colour-blindness argument: in multicultural Canada race does not limit or impede success. As Nigel stated, when asked about his positionality in schools that were predominantly White,

> Let me start off by saying this: I go any which way and I can go into any place and I just go and focus on what it is I have to do. As far as cultural implications I didn't see it or think about it. Or maybe I didn't have the time to think about it. So, I didn't see it *per se*. (July 30, 2009)

During the interview with Nigel I tried in many subtle ways to ask if he experienced any racism. As a Black male in a White, female dominated profession (he was 1 of 3 males becoming a primary-junior teacher) I anticipated hearing stories of discrimination, particularly because of the location and demographics of Nigel's practicum schools in predominantly White, homogenous schools. My own intuition and knowledge of counter-stories from my family were certainly informing my perceptions. Nigel has been in Canada since before he began high school and also works in the school system as an educational assistant. Through our conversation, I ascertained that Nigel was very conscious of professional constraints as he chose his words carefully when asked to speak about the teaching profession. I, too, was treading cautiously and using coded language around race such as "in a homogenous school" or terms such as "cultural representation" as I attempted to broach the topic of racism that he might have experienced. In an attempt to press Nigel with respect to the issue of race, I specifically asked if in his placement schools "with all White teachers, surrounded by White kids, did they respond alright to you? Did you have any challenges that way?" Nigel immediately responded,

> I had none what-so-ever actually. No, I stand corrected, I did have one, I did have one. In my initial placement, there was girl in Grade 2, she had issues with what I looked like, actually. She used a term, I'm trying to think, it was something almost like, the word she used was reminiscent of, or was indicative of, her using terminology that is not quite hers, it had come from home. I'm trying to think of what exactly it was she'd said. We had to come to an understanding where, I made a decision and my Associate was very good, you know, she just, you know, let's move on, she didn't make an issue of it, she didn't make an issue of anything. We just sort of went about our merry ways. But the student, every time she came to work with me, I found her to be very defensive, so I mean I just developed the strategy of working with her whereby it was as limited as necessary. I mean, she was a student in my class that I had to work with, but I'd provide her with the work and I was there to answer her questions and be of assistance to her. I would give her instructions but where necessary I would get a buddy to work with her. One of the kids I'm going to encounter in my classroom, who potentially, for one reason or another would have difficulties working with me. So, I just find ways to work around it and I think working around with her was finding a buddy that, they sat in pairs so I would have one of her seatmates assist her with assignments and things like that. (July 30, 2009)

Reading and re-reading Nigel's counter-story still haunts me. I did not intend for my question to suggest that he had been a victim of racism but he may have heard my question this way and perhaps the idea that I assumed he would have experienced racism positioned him as victim. It was at this point I was recognizing I was making assumptions about his truth claims, imposing my reading of his world. I admit, in the moment, I was in disbelief that he could have not experienced any negative interactions. I was also conscious of the fact that I had not outwardly named what I was asking about as *racism*. I did not press him to remember the word or phrase the girl said to him. I believe he did remember the words. Nigel constructs this counter-story as a "vague recollection" which I interpreted, perhaps erroneously, as his preference to erase the incident. While Nigel believes the girl was repeating something she heard at home, the content of what she said has not been addressed. Nigel's inability to recount what name the child had called him may stem from being conditioned to maintain calm and develop strategies, such as ignoring racist innuendos, in order to be successful in school. But it also permits Nigel to assert his own agency, to try and maintain control over his positioning. Perhaps Nigel chose not to reveal the name on purpose. Articulating a racial slur draws more attention to the racism. By not identifying the name he was called, it may be easier for him to position himself as moving past it. Whether the words are repeated or not does not alter his truth claim.

In sharing the incident with me, I perceive Nigel positioning himself as having the power to determine his response and it is this critical moment, or series of moments, that shed light on radical-reflexivity. I needed to go further than challenging his truth claim; I needed to consider the situated nature of the event and take into account the cultural, historical, and linguistic traditions that were informing this exchange. For example, navigating the Canadian school system means adapting to the "culture of power" (Delpit, 1995) and thereby consciously positioning yourself within the school hierarchies. Nigel began his first placement by making an error in judgement, in term of this positioning, as he describes it:

> One of the things I did that I thought would have been beneficial but in hindsight, was not. I came into the program, and told myself, 'I'm gonna check my ego at the door, whatever I knew, I don't know, and I'm here to absorb everything'. And I quickly realized that that was a silly thing to do. I was somehow denying myself. For example, when I went on my first practicum I had more classroom experience than my Associate but I took it as 'okay, she is the expert and I'm just here to learn. I'm that empty vessel, fill me up.' And that wasn't a very wise thing to do because I wasn't being as authentic as I possibly could have been. (July 30, 2009)

Nigel was working to navigate multiple layers of his identity: student, educational assistant and future teacher. As I coded the interview transcripts, I also used the lens of race to read and re-read Nigel's decision to be an 'empty vessel'. As Milner (2010) explains, "students of color are often misunderstood, exploited, abused, and targeted for not being acquainted with cultural norms different from their own" (p. 123). Challenging the culture of power (i.e. as a student teacher having more experience than the Associate teacher) or demonstrating his experience might get Nigel labelled as difficult or could reflect poorly on his evaluations. It was within his mindset of being an 'empty vessel' that Nigel had the incident with the student. Near the end of the interview, Nigel returned to the incident and stated the following,

> I think that, as I reflected on how things transpired with my first placement, I think about that student who had brought some ideas from home. I felt that I should have been able to reach her more than I did. I mean it's possible that I couldn't of, but I felt that I probably could have and it probably would have been a help. Had I said, 'okay this had happened and I'll be with you for the next few weeks and these are the things you're going to do'. I needed to demonstrate a bit more confidence. (July 30, 2009)

As I consider the implications of Nigel's counter-story and, in particular, his *telling* of it, I must also consider how I am *hearing* his story: in what ways is my own positionality interacting with his narrative? I am also the mother of a mixed-race child. Throughout the course of my daughter's schooling, she has had many experiences with racism. One experience was particularly poignant and I draw from it another dimension towards understanding Nigel's experience and my interpretation of his experience.

Counter-Story #2: Me Chinese

Eight years ago: I remember it was raining when I picked my daughter up from school. She thrust a stack of papers at me shouting, "Don't look at these. This is what people think about me." I shoved the papers inside my raincoat so they did not get wet. I thought it best to wait until we were home and dry before enquiring further. After we got home she proceeded to tell me what happened at school that day. My daughter was going to the back of the classroom to get something and overheard a group of boys singing this song:

>Me Chinese/Me no dumb/Me stick finger in Daddy's bum/Daddy go fart
>and me go zoom/That's how I get home so soon!

First off, in full disclosure, I must state that, at the time, I had to ask my
daughter to repeat the song so I could write it down. The incident happened
more than two months prior to my writing about it but the song was as fresh
as the day it was burned into her mind. She told me she was not sure I should
be writing it down because she did not want other people to be singing it.
To me, this is a poignant and pivotal moment in my learning. Her reaction
and experience with racism at school and her reluctance to have the words
of the "Me Chinese" song written down, mirrors my interpretation of Nigel's
reluctance to recall to the racist words used towards him. He knew I was
conducting research and recording the interview. Nigel put a positive spin
on a difficult situation and positions himself as a qualified and capable TC
who can reframe a situation and be successful in the classroom. The stack
of papers my daughter did not want me to read were "apology" letters the
boys were made to write to her. It seems that when she told the boys to stop
singing the song, they further mimicked her, so she went and did what was
within her power as an 8-year-old encountering an injustice: she told the
teacher. In the end, the incident was dragged out over several days, requiring
visits to the principal, phone calls to the boys' parents (made by the school),
and a rather unsatisfactory ending. When I had asked her about the incident
again, two months later, I was asking her, as I realize I had asked Nigel, to
relive a story of Othering and all the emotional issues associated with the
event.

Sadly, it was not the first such incident, nor the last. The previous year, when
my daughter was in choir practice, two boys behind her starting pulling on
their eyes and saying "me Chinese." When she came home upset from that incident my husband thought it best not to address the issue with the school. He
said he experienced the same thing when he was a child. The desire to work
within the culture of power is so strong. As Nigel said during the interview,
"you can't get along with everyone." There is the connotation that a racialized
person might not address racism in order to preserve the harmony. In both
my daughter's story and Nigel's, they are not in positions of power. Nigel was
a teacher candidate, pursuing a second career. He just wanted to finish the
programme and get his teaching certification. My daughter was an 8-year-
old in school, relying on the adult in the room to make the classroom a safe
place. Neither wanted to be constructed as difficult. Nigel has been put in a
position in which he is required to ignore and/or accept the racism implicit in
the situation, and dismiss the hurtful actions, again, not drawing attention to

the ways in which racism is perpetuated. My husband's own recollection that racist taunts were uttered to him at school and that it is best to ignore them bring out a rank ire in me. I try to keep these narratives at the forefront of my thinking as I conduct my research. I consciously work to employ multiple layers of understanding (Chia, 1996) and my privileged position gives me choice: when to speak, when to remain silent, when to go to battle, and, perhaps most importantly, when to listen.

Conclusion

As I conduct my research I consciously implement numerous lenses, practical and theoretical, through which to examine the data. I also work to hear and re/hear the counter-stories and narratives of teacher candidates who self-identify as immigrants. Naming oppressive situations and exploring the ways in which all stakeholders (including the researcher) are implicated is a fundamental component of this work. Immigrant and racialized teacher candidates in my classes are usually reluctant to tell their counter-stories to their prototypical counter-parts. Being able to listen to counter-narratives while examining my own biases and understandings is what I am striving for by taking a reflexive stance: I, too, am being transformed. By sharing the counter-stories it is possible that more people will begin to view the world of teaching through different lenses and ask the question, how are we preparing future teachers? How is the landscape of "teacher" changing? In what ways is the landscape staying the same? Of paramount concern, however, is how to make our universities and schools safe and accepting spaces so ITCs can tell their stories and so that their counter-stories can be heard to evoke systemic change.

Note

1   Solórzano and Yosso posit that counter-stories "are a method of telling the stories of those people whose experiences are often not told (i.e., those on the margins of society). The counter-story is a tool for exposing, analyzing, and challenging the marjoritarian stories of racial privilege" (p. 32). In contrast, majoritarian stories "privilege Whites, men, the middle and/or upper class, and heterosexuals by naming these social locations as natural or normative points of reference" (p. 28). Majoritarian stories may include the stereotypical ways in which people who are immigrants are constructed in the dominant discourse. A story may also be a majoritarian story because of what is omitted as well as what is misunderstood.

References

Bergerson, A. (2003). Critical race theory and white racism: Is there room for white scholars in fighting racism in education? *Qualitative Studies in Education, 16*(1), 51–63.

Boler, M., & Zembylas, M. (2003). Discomforting truths: The emotional terrain of understanding difference. In P. Trifonas (Ed.), *Pedagogies of difference: Rethinking educatoin for social change* (pp. 110–136). New York, NY: RoutledgeFalmer.

Causey, V., Thomas, C., & Armento, B. (2000). Cultural diversity is basically a foreign term to me: The challenges of diversity for preservice teacher education. *Teaching and Teacher Education, 16*, 33–45.

Chia, R. (1996). *Organizational anaysis as deconstructive practice.* Berlin: De Gruyter.

Cho, C. L. (2013). *Performing the innocent stranger: Exploring immigrant identities and education.* In C. Broom (Ed.), *Canadian Society for the Study of Education (CIESC)* (pp. 76–89). Kelowna: Citizenship Education Research Network (CERN).

Cho, C. L. (2016). No dreads and saris here: The culture of teacher education conformity and the need for diverse representation amongst teaching staff. In C. Schmidt & J. Schneider (Eds.), *Diversifying the teaching force in transnational contexts: Critical perspectives* (pp. 45–57). Rotterdam, The Netherlands: Sense Publishers.

Clandinin, D. J., & Connelly, F. M. (2000). *Narrative inquiry: Experience and story in qualitative research.* San Francisco, CA: Jossey-Bass.

Clifford, J. (1986). Introduction: Partial truths. In J. Clifford & G. Marcus (Eds.), *Writing culture: The poetics and politics of ethnography* (pp. 1–26). Berkeley, CA: University of California Press.

Cunliffe, A. L. (2003). Reflexive inquiry in organizational research: Questions and possibilities. *Human Relations, 56*(8), 983–1003.

Day, E. (2002). Me, my* self and I: Personal and professional re-constructions in ethnographic research. *Forum Qualitative Sozialforschung/Forum: Qualitative Social Research, 3*(3), Article 11. Retrieved from http://nbn-resolving.de/urn:nbn:de:0114-fqs0203117

Dei, G. J. S., & Kempf, A. (Eds.). (2006). *Anti-colonialism and education: The politics of resistance* (Vol. 7). Rotterdam, The Netherlands: Sense Publishers.

Delpit, L. (1995). *Other people's children: Cultural conflicts in the classroom.* New York, NY: The New Press.

England, K. (1994). Getting personal: Reflexivity, personality, and feminist research. *Professional Geographer, 46*(1), 80–89.

Foucault, M. (1977). *Discipline & punish: The birth of the prison.* New York, NY: Vintage Books.

Johnson-Bailey, J. (1999). The ties that bind and the shackles that separate: Race, gender, class and color in a research process. *International Journal of Qualitative Studies in Education, 12*(6), 659–670.

Ladson-Billings, G. (2005). Is the team all right? Diversity and teacher education. *Journal of Teacher Education, 56*(3), 229–234.

Milner, H. R. (2010). What does teacher education have to do with teaching? Implications for diversity studies. *Journal of Teacher Education, 61*(1–2), 118–131.

Myles, J., Cheng, L., & Wang, H. (2006). Teaching in elementary school: Perceptions of foreign-trained teacher candidates on their teaching practicum. *Teaching and Teacher Education, 22*, 233–245.

Nagar, R., & Geiger, S. (2007). Reflexivity, positionality, and identity in feminist fieldwork: Beyond the impasse? In T. Barnes, E. Sheppard, J. Peck, & A. Tickell (Eds.), *Politics and practice in economic geography* (pp. 267–278). London: Sage Publications.

Putnam, R. T., & Borko, H. (2000). What do new views of knowledge and thinking have to say about research on teacher learning? *Educational Research, 29*(1), 4–15.

Reger, J. (2001). Emotions, objectivity and voice: An analysis of a "failed" participant observation. *Women's Studies International Forum, 24*(5), 605–616.

Solórzano, D., & Yosso, T. (2002). Critical race methodology: Counter-storytelling as an analytical framework for education research. *Qualitiative Inquiry, 8*(1), 23–44.

Sue, D. W., Capodilupo, C. M., Torino, G. C., Bucceri, J. M., Holder, A., Nadal, K. L., & Esquilin, M. (2007). Racial microaggressions in everyday life: Implications for clinical practice. *American Psychologist, 62*, 271–286.

Thompson, A. (2003). Tiffany, friend of people of color: White investments in antiracism. *Qualitative Studies in Education, 16*(1), 7–29.

CHAPTER 19

Reflexive Inquiry as a Scaffold for Teacher Identity Exploration during the First Year of Teaching

Dana Vedder-Weiss, Liel Biran, Avi Kaplan and Joanna K. Garner

Teachers' experiences during the early years of teaching are crucial for their motivation, learning, decision-making, and retention in the profession (Cochran-Smith, 2004; Hong, Greene, & Lowery, 2017). Unfortunately, it is all too common for these experiences to result with the decision to leave teaching, with attrition during the first few years reaching as high as 50% in some contexts and subject domains (Heikonen, Pietarinen, Pyhältö, Toom, & Soini, 2017; Ingersoll & Strong, 2011; Mansfield, Beltman, & Price, 2014). Various strategies have been employed to try and mitigate this issue, including providing mentorship to first year teachers, creating professional learning communities, and engaging teachers in professional development (Burke, Aubusson, Schuck, Buchanan, & Prescott, 2015). While such external supports are crucial for creating environments that promote a better experience for early career teachers, they often neglect a central feature of that experience – teachers' professional identity (Hong et al., 2017). Teacher identity is viewed as providing the teacher with a frame from which to interpret events relative to the self and make decisions about action (Beijaard, Meijer, & Verloop, 2004). Arguably, a teacher's interpretation of early years experiences as involving satisfactory environmental support, and as implying sufficient personal teaching efficacy and value, is framed by the sense of who he or she is and want to become as a teacher. As an important mediator of teachers' experiences and actions, the formation of different teacher identities may manifest in quite divergent responses to similar circumstances and professional trajectories. Therefore, interventions in teacher identity may promote constructive interpretations of such circumstances and could lead to more satisfaction and wellbeing, better instruction, and higher retention. However, there are many different definitions and perspectives on teacher identity and, correspondingly, different approaches to interventions that facilitate teacher identity.

In the current chapter, we employ a conceptualization of teacher identity that integrates the interplay between identity's contextualized and culturally-negotiated nature with the agency of the person in exploring and forming a sense of identity. The *Dynamic Systems Model of Role Identity* (DSMRI;

Kaplan & Garner, 2017, 2018) views identity as based in the social-cultural roles that the person occupies and negotiates continuously within her lived contexts. This perspective suggests that early career teachers may benefit from being encouraged to explore their professional identities through constructive personal reflections on their experiences and professional practice and through considering the implications to who they are and want to become as teachers. Moreover, the model itself can serve as a scaffold for such a systematic identity exploration process (Kaplan & Garner, 2018).

In this chapter, we operationalized early career teachers' identity exploration as reflexive inquiry – scaffolding and encouraging the teachers' engagement in a systematic process of gathering and analyzing self-relevant data about their environments, personal experiences, and professional decision-making in order to generate greater self-understanding of their realities and themselves in it as teachers (Lyle, 2009). Here, we report on a yearlong reflexive inquiry process by one first-year teacher of elementary science in a democratic school in Israel. We begin by explicating the identity model that served both as the theoretical framework and the scaffold for the reflexive inquiry, follow to describe the context and the teacher, and then discuss the principles guiding the design of the reflexive inquiry and how they were operationalized. Finally, we describe insights from the inquiry and conclude with thoughts about using a teacher identity model as a focus and scaffold to promote constructive identity exploration and formation among early career teachers.

Teacher Professional Identity as a Complex Dynamic System

Increasingly, scholars, teacher educators, and teachers recognize the central role of identity in teachers' experiences, motivation, and decision-making (Hong et al., 2017; Schutz, Hong, & Cross, 2018). A teacher's professional identity is considered to involve and frame the teacher's conception of the teacher role, motivation for teaching, instructional practice, interpretation of teaching experiences, willingness to change, as well as the trajectory of her professional learning (Beauchamp & Thomas, 2009; Beijaard et al., 2004; Olsen, 2010).

While teacher identity has been defined and studied in multiple ways and from various perspectives, definitions seem to converge on the understanding that teacher identity is meaning-based, and that, while it involves the unique teacher's personal background, it is also highly contextualized, dynamic, and mediated through social interactions (Beauchamp & Thomas, 2009). Yet, the multiplicity of perspectives and vague definition of teacher identity present challenges to scholars and educators in integrating understandings across studies (e.g., studies that concern teachers' ethnic identity, subject matter identity, gender identity, self-efficacy, in urban and rural settings), and in deriving practical insights from the literature.

In a recent model, we relied on assumptions of the complex dynamic systems approach to integrate insights from multiple identity perspectives (e.g., social-cultural, psychosocial, social-psychological, social-cognitive) into a model of identity that captures the rich, contextualized, dynamic, and social-cultural nature of identity while anchoring it in established concepts and processes. This model allows us to bridge insights across people and contexts while maintaining an emphasis on individuals' unique identity features (Kaplan & Garner, 2017). The complex dynamic systems' assumptions that most pertain to the conceptualization of role identity include: the dynamic and continuous self-emergence of role identity; the interdependence of the various role-identity elements and, hence, the irreducibility of role identity to its constituting parts; the non-linear and non-deterministic nature of identity change; the embeddedness of identity in contextual-cultural as well as individual-dispositional characteristics; and identity's unit-of-analysis of the person in her context, and its dialogical relations with other systems within the person (i.e., other role identities) and outside of the person (i.e., role identities of other people such as students, colleagues, supervisors, and of organizations such as the department, school, and education system).

While based on complexity assumptions, the Dynamic Systems Model of Role Identity (DSMRI) is premised on the rather simple notion that, in any particular situation, people act in order to pursue a certain goal in light of their perception of the reality of the situation and themselves within that reality. This seemingly simple premise serves as an anchor to a conceptualization of teacher identity as a complex dynamic system consisting of four contextually and dynamically constructed and interrelated components that correspond with different elements of the premise (see Maehr, 1984; Maehr & Braskamp, 1986): ontological and epistemological beliefs; purpose and goals; self-perceptions and self-definitions; and perceived action possibilities (Kaplan & Garner, 2017, 2018).

Ontological and epistemological beliefs concern the teacher's perceptions of the reality within which she lives, and her sense of certainty about these perceptions. Such beliefs include characteristics of people (e.g., students, colleagues, administrators), institutions (e.g., the school, district, education system), societal structures and processes (e.g., societal values, group dynamics), and causal attributions (e.g., nature of student ability, causes of students' behavior, success, and failure) that serve the teacher in constructing an understanding about the nature of events. *Purpose and goals* refer to the teacher's understanding and setting of the overall purpose for her role as well as the more specific goals that she pursues in teaching. *Self-perceptions and self-definitions* concern the teacher's construction of herself in the role – self-perceived attributes, characteristics, and group memberships that are salient to who she is as a teacher. Finally, *perceived action possibilities* refer to the actions that the teacher perceives are available and unavailable to her for pursuing her goals in light of her perceived reality and herself in that reality. All four of these components are interdependent, and continuously emerge while being framed by the context and the subject domain of teaching, mediated by social interactions and negotiations that employ cultural meanings, and influenced by the teacher's implicit dispositions.

The DSMRI depicts teacher identity as involving three facets: content, structure, and process. The *content* in the role-identity components may differ among different teachers, and may change for a particular teacher over time. Teachers may have more, less, or different knowledge about their environment, goals for teaching, self-knowledge and personal definitions as teachers, and perceived strategies and actions in their teacher role. Different content (e.g., self-perceptions, goals) may also rise or fall out of salience depending on situational or personal circumstances. The *structure* of the teacher's identity may also differ between teachers and change over time for a particular teacher – elements within the four components (e.g., various self-perceptions, goals, or action possibilities) can be in harmony or in tension with each other, components can be more or less aligned, and the teacher role identity may be more or less integrated with other meaningful role identities of the person (e.g., parent). For example, the content of a teacher's self-perception may change with time as she builds more confidence in managing her classroom. The structure of her identity would also change as her self-perceptions as having high efficacy in classroom managements aligns with more student-centered goals and instructional practices. Finally, the *process* of identity formation can characterize different teachers and change for a teacher across time. The teacher may have formed her identity primarily through socialization and identifications with significant others, through active and agentic identity exploration, or by avoiding identity issues and passively assimilating goals, self-definitions, and actions from the particular situational directives.

The DSMRI suggests that, relative to veteran teachers, among early career teachers, teacher identity is likely to be characterized by less content (e.g., fewer ontological beliefs, goals, and action possibilities) and more fragmented structure (e.g., less alignment among role identity components). Particularly among first year teachers, the relatively thin and fragmented teacher role identity is likely to manifest in confusion, identity tensions, uncertainty, and lower capacities for systematically and constructively framing, processing, and interpreting the meaning of events in ways that promote identity growth and integration. Therefore, particularly among first year teachers, reflexive inquiry with scaffolds that promote agency and systematic engagement in self-relevant data collection, processing, and interpretation, is likely to contribute to constructive identity exploration and formation.

Reflexive Inquiry with the DSMRI to Scaffold Teacher Identity Exploration

The objective of the current study was to scaffold the professional identity exploration and formation of a first year teacher in order to promote his adaptive identity exploration and formation. A second goal was to contribute to the conceptual understanding of the professional identity formation of teachers during the first year of teaching and how it relates to interpretation of experiences, decisions about instructional approach and strategies, and commitment to the profession.

Context and Procedure

The study involved a collaborative project between a science education researcher (Dana) and a beginning Israeli science teacher, Liel, during his first in-service year in a K-12 democratic school (a school emphasizing teachers' and students' autonomy and participation in school management; Vedder-Weiss & Fortus, 2011). Specifically, the study focused on Liel's experience instructing a weekly 3-hours mixed-aged science class that was selected because it involved particular challenges for him. The collaboration was designed to implement four principles for promoting the teacher's (and his students') identity exploration – promoting perceived self-relevance, triggering identity exploration, promoting sense of safety, and scaffolding identity exploration strategies (Heffernan, Kaplan, Peterson, & Newton, 2017; Kaplan, Sinai, & Flum, 2014). Liel had the agency to select and explore the events he perceived as most relevant and meaningful to his experiences and identity as a teacher and, hence, the content was self-relevant and involved triggers to his identity exploration. Therefore, Dana focused on providing Liel a sense of safety and scaffolding his identity exploration through scheduling a weekly reflection session, teaching him about the DSMRI, observing and conversing about his teaching, and using the DSMRI in conversations and correspondence as a guide for systematic self-reflection, interpreting experiences, and considering their meaning to his professional identity content, structure, and process of formation.

The collaboration involved collection of multiple forms of data, including: weekly reflective journal entries that Liel wrote during the academic year; participant-observations by Dana of 75% of the class meetings; Dana's field notes that she shared with Liel; electronic communication between Dana and Liel throughout the year; and two in-depth interviews that Dana conducted with Liel, one early in the year and one towards the end of the year.

Here, we emphasize the reflexive inquiry aspect of this collaboration and highlight Liel's own analysis of the data, which he originally wrote as part of a paper for a course in a teacher college. Liel used the DSMRI as he read through his journal, identified meaning units in the data that corresponded with the model components, sought indications for alignment and misalignment between components of the role identity and for changes in these components and their interrelations, as well as personal and environmental events that coincided with these changes. He then reflected on personal understandings and decisions he arrived at through his journal writing, interactions with Dana, and the process of analyzing his own journal using the model.

Liel's Reflexive Analysis

Liel noted very prominent fluctuations in his role identity components throughout the academic year. These fluctuations highlighted Liel's continuous identity exploration, which included continuous learning, external and internal negotiation of ontological beliefs about the nature of students and the school, reconsideration and redefinition of goals for his students and for himself, and reflection and exploration of self-perceptions and action possibilities that were triggered by events he experienced as involving negative emotions and identity tensions. Liel identified five general themes around which he explored his identity during the year: the sub-role identity of being a mentor (a particular role for teachers in democratic schools that is different from the traditional role of a teacher); ontological beliefs concerning students' social behavior; ontological beliefs concerning students' academic motivation and learning; self-perceptions and self-definition of himself as a teacher; and negative and positive emotions and energy, or stamina, he experienced in the teaching role.

Liel identified classroom management as the most significant content around which he explored his teacher role identity during the first year – a topic of concern to many first year teachers. Liel's identity exploration around classroom management began with a strong sense of discrepancy between his initial expectations that students in a democratic school manifest responsible citizenship and proper social behavior, and the students' behaviour he actually encountered in the classroom. Liel's initial ontological beliefs were that students in a democratic school, where they have autonomy and are co-participants in school governance, exercise self-discipline, and have a sense of inner boundaries and respect for classroom norms. Therefore, he was caught unprepared by the students' inattention in class and their disregard for lesson regulations and for the school's cultural norms of responsible civic behaviour. As a consequence, Liel found himself adopting authoritarian classroom management actions used by other teachers in the school, such as giving children warnings and sending them out after three such warnings, which he experienced as standing in tension with his goals and self-perceptions of values as a teacher. In his systematic reflection on his journal entries, Liel identified a strong misalignment between these action possibilities and his self-definition – he did not want to define himself as a disciplinarian *"I came here to be a respecting enabling person, who encourages dialog ... It was hard for me to 'put on' the role of a strict disciplinarian."* This led to deeper reflection and critical personal inquiry regarding a shift he noticed in his identity as a result of enacting these practices. He also noted a growing alignment between these actions and his goals for students' learning, his emerging ontological belief that the context requires establishing and enforcing behavioural boundaries, and persisting tensions within his self-perceptions between feeling responsible for students' learning and behaviour and valuing mutual respect, decency, and collaboration. Identifying such tensions in his self-perceptions triggered identity exploration around questions of personal ontological beliefs such as "what is my boundary for a student behaviour to be considered out of line," and around action possibilities such as "how should I respond in such and such a situation?"

Liel's analysis of his journal highlighted fluctuations in his perceptions and emotions, as well as in his acceptance of the necessity of using actions such as sending children out of the classroom in order to maintain order. At times he determined to be more authoritative, still recognizing the tension with some aspects of his self-perceptions. At other times, he perceived himself to be inconsistent, reflecting on the ontological possibility that students perceive him as given to manipulations. He analyzed these experiences to reflect identity exploration with the following words:

> It is possible to see the issue of boundaries with which I struggled during the first year as a continuous internal battle – like rope pulling or a seesaw. The moving force, the "gravity," is the collection of values in my self-perceptions, and their [the values'] aligned goals: mutual respect, listening, dialogue, personal growth and learning. And, without giving these up, I am trying to maintain balance and not to fall to either of two poles:

rigid discipline that produces a mere "forced sense of calm," or anarchy
that allows free action without any overall authority.

Liel then reports on his search for action possibilities that would allow resolu-
tion of these identity tensions. He describes a collaborative discussion with the
students about discipline, asking them to think together about ways for creating a learning-oriented atmosphere in the classroom, and about alternatives
to sending students out of the classroom in response to misbehaviour. The
attempt proved unsuccessful, as the students subsequently misbehaved in that
discussion, and Liel stopped the lesson. He continued to search for action possibilities aligned with his self-perceptions and goals and decided to try having
students sign a behavioural contract. This too was unsuccessful as the students
did not abide by the contract. Finally, while writing in his journal, Liel had an
insight about a new action possibility: beginning the lesson with a brief science assignment, then allowing students who so chose to leave, and continuing the lesson with the students who want to stay and learn. Liel summarized:

> First, it was interesting to see that the new solution to the problem with
> discipline in the lessons came up while writing the reflection ... Second,
> one can see the attempt to maneuver within the terrain of action pos-
> sibilities, within [ontological beliefs about] the framework of autonomy
> that the school provides, in order to minimize the extent of the problem
> with which I've been dealing.

This solution worked, but only partially. Liel continued to explore a variety
of action possibilities (e.g., student-led lessons, field trips, incorporating games
and movies). Then, about a month and a half before the year's end, he pointed
to a change in his purpose and goals in the following journal entry:

> The idea is to (a) get them to be physically active, (b) afford them more
> social interactions, (c) connect the above with the topic of the day's exper-
> iment. There are not going to be deep conceptualizations, but they may
> have more fun, and they may come out with a more positive feeling about
> the topic and with a little insight into a scientific world that, perhaps, they
> could develop further in the future. It will be also nicer for me, and a social
> experience also makes a contribution. With an eye to my future as an edu-
> cator, it also helps me to develop tools to serve me in group-work.

Whereas Liel highlighted the redefinition of his goals in this solution, the
quote above involves all the other role identity components. He defined new

goals for his students, justified them with ontological beliefs that are appropriately epistemologically tentative, and harmonized these beliefs (and implied actions) with his own present and future personal and professional goals.

Finally, when reflecting on the entire body of journal entries, Liel noted the interdependence between the change in his ontological and epistemological beliefs about the students, his goals for his students and for himself, his action possibilities, and the non-linear but progressive improvement in his overall emotions and sense of himself as a teacher. His interpretation of the underlying reasons for this positive change was anchored in the greater alignment within his teacher role identity:

> Overall, despite the fact that I did not find answers to my questions about defining and properly implementing boundaries, through changes in the various components of ontological beliefs (narrowing the gaps between expectations and reality), goals (redefining), actions (examining new possibilities) and self-perceptions (development of inner strength and emotional containment), one can assume that I've learned to minimize the friction in these conflict zones.

Four years later, Liel is a full time science teacher at the same Democratic school, where he is fulfilling additional roles with increasing leadership responsibilities in the community.

Using the DSMRI within a Reflexive Inquiry During the First Year of Teaching

In his systematic and thorough analysis of the factors that contributed to his experience of positive change during the first challenging year in teaching, Liel pointed to an integration of the autonomy provided to teachers within the democratic school to experiment with a variety of action possibilities, the tremendous support he received within the school and outside of it, and personal characteristics of experience and maturity. He summarizes his analysis, however, by pointing to the multiple benefits he experienced from the reflexive inquiry. The analysis highlighted to him the power of reflective writing as affording insights that lead to personal change during the writing and following the analysis. The inquiry itself, he wrote, clarified the broader picture of the intensive first year: "*From the analysis of the materials, I learned about the path I've treaded, I understand better where I am on the developmental trajectory, and I draw encouragement from that in order to continue.*" He attributed the depth of his reflection to the understanding that it was all part of his personal inquiry. Finally, Liel also commented on the DSMRI as a scaffold, noting that it *"provided a structured framework, relatively simple for application, for organizing a very large mass of words into clear categories."* Appropriately, Liel acknowledged the fuzziness of the analytical process using the DSMRI and the need for additional analyses and their corroboration by other researchers for more robust and trustworthy conclusions regarding his development. Yet, he also noted how the model eased the identification of patterns across time, clarified the interdependence between the various identity elements and components, and helped to elicit themes and trends.

In summary, this study illustrates how the DSMRI can serve as a conceptual tool and a scaffold in the reflexive inquiry that supports a teacher's systematic identity exploration as he copes with the challenging experiences during the first year of teaching. Such a scaffold for reflexive inquiry has the potential to promote the teacher's agency and competencies in exploring and forming a more aligned teacher role identity. The insights further suggest that a reflexive inquiry that uses the DSMRI might also be useful in teacher education and other contexts of teacher change, like internships, professional development programs, and school transitions.

References

Beauchamp, C., & Thomas, L. (2009). Understanding teacher identity: An overview of issues in the literature and implications for teacher education. *Cambridge Journal of Education, 39*, 175–189.

Beijaard, D., Meijer, P. C., & Verloop, N. (2004). Reconsidering research on teachers' professional identity. *Teaching and Teacher Education, 20*, 107–128.

Burke, P. F., Aubusson, P. J., Schuck, S. R., Buchanan, J. D., & Prescott, A. E. (2015). How do early career teachers value different types of support? A scale-adjusted latent class choice model. *Teaching and Teacher Education, 47*, 241–253.

Cochran-Smith, M. (2004). Stayers, leavers, lovers, and dreamers: Insights about teacher retention. *Journal of Teacher Education, 55*, 5, 387–392.

Heffernan, K., Kaplan, A., Peterson, S., & Newton, K. J. (2017). Integrating identity formation and subject matter learning. In E. Lyle (Ed.), *At the intersection of selves and subject* (pp. 53–61). Rotterdam, The Netherlands: Sense Publishers.

Heikonen, L., Pietarinen, J., Pyhältö, K., Toom, A., & Soini, T. (2017). Early career teachers' sense of professional agency in the classroom: Associations with turnover intentions and perceived inadequacy in teacher–student interaction. *Asia-Pacific Journal of Teacher Education, 45*(3), 250–266.

Hong, J., Greene, B., & Lowery, J. (2017). Multiple dimensions of teacher identity development from pre-service to early years of teaching: A longitudinal study. *Journal of Education for Teaching, 43*(1), 84–98.

Ingersoll, R. M., & Strong, M. (2011). The impact of induction and mentoring programs for beginning teachers: A critical review of the research. *Review of Educational Research, 81*(2), 201–233.

Kaplan, A., & Garner, J. K. (2017). A complex dynamic systems perspective on identity and its development: The dynamic systems model of role identity. *Developmental Psychology, 53*(11), 2036–2051.

Kaplan, A., & Garner, J. K. (2018). Teacher identity and motivation: The dynamic systems model of role identity. In P. Schutz, J. Hong, & D. Cross (Eds.), *Research on teacher identity and motivation: Mapping challenges and innovations*. New York, NY: Springer Publishing.

Kaplan, A., Sinai, M., & Flum, H. (2014). Design-based interventions for promoting students' identity exploration within the school curriculum. In S. Karabenick & T. Urdan (Eds.), *Motivational interventions* (pp. 243–291). Bingley: Emerald Group Publishing Limited.

Lyle, E. (2009). A process of becoming: In favor of a reflexive narrative approach. *The Qualitative Report, 14*, 293–298.

Maehr, M. L. (1984). Meaning and motivation: Toward a theory of personal investment. *Research on Motivation in Education, 1*, 115–144.

Maehr, M. L., & Braskamp, L. A. (1986). *The motivation factor: A theory of personal investment*. Lexington, MA: Heath & Co.

Mansfield, C., Beltman, S., & Price, A. (2014). 'I'm coming back again!' The resilience process of early career teachers. *Teachers and Teaching: Theory and Practice, 20*, 547–567.

Olsen, B. (2008). Teacher identity as a useful frame for study and practice of teacher education. *Teacher Education Quarterly, 35*(3), 33–46.

Olsen, B. (2010). *Teaching for success: Developing your teacher identity in today's classroom*. New York, NY: Routledge.

Schutz, P., Hong, J., & Cross, D. (2018). *Research on teacher identity: Mapping challenges and innovations*. New York, NY: Springer International Publishing.

Vedder-Weiss, D., & Fortus, D. (2011). Adolescents' declining motivation to learn science: Inevitable or not? *Journal of Research in Science Teaching, 48*(2), 199–216.